Dear Deb

I'm sure you'll

going through the book and

visiting the city.

A GUIDE TO THE
HERITAGE OF
HYDERABAD:

The Natural and the Built

Love!

Madh_

6 Sept 2011.

A GUIDE TO THE HERITAGE OF HYDERABAD:

The Natural and the Built

Madhu Vottery

Rupa & Co

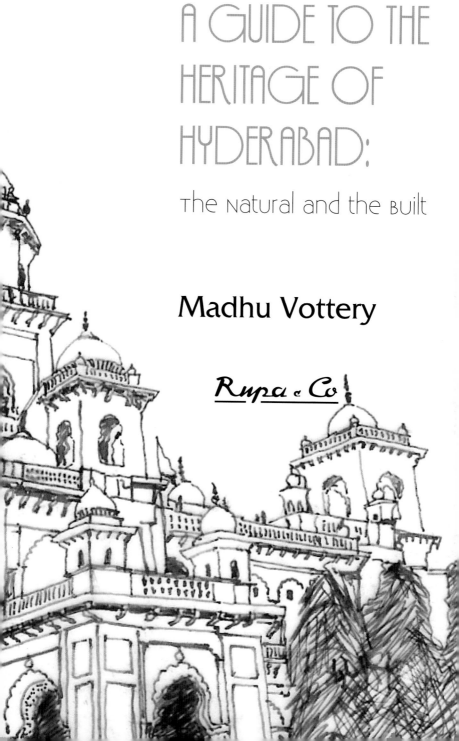

Published 2010 by:
Rupa Publications India Pvt. Ltd.
7/16 Ansari Road, Daryaganj
New Delhi 110 002

Sales Centres:
Allahabad Bengaluru Chandigarh
Chennai Hyderabad Jaipur
Kathmandu Kolkata Mumbai

Book design by Sonali Lal
(sonalilal@gmail.com)

Printed in India by
Gopsons Papers Ltd.
A 2&3, Sector 64,
Noida - 201301

Contents

Acknowledgements

I am grateful to Dr V.K. Bawa and Sri Sajjad Shahid from Centre for Deccan Studies, Hyderabad for their constant and much needed support and guidance.

I gratefully acknowledge all the help and support that I have received from Dr Reddy's Laboratories Limited, Hyderabad.

My sincere thanks to the officials of Hyderabad Metropolitan Development Authority, the Archaeological Survey of India and State Archaeology & Museums for providing me access to the data relevant to the listed and protected heritage structures of Hyderabad.

I must thank the staff and members of State Archives for letting me use their library.

I would like to express my gratitude to Sri S.P. Shorey, Sri M.A. Qayum, Sri Vikram Dev Rao, Dr Oudesh Rani Bawa, Sri Maheep Singh Thapar, Sri G.S.V. Surya Narayana Murthy, Sri Scott Kugle, Prof Ramesh Reddy, Sri Robert Simpkins, Smt Faruke Quader, Smt Anuradha Reddy, Sri Aminuddin Khan and Sri Bakhtiyar Dadabhoy for all their invaluable suggestions.

I gratefully acknowledge all the help I have received from Sri Jayesh Ranjan, Sri G. Kishen Rao and the owners, administrators and caretakers of different heritage sites.

My sincere thanks are due to Sri Narendra Luther, who has looked at the final draft of the book and suggested suitable changes. I convey my thanks to Dr George Michell for looking at the Chapter on Architectural Knowledge System and agreeing to write Foreword for the book.

I thank the team of Rupa for the successful completion of the work.

Last but not the least, I thank my family and friends for their constant support; and God, for bringing the opportunity my way to work on this project.

Team Members

Madhu Vottery, Prof Rajendra Vottery, B. Arvind and Hari

All the pictures are taken by the author's team (otherwise specified). The sketches are made by the author and B. Arvind.

The building drawings are manually sketched, otherwise drafted by the author.

Bohron ki sarai

Foreword

As one of the greatest of India's historical capitals, with chronological overlays dating back five centuries and more, Hyderabad's built and natural heritage has been inadequately served with a professional guidebook. Unlike Delhi and Agra, and even Calcutta (Kolkata) and Bombay (Mumbai), Hyderabad has until recently escaped the attention of architectural historians, in spite of the interest of previous researchers in the monuments of the Qutb Shahi founders of the city.

It is a pleasure therefore to welcome this volume, in which is presented for the first time, the entire heritage panorama of Hyderabad's historical environment, from the mosques, tombs, fortresses and waterworks established by the Qutb Shahi sultans and their family members in the 16th and 17th centuries to the palaces, shrines and civic edifices commissioned by the incomparably wealthy Nizams and their nobles in the 19th and 20th centuries.

More than 275 such sites and monuments surviving from these different periods in and around the city are described and illustrated in this volume. Nor is this coverage strictly limited to buildings. The author is also interested in the natural heritage of Hyderabad, especially the historical gardens, lakes and canals that are still preserved, if only incompletely.

The provision of city maps locating all these different sites, monuments and hydraulic features should prove invaluable, both to those citizens of Hyderabad who wish to be better informed about their own city, and to visitors from elsewhere. The author must be congratulated for assembling such an abundance of diverse data, and organising them in the most useable manner possible.

One theme that runs through this volume is the author's judgement about the present condition and historical value of Hyderabad's built and natural environment. While she is generous in her appreciative comments of this richly textured heritage, she is critical of the effectiveness of current efforts at conservation. Many of the city's historical sites and monuments are being

subjected to grave danger as Hyderabad undergoes rapid and unbridled development. Such threat remains a serious obstacle to the study and preservation of the built and natural heritage. I hope that this piece of work will provide useful ammunition for the daunting task of shielding sites, monuments and water features from destruction, especially those which until now have not benefited from the protection of civic and archaeological agencies.

The author has also argued for the appropriate re-use of historical sites and monuments in the city. If guided by enlightened and enforceable policies, there is no reason why such a strategy should not contribute to the preservation of the city's most significant features for the benefit of future generations.

George Michell
Architectural Historian

Preface

The idea of exploring the field of built-heritage first came to me when I noticed the negligence and gradual demise of many monuments in my home town, the historic city of Shahjahanpur, in Uttar Pradesh. I grew up in the neighbourhood of mosques, graves, tombs and gateways, visiting heritage components, also reading and discussing about them. My passion for the built heritage has become my profession now, after my Masters in Architectural Conservation. While visiting the different heritage sites in the northern and southern parts of India, during my education, and later, as part of my profession, the idea of documenting the city's heritage began to take shape. As I went to different heritage sites in Hyderabad, I tried to understand the administrative system of protection of these sites in the city. I had some idea of the administrative systems of listing and protecting of heritage at different places in the country; but learning about the administrative system of listing and protection of the heritage in Hyderabad has become a practical experience.

The role played in the field of heritage conservation by Government authorities, NGOs, and some individuals is a matter of appreciation. However, there is scope for further improvements in the system. I believe this book will add to the awareness of citizens, tourists and different organisations, and will be of great help to understand the significance of Hyderabad's heritage, leading to save and maintain it in the best possible way for generations to come.

Madhu Vottery

An ornamentation detail, Paigah Tombs

Chapter 1

A Few Introductory Words for the Reader

This chapter provides an insight into the past and the present of Hyderabad, and discusses the future of the city, treating heritage and development as two sides of the same coin.

The architecture of any region is mainly the result of the culture and the geography of that region. Over a period of time, as people move from one place to another, to fulfil their physical and spiritual needs, their culture travels with them and so does the architecture. Thus, cities which were the centre of power became the melting pots of different cultures and different types of architecture. Hyderabad is one fine example of such a city, with its remarkable mix of different cultures and architectural styles. Deccan Kingdom, initially ruled by the Kakatiya Rulers went into the hands of Khiljis, Tughlaqs and then to Bahmanis. The Bahmanis had five governors. One by one all of them became independent. In 1518, the Qutb Shahis of Golconda were the last one to do so. The rulers of this kingdom ruled from the Golconda fort (a mud fort built earlier by the Kakatiya kings). Mohammed Quli Qutb Shah founded a new city and gave it the name Bhagnagar. It was later called Hyderabad.

The history of Hyderabad is incomplete without a reference to its architectural heritage. Localities tended to grow around the structures that were being built in Hyderabad. This is quite evident even today; a single structure in Hyderabad often defines a complete site around it: Gulzar Houz, Charkaman and Ghode ki Kabr, for example. As the kingdom went mainly into the hands of two dynasties, the typology, the architectural style, and the technology of the buildings in the city registered a change. The architectural heritage components of Hyderabad reflect the period of their origin and the culture of their patrons.

The writer's attempt to understand the relationship between the history of Hyderabad and its heritage is shared with the reader in this guide book. The scaled road maps in the book are meant to facilitate visits to different heritage sites of the city. The book talks about the significance, the value and the architecture of each heritage structure. It also refers to the period in which it was built, by whom, and how. The visitor can quickly turn a few pages to look at the interior and exterior of a heritage building, and refer to a brief description of its surroundings. The sketches and maps guide the visitor to a historic structure via the neighbouring landmark buildings with a view to making him/her aware of the important aspects and significance of the surrounding area of the heritage site. The sketches are made with the help of archival pictures to describe the original form and façade of some of the heritage structures/components[1]. After discussing the historic structures and their sites, a brief note is given dealing with the different phases of the architectural history of the city with special reference to the construction/ornamentation techniques and various interior features characteristic of these phases.

The last chapter of the book is devoted to the various efforts that have gone into the conservation of the city's heritage structures: the efforts made by the local citizens, the administrative officers, the academicians and the conservation professionals to save the city's historic fabric. The book is written to serve the purpose of a guide-book, in addition to being a research work. Hence, an appendix has been added to the book to take care of its research aspect; the conservation aspects, and the lists of the built and natural heritage have been incorporated here. This is meant to spare the general reader an undesired overload of information. The pictorial index has been designed for a better appreciation of the unavoidable architectural terminology, the underline terms.

The names of the structures are directly taken from the list of HMDA and State Archaeology. To maintain a consistency in the work the other related names (of the people and areas) have been copied from these names.

THE FUTURE OF ARCHITECTURAL HERITAGE OF THE CITY

It is important to preserve the past of the city in the midst of the growing pace of present day development; the city should retain its identity. There is a need to monitor the balance between the past and the future of the city and to strengthen the ties between the two. It is advisable to remember that conservation is not just about protecting and preserving the past; it is also about making appropriate use of the valuable heritage resources available to us.

How to use this book:

This section is written for the benefit of the reader; complete information on each heritage component, along with its picture, makes it easier for the visitor to locate on site.

Chapter three of the book is about the immovable heritage of the city. The city is divided into seven circles[2] to visit the historic structures with ease. The discussion of the natural and the built heritage starts with Secunderabad—the north part of the city (easy to understand on the present map). Each circle provides a description of all the heritage components[3] sequentially with a system of walk/trip. One or more walks are designed in one circle for the convenience of the visitor. The number and the name of most of the heritage components are identified by different authorities and can be found on the map that indicates its location. The name of the surrounding area of a heritage site is printed on the city-level map also. If the component belongs to an architectural heritage or natural heritage precinct printed-map, it can be co-related with both the write-up and the maps. The numbers and the colour coding assigned to the components on the map indicate the level of their protection and the name of the authority/agency concerned with it, e.g. the Archaeological Survey of India, the State Archaeology, HMDA, etc. All the circles are numbered in an anticlockwise sequence.

For instance, if the readers look at Aza Khana-e-Zehra, they can look for its serial number and the route in the index. The number in this case is 88 and the structure is located at Dar-ush-Shifa in the Charminar area. One look at the Charminar Area level map (in Chapter III, Circle V) and the city level map will provide the information on the location of the site in question. For detailed information on the same component, the reader can refer to Chapter III, Circle V. The underlined terms have been discussed in the pictorial index.

Chapter IV deals with the construction system, the building materials, and the ornamentation techniques of different phases of history. The comparisons have been made between different buildings of the city for the better and easy understanding of architectural features.

Chapter 2

The History of the Heritage of Hyderabad

This chapter deals with the evolution of the historic areas of the city, reconstructing chronologically, the city's architectural history, layer by layer.

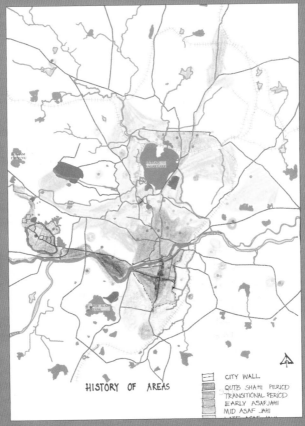

HISTORY OF AREAS

CITY WALL
QUTB SHAHI PERIOD
TRANSITIONAL PERIOD
EARLY ASAFJAHI
MID ASAF JAHI

Note: The following map delineates links between different heritage structures / sites that have come up over a period of time.

The history of the heritage of the city, to a large extent, is contributed by the natural heritage. The natural heritage of the city gave birth to the architectural heritage and hence both of them are inseparable. This natural heritage[4] comprises the rocks, the water bodies: the man-made and natural and the gardens/parks, trees. The rocks gave strategic locations to the forts and palaces. The gardens gave the beautiful and comfortable environment for the nobles and common man. The water bodies gave life to the city.

The rock heritage of the city belongs to one of the oldest rock systems of the world. A number of rounded and smoothed boulders standing one over the other, and in groups, creating unique compositions, surprise the visitors. The rocks of the city have witnessed each and every phase of the city's past. These rocks have weathered in an astonishing manner and present the appearance of the Ice action[5]. They are the result of a geological process known as sub-aerial denudation. These natural compositions are quite vulnerable and are now falling prey to Hyderabad's growing density. Some of them (refer to the appendix) have been identified by the HMDA, and listed under the natural heritage[6].

The water bodies and gardens of the Deccan together gave life to the city dwellers. The tradition of formal gardens was established by the Bahmani rulers and flourished well in Qutb Shahi period. The origin is traced back to Iran by the scholars of history. After the Qutb Shahis took over the Golconda, they observed the networking of water bodies in the kingdom created by their predecessors. They discovered the water body (today's Durgam Cheruvu) hidden behind the city's hillocks. Building upon the existing resources, they added to the traditional and indigenous practices of storing and transporting water. Not only the Qutb Shahi, Asaf Jahis also worked in the same direction; after the floods of 1908, walls were built on that stretch of the Musi, dividing the old city from the northern suburbs. Roads were built along north and south bank of the river, and gardens and parks were laid at a greater length. One of the parks crossing about 16 acres from Mussalamjung Bridge to the Afzalgunj Bridge and beyond contains a large tamarind tree that saved the life of nearly 200 persons who clung to it during the flood of 1908. Over a period of time most of these gardens have disappeared, only the names are left.

With a general understanding of the natural heritage, we move to understand the city's history of the built heritage. The remarkable point in the history of Hyderabad starts from the Fort of Golconda, standing amidst the natural rocks in the south-western part of the city. The oldest monuments of the city are found in and around the fort. After the downfall of Bahmanis in 1518, it became the capital of Qutb Shahi Rulers (1518-1687). During this period, the fort was further strengthened. Sixteenth century Golconda was not only a major marketplace but also the very important resting place along the famed Goa-Machlipatnam trade route. The entire stretch of Hyderabad from Gandipet-Janwada in the west to Saroornagar-Hayatnagar in the east is rich in ancient structures such as fortresses, moats, temples, mosques, tombs, carvansarais, etc., which date back to Qutb Shahi period.

The fourth Qutb Shahi king, Mohammed Quli shifted his palace from Golconda to the south of the Musi River as the fort was getting congested. He planned the city with Charminar as its centre and four roads perpendicular to each other, dividing the city in to four parts, within a fort wall. About two-fifty feet to the north of Charminar are Charkaman (1592) and the famous garden complex bordered by the *Kamans* or the four gateways. In the north-east was built the Dar-ush-Shifa, the first General Hospital in 1595. Shifting of the palace complex gave way to the building activity in this new area, which continued till the fall of Qutb Shahi dynasty, to the Mughal Emperor Aurangazeb. Before the downfall of the Qutb Shahi dynasty in 1687, the suburbs Khairatabad, Lingampalli and Naubat Pahad came up. The majestic Qutb Shahi palaces near Charminar are said to have been destroyed by the victorious Mughal army. Between the years 1687-1724, Hyderabad remained under Mughal control. The Mughal Governor ruled from Aurangabad, and was known as the *Subedar* of Deccan. In 1724, the Mughal king started building the city walls to defend against Maratha attack. As the Mughal Empire decayed and began to disintegrate, the then *Subedar* became independent. The construction of the city walls was completed in 1740.

The Asaf Jahi kings built their palaces in the south west of Charminar – beginning with the Chowmahalla. The major construction activity came after 1763, when Nizam Ali Khan, Asaf Jah II, shifted his capital back to Hyderabad. Now, localities like Begum Bazaar came up outside the walled city. In 1770, Hyderabad once again became a major capital city, now ruled by the successful Nizams of the Asaf Jahi dynasty. In 1798, Subsidiary Alliance for military and political cooperation was signed between the Nizam and the East India Company. Thereafter, in the north of the city, a British cantonment was established, followed by the British Residency in the year 1805 on the north bank of the River Musi. The area on the north, earlier not populated but now coming up, was called Secunderabad, after the name of Nawab Sikander Jah, the third Nizam. This followed the growth of the new area on the north of the river including the construction of the churches, convents and other civic structures in the European style. Secunderabad became the major sports centre and a hub of social activity.

Both Secunderabad and Hyderabad are linked by Hussain Sagar Lake. The Puranapul was the only bridge over Musi, built in 1578. The British Residency was required to be connected to the south part of the river. To do this a new bridge was built in 1839, known as Chaderghat Bridge. Another one, Afzalgunj Bridge (known as Nayapul today), was constructed in 1857-61. One more major event in the building history of the city is the introduction of Rail Network in 1874. With a broad gauge line, the city was linked with Wadi; the metre gauge came later.

A major change was observed in the development of the city after the flood in 1908. The then Nizam Mir Osman Ali felt the need for the development of the city planning and Sir Vishwaishwaraiya, a great engineer from Mysore, was called in to work on the Water Management system of the city. This was followed by the constitution of the City Improvement Board (CIB) established by the Nizam VII in 1912. The city was surveyed extensively for the first time (1912-13). By then the walled city started getting congested. Nizam VII Mir Osman Ali Khan moved to the King Koti palace in the north (1890s). The nobility moved with the Nizam to settle in the areas of Himayatnagar, Hyderguda and Banjara Hills, which soon became associated with the upper class. The CIB worked for several public structures, such as, the educational institutions, the hospitals, the marketplaces, etc., not only in the city but in the whole of the Hyderabad State to give it a distinctive character. Other major works done by CIB was the removal of city walls for the decongestion of the city. In 1937, the second city survey was done.

Earlier in 1923, electricity was made available to the public and, with the establishment of the rail connection with Bangalore; the city was placed on the metre gauge map of India. Industrial development was another major achievement of this period.

From the history of Hyderabad heritage we move to the discussion of different areas of the city with their rich architectural and natural heritage in the chapter three.

Chapter 3

The Natural and Architectural Heritage of Hyderabad

This chapter deals with the heritage components of different localities of Hyderabad. It provides maps detailing the location of each heritage component and precinct. The features of these components, along with their pictures, have also been provided; to visit them sequentially, the city has been divided into seven circles:

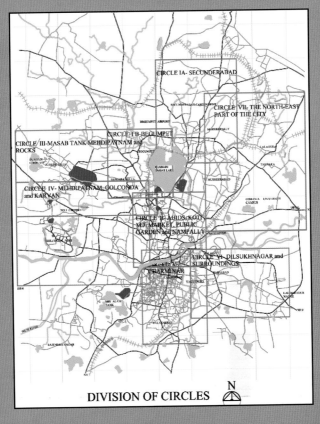

DIVISION OF CIRCLES

Circle I- Secunderabad and Begumpet
Circle II- The historic north of the city: Abids and the surroundings
CircleIII- Masab Tank, Banjara Hills and Jubilee Hills
CircleIV- Mehdipatnam, Golconda and Karvan
CircleV- The Walled City and surroundings
Circle VI- Dilsukhnagar and eastern part of the city
CircleVII- The north-eastern part of the city.

CIRCLE-1A
SECUNDERABAD: The Younger One of the Twin Cities

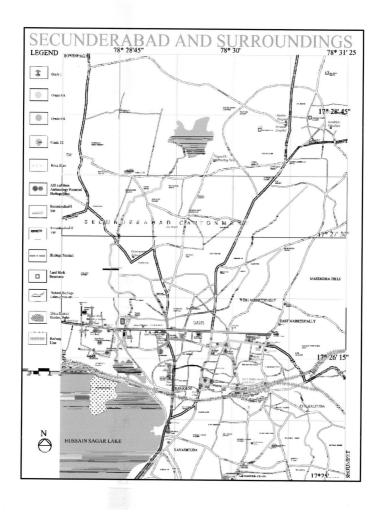

Monty's Hotel, Secunderabad

Secunderabad was founded in 1798 by the British, and was named after Nawab Sikander Jah, the third Nizam. The city is also referred to as Naya Shaher since it was a new city for the people already living in the walled city. Secunderabad mainly has the historic building typologies that were needed to start a European settlement: the churches, the residences, the schools, a club, a clock tower, etc. The Secunderabad Cantonment was one of the biggest cantonments of the British India that took the form of a British Settlement. It used to be the headquarters of the Hyderabad Subsidiary Forces.

The selection of the structures discussed in Secunderabad - I, II and III is based on the proximity of these structures to each other and alignment on the same road. The city of Secunderabad has some major roads, such as Sardar Patel Road, Sarojini Devi Road[7], Mahatma Gandhi Road-James Street, and Rashtrapati Road and Minister Road. They are all linked to the Secunderabad Clock Tower. Hence, the clock tower has become the most important landmark over the past several decades and has been discussed here first. The Clock Tower stands on the crossing of St. Mary's Road (north-south, leading to station) and Sarojini Devi Road (east-west).

SECUNDERABAD-I

The first section deals with the heritage components, located between the Clock Tower and the Secunderabad Railway Station.

Clock Tower, Secunderabad (Ref No. 2, Grade I HMDA, INTACH Awards 2005)

The Clock Tower was constructed in 1896. As one enters the city from the Secunderabad Railway Station, this is the most prominent landmark, boldly

expressing the European architectural style. Its clocks have now been repaired and the garden around it has been re-laid by the Greater Hyderabad Municipal Corporation. This site functions as a traffic island and the temple built on the same premises is a later addition. The Clock Tower stands on a square base plan. Among the main features of the Clock Tower, there is a unique element of a twin semi-circular arch heads (known as bifora also) with a keystone in the centre on all four sides of the clock tower. The surface is treated with ashlar masonry, a common feature of European structures.

Wesley Church Complex (Ref. No. N-6, Grade I, HMDA)

Towards the south of the clock tower there stands a modest structure in a big paved compound known as Wesley Church. The façade of the church is simple and composed of Gothic pointed arches. In the centre of the front façade two massive pillars and two pilasters hold the entrance hall. The interiors of the church are architecturally richer than its exteriors. The ceiling in the shape of a vault is composed of a series of pointed arches, supported on the console brackets and tie bars. The round ventilators with multi-layered mouldings are providing symmetry to the exteriors and the interiors. Rev. Burgess and Rev. Benjamin were the people who started this church in 1916.

One can go around the clock tower and take the road to the east, Sarojini Devi Road; 300 metres from the Wesley Church is St. Mary's Church.

Wesley Church

Wesley Church interior view

St. Mary's Cathedral (Ref. No. 26, Grade I, HMDA, INTACH Awards 2007)

It is a magnificent and a major construction of the nineteenth century in Secunderabad and is located in the St. Ann's School Complex, Sardar Patel Road. The orphanage and the school were opened under the care of three Italian nuns in the year 1859. The church structure was built around 1860-65. The façade of the church is donned with pointed arches, windows, turrets and buttresses. It is one of the landmark structures of Secunderabad. The giant Pieta statue in the courtyard of the church is a recent addition.

St. Ann's School, which shares the same campus with the church, has earned a big name for itself in quality education for Girls in the past several decades. In the later additional list issued by HMDA, the presbytery of St. Mary's Church is also added in Grade IIB.

St. Mary's Presbytery, St. Ann's School (Ref. No.N-7, Grade I, HMDA)

St. Mary's Presbytery stands on the same campus of St. Mary's Church, has also been added in the Grade IIB of the second heritage list issued by the

Development Authority. The presbytery was built in 1946 by an Italian priest and has been serving as the residence of the presiding parish priest of the church. The structure is simple looking, single storeyed, yet elegant. It has stone façade and is accessed from the church courtyard. There is a small garden surrounding the presbytery and small statues depicting the life of the Christ welcome the visitor.

St. John's Church (Ref. No 27, Grade I, HMDA, INTACH Awards 1998)

This church is situated on the East Marredpally Main Road, at the crossing, opposite St. John's High School. It is an Anglican Church, founded by Missionaries from England, almost 120 years back. Raja Ram Gopal Bahadur, the great philanthropist also contributed for the construction of the church, and later (in 1923) paid for its belfry too. St. John's Church was also known as the Church of England. The church has a European style of façade with semi-circular arches and pilasters. On the east and south side of the site of St. John's Church there are other Christian missionary schools: St. John's High School, Wesley Girls High School and St. John's Junior College.

The rich wooden ceiling, the altar and the pews (the long wooden seats) of the church have recently been repaired, under a restoration scheme. The church received INTACH Heritage Award in 1998. The exterior finish and landscape of the church give it a well-maintained look.

From the St. John's Church one needs to go to Patny Circle, RP Road to visit some more structures. The RP Road has some streets perpendicular to it leading to Shivaji Nagar.

P. Ramchandra Pillai Memorial Hall, CV Padma Rao Memorial Hall and Muthiala Raman Memorial Hall at Mehboob College (Ref. No. N-3, 4, 5 all three in Grade IIB, HMDA)

Gateway Mahboob College

Mehboob College was established in 1862 by one of the renowned Mudaliar businessmen. It stands on the starting of RP Road, right on Patny's Circle. It was meant to provide an alternative to St. Ann's School. It was also the first English medium school set up by the locals to promote teaching in English. At a later date, the sixth Nizam, Mir Mehboob Ali Khan decided to help the school with generous donations. In acknowledgement of his generosity, the school was renamed as Mehboob College. Different halls in the premises were named after the great celebrities of the city who had contributed to the cause of education. Three halls among these have been listed by the HMDA.

The entrance to the Mehboob College is through a gate which has a semi-circular arch enframed with round pilasters and topped with a simple yet elegant crown moulding. Further down, there exists another gate which exhibits different architectural features. It carries a semi-circular arch enframed with rectangular pilasters and is flanked by a scroll on either side. The gate is topped by an element similar to pediment with lime stucco in it. On either side of this gate stands a structure – CV Padma Rao Memorial Hall on the right and P. Ramchandra Pillai Memorial Hall on the left.

D Lakshmaiah's Residence (Ref. No. 95, Grade III, HMDA)

D Laxmaiah's Residence is located in Sivaji Nagar (near Doklama ki Gudi) in Secunderabad .To the west (left side) of the RP Road, there is a street that leads to Old Jail structure (re-used as market). Opposite this Old Jail structure, there is another street. Here stand two residential structures, close to each other, retaining the vernacular character of Secunderabad. The commercial spill over of the RP Road has reached up to this street. These heritage structures appear in a poor state of repair, and the haphazard electrical supply lines have affected their character in a major way.

D Lakshmaiah's Residence is a small and humble two-storeyed structure. The entrance door made of wood is surrounded by two semi-circular pilasters, topped by two brackets on the capital. The brackets support a lintel, known as 'hood'. On the right end of the property, the structure forms a smooth corner and here one can see the steel girders in the ground floor slab of the cantilevered part. Simple moulding around the window is designed in lime. The space between the hood and the door moulding is decorated with ornamental pattern of flowers. The first floor *chajja* has Manglore tile roofing that slopes towards the road side and is held on wooden posts topped with carved brackets.

The street opposite to the Monda Market, perpendicular to RP Road, goes to the Mahankali Temple – a 140-year-old temple of Goddess Kali. The area surrounding the temple has quite a few residential structures built with vernacular architecture; they contribute to the interesting street facade of

General Bazaar. The *Bonalu* festival (June-July) celebrated here is famous all over the city. The festival lasts over a fortnight.

D Pentaiah's Residence (Ref. No.96, Grade III, HMDA)

This residence is located next to D. Laxmaiah's Residence in Sivaji Nagar. This is another two-storeyed house in the category of vernacular architecture of Secunderabad with wooden posts, brackets, sloping cantilevered roof. *See picture to the right*

I Prakash Building (Ref. No. 17, Grade I, HMDA)

This structure is located in Shivaji Nagar, Secunderabad. The owner of this building is one of the leading businessmen of the city. The structure belongs to the category of the city's residential structures that are built in the vernacular style. This two-storeyed residence with its projected balconies, wooden brackets and cast iron railings in the façade, is easily identifiable amongst its modern counterparts. The beautifully embossed tiles seen in the ceiling, adds to the beauty of interiors, other than building's well-kept exteriors. On either side of the residence—on the ground floor—space has been left for the goldsmith shops. The ground floor level of the structure has jack-arched roofing.

Old Jail Complex, Monda Market (Ref. No. N-2, Grade II B, HMDA)

This jail was built in early 1930s. The structure could accommodate thirty-five prisoners–the small time criminals. The Jail was converted into a market after Hyderabad's integration with India.

It is a two-storeyed structure with a flat roof on top. The skyline of the structure is dotted with small domed kiosks at the parapet level. The horizontality of the structure is broken by the entrance, which projects out a bit in both the storeys. The ground floor has a verandah in front of the shops. The first floor has bigger space, as it includes the ground floor verandah. The windows on the first floor have simple yet elegant sloping projections, supported by the brackets. The first floor flat roof also has sloping projections, supported by brackets, at a regular interval, according rhythm to the modest structure.

Note: Adding following two structures to the trip may take more time if the visitor takes the option of walking.

Monda Market

Shyam Rao Chungi's Residence (Ref. No. 107, Grade III, HMDA)

This building is situated in Padmarao Nagar, behind new Gandhi Hospital, in Musheerabad. The area is known as Walker's Town. The entrance to the residence is from a huge porch of double-storey height. The porch has semi-circular arches. The building stands on a rough finished stone plinth. The parapet of the porch is simple, and a small crowning member with lime stucco work is inserted in front. The structure has a symmetrical plan with a central polygonal tower. The tower is

topped with conical roof with imbrication[8] providing light and ventilation through the carefully planned openings in the walls and the roof. The elements of the structure – the openings, the parapet, the roofing are designed in the Gothic castle style. Some more structures of the city, such as the All Saints' Church of Thirumalgiri, the main entrance gateway of Mahboob Mansion, the Public Garden gateway and the Ritz Hotel, are also built in the same style.

During the Asaf Jahi period, when the British cantonment was established in Secunderabad, this structure was probably occupied by a British Officer.

One needs to come back on the main road, leading to Koti. The next structure is nearby.

Mushirabad Mosque (Ref. No S-4, Protected by State Archaeology and Museums)

It is located in the Mushirabad locality, at a short distance from the new Gandhi Hospital. The mosque can be approached by a lane on the right, opposite a small Goddess temple on the left, beyond the Police Station. This road is full of timber merchants' shops.

The mosque was built by the Qutb Shahi King, Abdullah Qutb Shah (1626-1672). This locality was a small village at that time. The locality slowly grew in

population, expanded, and was named Mushirabad some time after 1785. The entrance of the mosque is from the main gateway that has three pointed arches; the central one is bigger than the other two: one on either side. The gateway is guarded by four lofty looking, yet miniature minarets, with <u>annulated shaft</u>[9] in them. These minarets rise from the top of the gateway roof.

The original façade of the mosque is not visible from outside. It has five arches and two lofty minarets, one on either side. The mosque had an extensive open-to-sky courtyard, with nearly hundred enclosures, built as a caravanserai, placed symmetrically on the three sides around the original mosque structure. Three gateways were built around the courtyard. This courtyard is now covered by lately added two-storeyed pavilions. They have staircases on both the sides, transforming the site plan and spaces of this historic complex.

SECUNDERABAD-II
This section takes the visitor to the north of the Secunderabad Clock Tower, crossing the Parade Grounds, and on SP Road, leading to Begumpet (to be discussed in the next area)

Le Palais Royal (INTACH awards 2003)
Located in Secunderabad, the Le Palais Royal was built as a residential structure in 1930s by one of the city's *nawabs*. The actual name of the building is Ibrahim Manzil. The structure is presently used as a Function Hall. Some small permanent and semi- permanent structures have been built over a period of time to facilitate the re-use of the function hall without disturbing the original facade and form.

The structure stands in a fair condition, very close to Paradise Crossing, in the east opposite Gymkhana Grounds. The symmetrical front elevation has an inviting porch in its centre. The porch has a panel of three pointed arches. The either end of the structure is three-storeyed with a high <u>Mansard roof</u>, a common feature in the French palaces, with gabled openings facing all four sides. The heritage structure had a circular water body in front of it. A beautiful fountain with <u>gargoyles</u>[10] used to be there once.

The structure displays a combination of different roofing techniques. The main structure is covered with Madras terrace and Jack arched technique. The railings used in the different parts of the structure—made with different materials—appear to be lacing up the structure in the front. The doors, windows, and even the niches (refer to Chapter 4), contribute to the uniqueness of the structure, making it a romantic place for functions such as marriage ceremony.

Prem Chand's Residence (Ref. No. 106, Grade III, HMDA)

The structure was made by a local *nawab* in the year 1925. It currently belongs to one of the descendents of Raja Deen Dayal, the royal photographer in the Nizam's court.

This heritage structure is located on SP Road, behind the Kanchi Paramacharya Centenary Bhavan, on the right of the road if approached from Patny Centre (east side). The structure has a big garden in front. Due to the social and economic needs of the road side land, the structures have come up in front of the heritage structure. The front elevation of the building is hidden behind a multi-storeyed structure. Only a part of the structure is visible from the road now. One needs to go in the eastern direction and from the crossing take a right turn, under the flyover. At a distance of 100 metres is Paradise Crossing.

Picture courtesy: HMDA website

Parsi Dharamshala (Ref. No.1, Grade I, HMDA)

The Dharamshala[11] is located near the Paradise Hotel[12] and the Paradise Crossing. The Peroji Bai Hall and Jamsheed Ji Chenoy Hall were built in 1919, by the Chenoy Family. There are a number of other structures attached to the hall, connected by a long shelter stretching from east to west. The Jamsheed Ji Hall is a fine specimen of architecture. The façade of the structure beautifully reflects the European architecture elements.

The building continues to be used in the same way since the time it was built and stands in a fair condition due to regular maintenance. It can be accessed from the Paradise Crossing while moving towards the Prenderghast Road from east to west; it stands on the left side of the road, not very far from the Paradise Crossing.

This area is a hub of commercial establishments run by the members of the Parsi community. The Chermas' and Universal Bakery are amongst the most

famous. There stands the old Parsi Fire Temple, next to Chermas' Shopping Mall referred as Seth Vicaji Seth Merji Agiary, built 170 years ago. It is the oldest Fire Temple of the twin cities of Hyderabad and Secunderabad. Opposite side stands another Fire Temple known as Anjuman Dar-e-Meher. It was built by the Chenoy family during 1920-22.

Monty's Hotel (Ref. No.65, Grade II, HMDA)

The hotel stands on the crossing of the S D Road and Park Lane – on the north-west corner of the junction. It is also known as Montgomery's Hotel and was started during 1880-90 for the British officers staying in the Secunderabad area. The hotel was also known for its bar. The heritage structure has Gothic pointed arches, the doors and beautiful windows, with an ornamental wooden *tracery* on them. The steep-pitched roof makes it unique among its new neighbouring structures. On the first floor, the doors open into small size balconies, decorated with metal grill and supported by cantilevered ornamental metal brackets with an intricate pattern. These brackets stand on pilasters, on the ground floor. The massing of the building is reflected even in the original compound wall of the heritage structure. The monotony of the compound wall is broken by the composition of small towers and metal grill panels connecting the towers. The entrance is highlighted by the introduction of huge *pylons* made of brick and lime mortar.

Air and Land Warfare Building (Ref. No. 34, Grade II-A, HMDA), SP Road

Special permission is required from the Air Force Head Quarters, Delhi, before visiting the premises of this site[13]. Presently known as the College of Air Warfare (CAW), this structure was constructed by the Nizam's army and was later given to the British to form a part of the Secunderabad Cantonment. The college has a number of structures built in the courtyard. The roofing is done with the Manglore tiles. The height of the verandah is kept less than that of the roof of the rooms to provide clerestory light and ventilation. The building is landscaped beautifully and well maintained.

STRUCTURES ON THE MG ROAD

The Mahatma Gandhi Road (MG Road) is the principal commercial street of Secunderabad; it is also known as James Street. On the east side of MG Road is General Bazaar.

Lakshmi Paper Mart's Building (Ref. No. 97, Grade III, HMDA)

Standing right on the MG Road in the west, quite close to Ramgopal Police Station, is the Laxmi Paper Mart Building. It is an attractive, small and modest structure.

The <u>segmental arches</u> on top of the doors, on the ground floor, exhibit the European architecture influence. These doors, give a way to the low height seating on the ground floor facing the main road. The owners proudly display their cultural heritage through old pictures which have been framed and put neatly on the walls of the ground floor entrance hall. The efforts of the owners of retaining its original character are commendable.

Mohanlal Malani's Residence (Ref. No. 98, Grade III, HMDA)

Next to the Laxmi Paper Mart Building is Mohanlal Malani's Residence. The residence can easily be identified by its façade of five arches and five ventilators. The first floor balcony overlooks the road and there is a beautiful wood work done in the form of *jaalis* above the arches. Ground floor of the structure is put to commercial use. Behind the arches there is a series of five panelled doors (with <u>fanlight</u>) and elaborate lime moulding around them. The balcony railing is another important feature of the façade.

There is a street to the right of the structure (towards the north), where one finds the brackets supporting this roadside balcony. This heritage property has a few shops on the north side road also. The corners of the building are decorated with ionic pilasters. Two windows overlooking the main road in the front elevation, with the same features as the balcony, add to the beauty and simplicity of the heritage structure.

Clock Tower and the Police Station, James Street (Ref. No. 42, Grade II-B, HMDA)

Some of the clock towers in the city are individual structure, while the others stand as an integral part of some famous heritage component. The James Street Clock Tower stands in fair condition[14]. This famous landmark of the city stands on the busy road of James Street, on the western side. It is a police station. The clock tower was fixed over the structure in 1900 (during the period of Nizam VI) by Seth Ram Gopal, a philanthropist of Secunderabad. The tower is built with the European[15] architectural features. The Police Station structure has three semi-circular arches and Tuscan orders on the facade facing the street. The orders carry a band of *tryglyphs* and *metope* crowning the structure.

Saidani-ma-Saheba Tomb (Ref. No. S-42 Protected by State Archaeology and Museums)

This tomb stands on the left side of the MG Road. From here onwards, the MG Road is known as Tank Bund Road, locally known as TBR. The tomb belongs to the mother of the noble Abdul Haq Diler Jung, a high ranking officer in Asaf Jahi court. Diler Jung died in 1896.

The Tomb was built in the late nineteenth century, predominantly with Qutb Shahi features; a bit of European influence[16] can also be noticed on the surface of the walls of the first floor. The tomb is full of ornamentation done with brick and lime mainly; the skill of the master craftsmen is visible on the interior surfaces and on the exterior as well. The structure looks quite similar to the ones in the Paigah Tomb complex, when compared with different elements existing on both the sites. The facade of this tomb has a set of five multi-cusped arches: three placed in the centre and the other two on either side with a wall panel of lime fretwork. The apex of these arches bears a   flower-shaped element made with lime stucco.

The ground floor and first floor roof have a meticulously designed parapet, with various elements from different periods of architectural history of Hyderabad. The first floor walls display a panel of three arches with apex ornamentation[17] in exterior. The dome of the tomb structure rises from first floor roof top. It has a square base but the squinches, transform the plan of the dome to circle, creating a drum for the dome. There is a basement in which lies the original grave of Saidani-ma. The dome of the tomb is surrounded by four part minarets (complete minarets can be noticed in other Qutb Shahi structures of the city) with a miniature balcony. Four similar minarets standing on the first floor terrace complement the composition of different elements in the historic structure. The tomb stands at the entrance of a big graveyard, which is still in use. There are the remains of a *baoli* in the graveyard with a number of beautiful old grave stones.

A couple of years ago a complete chemical cleaning was done by the Department of Archaeology and Museums, to give this tomb its original character and glory. The tomb carries the architectural and religious and educational value. The students of architecture, history and archaeology can come here and learn about different elements and principles of design, along with historic building materials and history.

THE TANK BUND ROAD

The Hussain Sagar Lake was built in 1562. Currently, it is a favourite spot for the locals as well as the tourists. The grand statue of Gautam Buddha that stands in the lake waters is the main attraction. The Bund links – as well as divides – the twin cities of Hyderabad and Secunderabad. The road on the eastern side of the lake is known as Tank Bund Road, and another one which runs parallel to it with lake's retaining wall is known as the Lower Tank Bund Road. The Secretariat buildings, the NTR Park[18], the Lumbini Park and the

Boat Club (a part of Secunderabad Club) are all on the southern side. The Saidanima Tomb (across the road), the Sailing Annexe and the Sanjeevaiah Park are on the northern side. The two Kakatiyan arches, one at the starting point and the other at the end of the Tank Bund Road, present a good replica of the historic architecture of old. On the left of the road, to the east side, there are a number of statues of the great personalities who contributed to the making of Andhra Pradesh.

SECUNDERABAD III - THE CANTONMENT[19] and its surroundings

Secunderabad Cantonment practically took the form of an English Settlement. Eight thousand British troops and their animals quartered here. It was one of the largest Cantonments of the British India. *The boundaries of the cantonment extended up to Bolarum, covering an area of nineteen square miles* (Campbell, Claude A. 1898). At the north-east of the cantonment there are two granite hillocks. The one which is far is known as Maula Ali and the other one is Kadam Rasul. The Parade Ground is an important location of Secunderabad Cantonment. To the south of the Parade Grounds is a main road called Sardar Patel Road[20]. On the south this road is flanked by government offices. In the west this road leads to Begumpet.

Secunderabad Club (INTACH Awards 1999)

It is a well known landmark structure for the people of Secunderabad and Hyderabad. As one takes the road to the north of the Patny Circle, cutting across SP Road, and proceeds about a kilometre away on the same road, one can see to the right (east side) the high walls of the Secunderabad Club. The entrance of the club has on its either side a small green mound and a cannon.

The Club was previously known as the United Service Club. It was constructed by Sir Salarjung I in the nineteenth century. This structure served as a convenient meeting and resting place for him on his way to cantonment from Diwan Devdi (near Charminar). Later on, it was donated to the European Officers' Club. The main structure of the club looks lofty and graceful. The entrance to this part is through a porch with a flight of steps opening into the lounge. This lounge was earlier known as Men's lounge. The ambience of the club can be greatly appreciated by looking at the volume and scale of the lounge.

AOC Record office, Moti Mahal

This huge structure is located in the limits of AOC Catonment, Secunderabad. Moti Mahal was conceived by the fourth Asaf Jahi Ruler, Nasir-ud-Daula, for his beloved named Motiara. The building has a simple plan. A two-floor structure, standing on round pillars, is covered by roofing technique similar to Madras Terrace; the  huge halls of the structure are covered with trusses. The structure once served as the British Head Quarters. Later, in independent India, it served as the Head Quarters of General J.N. Chowdhary[21]. It also housed the British Military Hospital for some time for which the hand-operated lift was installed here. Since 1953, it is with the AOC. Permission from the AOC Head Quarters is required for visiting this structure.

Military Hospital

A historic gateway(presently locked) inside Military Hospital

The British officers camped in some area in Secunderabad cantonment during the first war of independence (1857). It all started in haste – a temporary camp of tents, with a circular trench and embankments. The site, which was put up in a hurry, slowly took a permanent shape and was called Military Hospital. Some most important and original features of this hospital are: a church, three arched gates (refer to the sketch), water towers, ammunition magazines, and the officers' quarters. Additions and alterations have taken place over a period of time. The site of the Military Hospital continues to be used as a hospital. One of the water towers (presently used as pharmacy and barber shop) of the complex has received the INTACH Awards in 1998.

The Officers' Mess

This is a large structure and currently falls within AOC limits. It used to be the only Officers' Mess in South India at the time of the British rule and has the distinction of having entertained the British and foreign royalty.

The Officers Mess has one of the most beautiful and well-maintained lawns of the Secunderabad Cantonment.

All Saint's Church, Tirumalagiri (INTACH Awards 2002)

The church structure is located in Tirumalagiri, on the left (in the north) of All Saints' Road, five hundred metres further down the Tirumalagiri Crossroads. The church was constructed in 1860 and stands amidst the mature green trees and well maintained garden. It has a long central nave[22] with a sloping roof and two aisles, one on either side of the nave, also with sloping roofs. The crenellated parapet, the spires and the pointed arches collectively qualify its style as the Gothic Church architecture.

Military Reformatory, Tirumalagiri (INTACH Awards 1997)

This structure was built in 1870 to serve as a jail for the British Indian Army. The form of the jail reminds us of the Kaala Pani[23] Jail in Andaman. The structure has both the architectural as well as historical value. It is currently maintained by the army. It is also known as Windsor Castle, located in Tirumalagiri.

Gun Rock, Tirumalagiri (INTACH Awards 2002)

This structure, a water tank, stands on a hillock, close to the Lal Bazaar Crossing, in the eastern direction. It is visible from the main road. A pleasurable walk on the meandering pathways takes the visitor to the hillock. This outcrop of rocks came to be known as Gun Rock, when in 1836, the Secunderabad Contingent mounted a cannon to protect their first permanent settlements in the Tirumalagiri, Bowenpally and Bolarum[24] areas. Gun Rock provided an ideal location for a reservoir fed by the waters from Jeedimetla and Hashmatpet. This ensured a reliable supply with gravity flow. The British engineers have modelled the structure as a castle.

Lal Bazaar and Garrison Wesley Church

Lal Bazaar is famous for selling the military uniforms, their accessories and for catering to the daily needs of the residents of this area. It is a small stretch of road lined with articulate vernacular structures on either sides housing shops and residences. The bazaar starts at the crossing and ends at the post office and Wesley Church.

Standing at the end of the vernacular fabric of Lal Bazaar is the 120 years old Church, known as Garrison Wesley Church. The main road - State Highway No.1 (Cariappa Road) – from Lal Bazaar Crossing leads to Alwal and Bolarum. Alwal lies on the left side about 2.5 km from Lal Bazaar; Bolarum is another 3 km ahead further down the road. One can walk from the Lal Bazaar crossing to the Gunrock and back to see the market ending at the Garrison Church. The visit can be extended further to see the heritage components of Alwal and Bolarum (listed below).

Venkateshwara Temple, Old Alwal[25] (Ref. No. 89, Grade III, HMDA)

The Venkateshwara Temple is quite famous and is located near the Alwal Municipal Office, at a distance of 300 m from the Alwal Bus Stop (on Alwal-Tirumalagiri Road). The temple was built sometime between 1823-1843 by Maharaja Chandulal, the *Diwan* in the Nizam's Court. It is situated inside a walled courtyard. Next to the temple entrance there is an old water tank. A small temple which is part of the original temple complex houses a six inches small statue of Gundam Balaji in *Swayambhu* form[26]. This structure is said to be an oldest part of the complex, stands overlooking the water body. In 1996, when the structural condition of the temple was found to be very poor, part of the temple with single *shikhara* (the tower) was reconstructed. Presently, that same part stands with three *shikharas* devoted to different Gods and Goddesses.

There is a big wooden chariot – *Ratha* to carry the deity in religious processions.

There is also a temple of Lord Shiva (possibly of the same period) with a stepped water tank, enclosed by a wall. Entrance to the Shiva Temple is, visible from the above said temple.

Trinity Church, Bolarum (INTACH Awards 1997)

This church was built in 1846 in Bolarum on a donation from Queen Victoria. The land for this historic church complex was donated by the Nizam's Government during the Residency of General Frazer. The church was the place of worship for the British army officers and their families, following an Anglican way of worship. The interior of the church adorns the tablets of the loved ones of the British Army officers. The church is designed in the Gothic style of architecture. The white spires and the stained glass windows dominate the architecture of the church. The church has the original pews (the church seats), which, despite the passage of time, have retained their sheen. The stained glass at the altar, the pulpit and the bell are all in their original shape.

The cemetery next to the church also dates back to the mid-nineteenth century. It buries the history and the memory of the British officers and their loved ones of the time. The oldest grave is of John Alexander, who was an officer of the Hyderabad Contingent and died on 7 April 1851.

From Secunderabad we move to the next Circle IB-Begumpet.

CIRCLE IB

BEGUMPET AND SURROUNDINGS

Basheer-un-Nisa Begum, daughter of the Nizam II, received lands from her marriage to a Paigah noble. This village came to be known as Begumpet, located in the north of the Hussain Sagar Lake. Begumpet is famous for its airport, which used to be the only airport of Hyderabad, until the Shamsabad Airport came up. The structures discussed in this trip are from the Asaf Jahi period. The trip is planned to take the visitor to the magnificent structures patronised mainly by the Paigah nobles of the Asaf Jahi court. The first structure in this trip is the Vikhar-ul-Umra Palace.

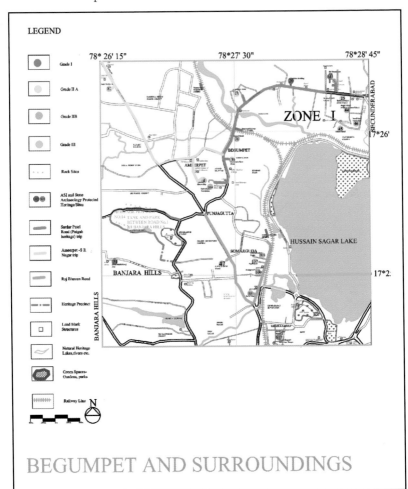

BEGUMPET AND SURROUNDINGS

Interiors of Devdi Nazir Nawaz Jung

Paigah Palace (Vikhar-ul-Umra Palace) (Ref. No.44, Grade IIB, HMDA)

Currently, the US Consulate office is located in this celebrated palace of the famous Paigah noble Iqbal-ud-Daula (Sir Vikhar-ul-Umra). It was constructed in 1890. Taken over, restored and extended by the Hyderabad Urban Development Authority, it is one of the most beautiful palaces of the city. After taking it over, HMDA got a new office complex built at the back of the heritage structure, setting an example for the good re-use of heritage structures.

Surrounded by a huge garden, the palace stands in the street off the Begumpet Main Road, opposite Hotel Tulip Manohar. A flight of huge steps starting from the mighty porch leads to a large entrance hall with two big elliptical arches on the walls parallel to each other. The palace is two-storeyed and the approach to the first floor is through a beautifully made wooden staircase, characteristic to Hyderabad's grand palaces.

The doors of the palace are unique, the pattern on them matches with the main elevation of the heritage structure. The heritage structure has a beautiful fountain in front and a garden in the entrance courtyard. This garden is a part of the original palace. The US Consulate authority has made many changes at site level and the building level, since they took over the heritage structure from HUDA (the earlier name of HMDA). The permission of the current authority is required before visiting the premises.

Spanish Mosque (Ref. No. 25 Grade IIA, HMDA)

Constructed by Iqbal-ud-Daula, the Paigah in 1906, the Spanish Mosque is a copy of a mosque in Spain and the only one of its kind in the country. It was once within the compound of the Paigah Palace (discussed above) at Begumpet. Today, it stands right on the SP Road with a 6 feet high compound wall, astonishingly unique in style. The mosque is famous for the uncommon shapes of its components, and resembles a church. Its Moorish arches in the elevation, a well proportioned porch, the octagonal domes and the minarets with sharp brass finials make the structure admirable. The central dome of the mosque stands on a square base and rises in the shape of a sharp pyramid (above the level of the main roof). The roof of the mosque is of Jack arch type made with iron girders, brick and lime.

The ownership of the mosque rests with the descedents of the same Paigah family. It is one of the best maintained mosques of the city, existing in its original shape even today.

Devdi Nazir Nawaz Jung (Chiran Fort Club) (Re.f No. 46, Grade IIB, HMDA)

Devdi Nazir Nawaz Jung is another good example of the re-use of a heritage structure. On SP Road, the left turn for Paigah Palace (the present US Consulate Office) leads to the dead end of this street; on the left stands the *devdi*: the majestic palace of Nawab Nazir Nawaz Jung. The palace was built by the Paigah noble Iqbal-ud-Daula in 1890s. Only one half of the *devdi* is being used as Chiran Fort Club, the other one is in residential use.

The plan of the *devdi* comprises the inner courtyards that add to the club environment. The structure presents a mix of ornamental features from different architecture styles. Transitional spaces of the *devdi* are adorned by a set of odd number of multi-cusped arches. There is a floral pattern on the apex, and at the springing points of the arches. There are single and coupled columns with fluted and plain shaft. These columns, often standing on the ground and sometimes on the pedestals, adorn the space. They add the fourth dimension-time to them: the era gone by. The inner courtyards with their palatial settings serve the need for an open air space. At some places there are semi-circular arches and ogee arches, surrounding a door and adorned with lime moulding. These mouldings are provided on the walls: around all the doors, windows, ventilators and the arches forming a rectangle. Different patterns of moulding and parapet design are adopted from the British architecture. The joining of wall and ceiling is highlighted by giving two bands of decorative plaster work close to the beam level and above the arch panels.

The efforts made by the present owners to retain the grandeur and original ambience of the *devdi*, are truly commendable.

Vikhar Manzil (Ref. No. 45, Grade IIB, HMDA)

The palace is situated in Prakash Nagar on a hillock. It is also known as Razzack Garh, after the name of its builder Mr Abdur Razzack, who was ADC to Vikhar-ul-Umra. Vikhar-ul-Umra bought it back from Abdur Razzak.

Entering from a lower level one comes up into an open ground with a fortified structure in front. Standing on a rusticated stone finish plinth the porch has barbicans (the fortified turrets) symmetrically designed on its four sides. The porch has three arches including the one in the centre-the entrance arch. These are tri-foliated arches[27], within the pointed gothic arches, rising from a Doric capital. The lower level has   semi-circular arches with rusticated stone finish. The roofing is done with Madras Terrace technique (with brick edge laid on the wooden joists). The louvered wooden doors and windows have beautiful moulding in lime surrounding their main post.

To go to the next structure one needs to come back on the SP Road and cross the road. There is a street next to Hotel Tulip Manohar, and Shakti Gas Agency. In this street stands Sir Ronald Ross Building.

Sir Ronald Ross Building (Ref. No. S-43, Protected by Department of Archaeology and Museums, INTACH AWARDS 1998 citation)

This is the place where the noble laureate Sir Ronald Ross discovered the Malaria parasite in 1897.

The structure has been restored with the financial assistance from the British Council and is presently being used as the INTACH office. A museum is proposed to be set up here in memory of Sir Ronald Ross. The structure has Mangalore tile roofing. Being located on a site full of mature trees, it provides a cool environment to its users.

Allauddin's Building (Ref. No. 20, Grade I, HMDA)

While travelling from Secunderabad to Begumpet, on the SP Road, one sees this structure on the right just before the shopping mall, 'Shopper's Stop'.This is the residence of the family of Sri Ghulam Allauddin and sons[28].

The structure displays a different architectural style[29] in the façade, done with coloured glass and intricate metal frame and grills. A very well ornate staircase stands out of the structure making the view of the house more interesting among the similar looking glass façade structures, on either side of this road. The entrance to the residence is through a line of beautiful flower pots, which leads to the marble steps. Here stands a beautiful water fountain, meant to give coolness to the courtyard which is covered with thick foliage of mature trees, bushes and creepers. This garden prevents much of the noise of the traffic on the busy road from reaching the house. The rectangular verandah serves as the entrance to the other spaces of the house. Its roof displays Madras terrace technique. The house is designed to provide for the natural light and ventilation in its every space.

Owner's permission is required before visiting the heritage premises.

Hyderabad Public School (Ref. No. 43, Grade IIB, HMDA)

Originally known as Jagirdar College, this institution was established in 1923 for educating the sons of *Jagirdars* and *Zamindars* (the landlords). After the abolition of *Jagirdari* and *Zamindari* system in 1949, it was affiliated to the Indian Public School Conference in 1951 and renamed as Hyderabad Public School in 1953. This heritage structure is one of the icons and landmarks of Hyderabad. The big palatial setting of the school is visible from the main road, on the way to Punjagutta Crossing from Secunderabad, before the Begumpet Railway Station flyover, on the right.

The pathway to the school structure from the SP Road entrance leads to a vast open space amidst the city's commercial spine. The main entrance to the school

is from a big flight of steps. Thus standing on a high podium, the structure welcomes the visitor to the elements of Indo-Saracenic architecture of Hyderabad. The shape of the domes here is similar to the ones seen in Unani Medical College, and Osmania General Hospital at Charminar. The smaller domed kiosks around the big dome appear to be complementing it. The structure is symmetrical to the main entrance axis. The pointed arches in the corridor (mostly odd in number) add to the horizontality of the heritage structure. The landscape around the structure is meticulously maintained and the campus is full of mature green trees.

The permission to visit the heritage structure can be obtained from the Principal of the School; the visiting hours are up to five o'clock in the evening after the school hours.

Vilayath Manzil (Ref. No. 76, Grade IIB, HMDA)

The present Country Club Building (low rise, old block) was once the *devdi* of Nawab Wali-ud-Daula Bahadur. He was the second son of Paigah noble Sir Vicar-ul-Umra Bahadur, and was born in 1877. Construction of the *devdi* continued through different periods - one of its wings was constructed between 1910 -1913 and the other, between 1920 and 1925. The structure has semi-circular arches with beautiful moulding and a keystone in the centre. The ground floor roof is kept flat whereas the first floor has got sloping roof with a pointed tower in one of its corners. The heritage building has been re-used as the Country Club for 15-20 years now. Some ancillary structures have been built around the Heritage structure (for the use of the club) over a period of time. The structure stands very close to the Lifestyle Store in Begumpet on the SD Road, and has a huge lawn with lush green grass, which perfectly serves the purpose of the club.

The permission to visit the structure can be sought from the club authorities.

Greenlands Guest House (Ref. No. 136, Grade III, HMDA)

The Greenlands Guest House stands on the SP Road. The plinth of the heritage structure is in stone. The heavy mouldings, the round columns and semi-circular arches borrowed from the Classical architecture have taken quite a simple look. These heavy mouldings adorn the parapet and the *chajja*. This character makes the structure to be a part of Classical Revival architecture in India. Presently it is being used as the HMDA office[30], earlier it had functioned as a government guest house. The rocks in the premises of the built heritage are very pleasing. Quite a few of them have been lost in the widening of the road. The fibre glass vault, on the roof of the porch facing the road, is a later addition to the heritage structure.

IAS Officers' Association (Ref. No. N-10, Grade IIB, HMDA)

The structure stands in a calm and green site. It can be accessed by walking into the lane of Chief Minister's residence and after crossing a few government buildings. On the right side of the same lane one finds the site of IAS Officers' Association building, a hundred-odd years old structure, standing in a good physical condition. Entering the complex one can see a swimming pool on the left and the well-maintained garden on the opposite side. The entrance to the main block is from a porch standing with round coupled columns and semi-

circular arches. The structure is covered with Jack arched roofing. The building functions as a meeting and gathering place for the local IAS officers. The permission of the concerned authority is required before visiting the premises.

After visiting this site one can go to Nizamia Observatory and then to Fakhrul Mulk's Tomb and Kukatpally Burj. Going to Raj Bhavan Road is another option.

THE RAJ BHAVAN ROAD

The Begumpet locality ends at the Railway Station; the road beyond the Greenland Crossing in the west leads to Ameerpet – the education and training hub of Hyderabad. The SP Road connects to the Raj Bhavan Road towards the east (avoiding the west side road to Ameerpet) at the next crossing.

Bella Vista -Administrative Staff College of India ASCI (Ref. No. 58, Grade IIB, HMDA, INTACH Awards 2000 and 2008)

The building received INTACH heritage award in the years 2000 and 2008. It stands on Khairatabad[31] Crossing. In 1931, the Bella Vista Palace[32] received the bride of the Prince of Berar, Azam Jah, son of the last Nizam Mir Osman Ali Khan.

After Independence the Government of India occupied the place. Later on, the college was set up on the model of the Staff College at Henley on Thames

River in England. The front lawns of today's date used to be full of dense shady trees in past. The structure is huge and has a number of entrances in the front and at the back. The main entrance has a massive wooden staircase with a beautiful wooden railing, of a monumental scale. The doors and the windows on the external facade of the structure contribute to the large linear elevation, resulting into visual rhythm. The front doors are made to look both festive and imposing. The living rooms of the prince are now being used as the rooms for the faculty. The architecture of the building has its origin in Europe and has an acquired local flavour.

Dilkusha Guest House (Ref. No. 108, Grade III, HMDA)

Since 1905, this was the residence of Sir Akbar Hydri, the Prime Minister* of Hyderabad. Presently painted in white, the heritage structure provides plenty of cool breezes, as it faces the lake. The name *Dilkusha* means, 'the one that pleases the heart'. The structure fully justifies its name, with open plan, good ventilation and plenty of natural light. The guest house presently provides lodging to the state dignitaries, the MPs and MLAs. It has a garden in front with a drive-way around it.

College of Nursing (Ref. No. 109, Grade III, HMDA)

This small heritage structure is located on the Raj Bhavan Road, between Dilkusha Guest House and the Post Office. It used to be the residence of a *nawab*. The structure was later taken over by the College of Nursing almost forty-five years ago.

Just behind the gate of the college that opens on Raj Bhavan Road, there is a beautiful circular garden, crossing which one finds the Nursing College building. The permission to visit the structure   cannot be granted as the spaces inside are being used for the lodging of the nursing students who go to Osmania General Hospital for their training. The building is done mainly in Mughal architectural style. It stands on a stone plinth. The plan and elevation of the structure may look symmetrical, but it is not. The entrance is from the porch providing the access through a multi-cusped arch. The porch is covered with wooden roofing members and on top there are two domed kiosks/*chatris* enhancing the role of the porch. The roof of the porch has a *chajja*, supported by the small brackets. On the left side of the porch there is a room (with octagonal façade) with a bay window in front.

The roof to this part (with three sides of the octagon) is again done with *chajja* and brackets in the exterior. The door on the upper floor is covered with a quasi-dome supported by brackets. After crossing the porch there is a main hall which is the present administrative office of the nursing college. The skyline of the structure is dotted with small-domed *chatris*, which gives this heritage structure its unique identity.

The building right next to College of Nursing which looks quite similar to it, houses the Post Office.

Raj Bhavan Old Building (Ref. No. 137, Grade III, HMDA)

Raj Bhavan complex is used as the residence and office of the State Governor. The complex has two structures of heritage value. The older structure, known as Shah Manzil, was built about 120 years ago; the later one is said to have been built around 1930 and its architect was Mr Heinz. Shah Manzil appears to be similar to the College of Nursing and Post Office (discussed above), which are situated on the same side on the Raj Bhavan Road. The Shah Manzil has a beautiful flooring pattern made in mosaic (with coloured broken tiles). The structure has pointed arches and round columns with an ornamental capital and is covered with a roof, which is similar to the Madras terrace roofing technique, a combination of primary and secondary beams.

The architecture of the second structure, built at a later point of time, looks similar to the Jubilee Hall, with a big flight of steps, cantilevered roof, shape of arches, the lawn and the design of open and semi-open spaces.

Crossing these structures on the left of Raj Bhavan Road one reaches the Punjagutta Junction. Following three structures could also be covered in this trip.

Nizamia Observatory (Ref. No. 4, Grade I, HMDA)

It is situated in Punjagutta, near CESS Campus (Centre for Economic and Social Studies). It was considered as one of the best observatories in India, especially the Astrolab. The Astrolab was presented by Nawab Zafar Jung, son of Sir Khursheed Jah Bahadur a famous Paigah Noble (refer to the Clock Tower Fateh Maidan, Circle II, Ref. No. 91). The observatory played an important role in the first ever international project for collaboratively photographing and mapping the skies the 'Carte du ciel'. The observatory, which was the first to have catalogued and mapped both the northern and southern skies, now stands desolate and in ruins. Nawab Zafar Jung, who donated a   15-inch refractor telescope and an 8 inch astrograph, established the Nizamia observatory in 1908. It is another unique building typology in the list of other heritage components and needs to be restored on a priority basis. The ownership of the observatory lies with Osmania University, and is presently closed.

The instruments of the observatory were transferred to the Department of Astrophysics located at Rangapur many years ago and these two barrel-shaped domed structures are lying vacant at present.

Tomb Fakhr-ul-Mulk[33] (Ref. No. 82, Grade III, HMDA)

The site is situated on SR Nagar Crossroads, two kilometres from Punjagutta Circle on the way to Kukatpally. It is the burial ground of Nawab Fakhr-ul-Mulk-II, his wife and the other members of his family. Nawab Fakhr-ul-Mulk[34], a famous noble of the Nizam's court, was born in 1857. He was a member of the Executive Council of the Nizam's Government and later became the vice-president of this Council. He was also made the in-charge of the Court of Wards. The *nawab* died in 1933. He and his wife started constructing this tomb ground much before their death. He is known for the marvellous construction of the Errum Manzil at Khairatabad. The site can be easily identified from the road by the skyline of the rising domes with sharp brass finials, and small minarets surround the big dome, right next to the SR Nagar Bus Stop. The necking of the dome is decorated with lotus petals.

Made with granite stone blocks, the tomb belongs to the group of City Improvement Board Style structures.

13 b) Ancient Gateway, Kukatpally

The gate can be seen on the main road NH 9, on the same road (from Punjagutta Circle to Kukatpally). The gate stands on the right, near the bus stop and opposite the Music World - a CD store.

The gateway has two multi-sided bastions flanking a huge pointed arch. The bastions have crenellated parapet and the oriel windows. Below the parapet are small brackets from Rajasthani architecture. The structure appears to be of early Qutb Shahi architecture.

Presently, the BJP city Party Office is located in a new structure abutting one bastion of the ancient gateway. The condition of the gate is fair, even after standing in the busy area.

The next locality is Circle II - Abids, the commercial hub of the city. Not many people are aware of the good density of the heritage structures in Abids and its surrounding areas.

CIRCLE II

THE NORTH OF THE CITY: KOTI, ABIDS, MJ MARKET, PUBLIC GARDEN, NAMPALLI AND SURROUNDINGS

The twin cities of Hyderabad and Secunderabad are connected by the Hussain Sagar Lake. The area between the southern limits of the lake and the Musi River (known as north of the city) grew up as a result of the growing congestion in the walled city. The main attraction of this trip stands in Koti locality – the British Residency.

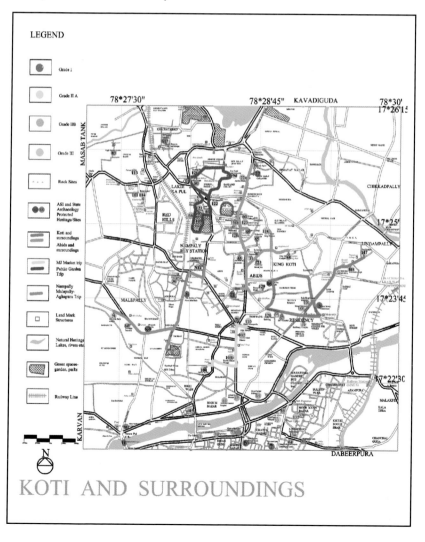

KOTI AND SURROUNDINGS

Moazzam Jahi Market

The Tank Bund Road bifurcates at the Liberty Junction. From here both the roads go to Moazzam Jahi Market (MJ Market), one via Gun Foundry Abids and the other via Nampalli-Public Gardens. Liberty Crossing, Bashir Bagh, Gunfoundry, Abids, MJ Market are situated on both the sides of the first road, while Adarsh Nagar - Hill Fort, Secretariat, Fateh Maidan, Public Garden, Nampally are situated on the second road. These roads meet again at Mozzam Jahi Market Crossing, lead to Afzalgunj[35] and end at Nayapul on Musi River.

The heritage structures of some of these localities have been discussed here.

I) KOTI and Surroundings

The area developed around British Residency (locally known as Kothi) was known as Koti. The British Residency had fortified wall around it with four huge entrance gateways. The influence of the European architecture of the Residency Complex can be distinctly noticed on several structures in the area; in a trip to Koti the visitor will experience the essence of European architecture in structures built on the Deccani grounds by local masons (designed by

Europeans mainly). There are some vernacular structures as well in Koti area, belonging to the community of traders, the Gujaratis and the Marwaris of Hyderabad.

Clock Tower, Sultan Bazaar (Ref. No. 5, Grade I, HMDA)

British Residency was constructed in the North of the River Musi in 1805. The clock tower was built several years later in 1865. At present, it stands in the busy

locality of the Sultan Bazaar and goes quite unnoticed because of the buildings that have come up right next to it. Structurally, it is quite simple. It has a square shape base. Each side of the clock tower has one semi-circular arch made in lime masonry with a simple version of keystone[36] and moulding on it. The clock tower rises to another level getting a little narrower than the base level. The top level is decorated by the simple crown moulding over which the parapet stands. Below the moulding, there is a clock on each side. The clock tower is an important feature of the city's history of the British establishment in the north (part of the city); it deserves proper maintenance and care.

Residency Complex (Ref. No. 49, Grade IIB HMDA)

There is an interesting anecdote about how the British Resident Major Kirkpatrick obtained the second Nizam's permission to construct this huge complex. The plan of this complex which the Major first presented in the Nizam's court was on a bigger sheet. Unaware of the scale of the drawing the Nizam rejected the plan of the structure as it required a huge area of land. The prime minister of Nizam Mir Alam, advised the Resident to change the scale of the drawing (keeping the same proposal). Hence, the second plan of the same proposal on a much smaller sheet[37] received the Nizam's approval. It was designed by P. Russel of the Royal Engineers in 1805, under the joint supervision of Raja Kanda Swami Mudaliar and the then Resident Major Kirkpatrick.

The chief entrance to the building faces north. There is a broad and open flight of marble steps leading up to a beautiful portico formed with six tall

Corinthian columns, fifty feet height. The construction of the 2.5 lakh square feet British Residency initiated an architectural movement in the construction of the palaces and mansions in the city of Hyderabad. The product of this movement was the Falaknuma Palace, the Paigah Palace, the Errum Manzil, to name only a few.

The first time visitor to the Residency Complex is likely to be surprised by the monumental scale. The length of pillars, their capital, the ceiling decorations, the wooden flooring, huge mirrors with golden borders around are all quite amazing. This structure is a true representation of the elements of European architecture, mainly the classical architecture.

There used to be a model (scale 1:10 approximately) of the British Residency main block built in brick and lime, in the open space of the garden in the complex: only the remains of this model can be noticed at present.

E.N.T. Hospital (Ref. No. 67, Grade IIB HMDA)

The ENT Hospital building stands in the busy locality of Bank Street Koti. It was formerly known as Pestonji ki Kothi and was built by the famous Parsi Bankers, Pestonji and Company, who supervised the revenues of Berar from AD 1839 to1845. Later, the building was then occupied by Raja Pratap Girji and was known as Pratap Girji Palace. It is now the E.N.T. Hospital.

The structure reflects the taste of its builder. The entrance is from the main road, the Bank Street, through a pair of bold entrance pylons. The pylon is a composition of four round columns capped with a beautiful crown joining all the four columns together, with a band of <u>metope</u> and <u>tryglyphs</u> made in lime on all the four sides.

The building is greatly influenced by the European architecture. The lower storey of the main structure has horizontal lines to imitate the stone masonry. The porch on the ground floor stands on four rectangular columns with rusticated stone finish plinth. On the first floor there are four fluted columns supporting a pediment, forming an integral part of the main façade of the building. The entrance to the heritage structure is from the porch. There are huge halls on both the floors, with their walls covered with ornamentation. The glass panels in the doors have beautiful etching of a flower vase. The ground floor hall which is at present used as an Out Patient Department (OPD) for the hospital has wonderful marble statues, towards the main staircase. This marble staircase has a marvellous baluster at the ascending level. The walls around the staircase at the lower storey are panelled with marble slabs. The beauty of the panelled doors here can be compared with the ones in Paigah Palace (the present US Consulate). The panels are made of wood and patterned with flowers and vase, with <u>festooning</u> around them. The hinges of the doors are big and made in brass. The roofing here is done with jack arch and Madras terrace technique. The doors of the first floor hall have around them ornamental plaster work done in lime.

Central Bank Building (Ref. No. 120, Grade III, HMDA)

The complex of the Central Bank Building is situated in the Bank Street area of Koti. The building belonged to the Raja Dubbak Samasthan (Siddipet Taluq, Medak District). There are three buildings in the area which have in them the Central Bank and the Neonles' Tutorial College. The structures are two-storeyed and display western architectural vocabulary.

From Bank Street one needs to go to Tilak Road to visit the Parsi Fire Temple[38] from there to Sultan Bazaar for some of the modest vernacular architecture structures.

Parsi Fire Temple (Ref. No. 86, Grade III, HMDA)

Built by the Chenoy Family, it is one of the three Fire Temples of Hyderabad (one at the Paradise Crossing, next to CHERMAS' store, and another, opposite Asrani Hotel). Before this, there was no temple in this locality. On community's request Lady Bai Manikbai generously agreed to build a temple (known as

Agiary); the temple was completed in 1904. The architecture of the temple is influenced by the European architecture constructed in the surroundings. The top of the temple displays HUMTA HUKTA HAVISTA which mean 'good thoughts, good words and good deeds'– the motto for the Parsis. The entrance to the *Agiary* is from a flight of steps in the courtyard. The entrance hall stands on round columns, with square base. The roofing of this hall is done with a combination of primary and secondary beams.

All important Parsi festivals are celebrated here. There is a library in the campus – in addition to the lodging facilities – for the members of the Parsi community. The plan of the temple is simple and composed of rectangles. The entrance steps that lead to the verandah, crossing the verandah is the space for worship. Daily *puja* is performed here in the main hall. The non-Parsis are not allowed inside the temple.

Nanu Bhai G. Shah's Building (Ref. No. 100, Grade III, HMDA)

Owned by one of the leading business families of Hyderabad, the building is located close to the Hanuman temple of Sultan Bazaar. The heritage structure is double storeyed and presently houses shops on the ground floor. The exact date of the structure is not known but it is believed to have been built about 100 years ago. The ground floor with its round <u>fluted columns</u>, the first floor with its iron railings and the second floor with its brick and lime railing, lend the building the city's vernacular architectural touch.

Raja Bhagwandas Building (Ref. No. 101, Grade III, HMDA) *Refer to the picture to the left*

This is a huge three-storeyed building located in the south of the Sultan Bazaar Crossroads. The structure is almost 100 years old, built by the family of the famous businessman Raja Bhagwandas[39]. In the past they were the noted Royal Jewellers of the Nizam. Once been a landmark, this structure lies uncared for today, amidst the commercial set up of the busy Sultan Bazaar Street. The heritage structure planned with an internal courtyard, provides the breathing space in today's congested locality of the Sultan Bazaar. The ground floor is used commercially. Both, the first and second floor, are rented out for residential use.

From Sultan Bazaar a road goes to Lingampally via Badi Chawdi and Kachiguada Crossing; here stands the Panjmahalla and Parwarish Bagh.

Panjmahalla, Lingampally (Ref. No. 117, Grade III, HMDA)

Panjmahalla is a palace complex, situated inside the gateway standing on the road in Lingampally locality, about 300 m away from Nruptunga Junior College in the eastern direction. This complex belonged to the Nawab of Machli Bunder and then to the Nizam. The street façade of the palace complex adds a historic character to this locality. Some of the space in this is used for functions. Some temporary structures are built here for this purpose.

Parwarish Bagh (Ref. No. 118, Grade III, HMDA)

Parwarish Bagh was the property of Nawab Moinuddaula[40], a Paigah noble from Amir-e-Paigah Asman Jah's family. The property is named after Parwarish-ul-Nisa Begum[41], the wife of Sir Asman Jah Bahadur, who was born in 1839. Thus, the property is almost 150 years old. There is a huge gate on the road which leads to the palace complex. A mix of different architectural styles can be seen in this complex.

From the roadside, one can see the stone plinth and Gothic arches surrounded by Ionic pilasters on the lower storey. On the upper storey there are gothic-pointed arched openings with Ionic pilasters. The openings have the wooden louvered doors with ventilators on top. There are glass panels fixed in the wooden tracery of these fixed ventilators. On the parapet there are barbicans, giving a defensive look to the structure. The main entrance to the complex is through a semi-circular arch enframed by engaged Doric pilasters. The structure stands opposite to (south of) Nruptunga Junior College, in Lingampally. The road on which the structure stands is parallel to the road leading to Kachiguda, from Kachiguda-Narayanguda Crossing.

ABIDS and surroundings:

Today's famous shopping hub of the city, the Abids Market was started as, 'Abid's Shop'. This shop was owned by Albert Abid, a Jew. He was a valet and steward-in-charge of the wardrobe of the sixth Nizam, Mir Mehboob Ali Khan. Abid owned the shop on today's Abids Crossing (near MPM Mall). A trip to Abids and its surroundings, i.e. Abids—Gunfoundary—Bashirbagh (located on the same road), takes the visitor to the residences, churches, clock towers, educational institutions and a club. Some of them have been put to re-use after independence as per the needs of the city. This trip can be taken from Liberty Crossing, if one is coming from the north of the city, i.e. Secunderabad.

The first building in this trip is Gandhi Medical College structure, standing close to the starting point of the Bashir Bagh flyover, on the left (east). The Lady Hydri Club is another structure standing in the same premises as Gandhi Medical College.

Gandhi Medical College (Ref. No. 22, Grade I, HMDA)

In 1890, this was the property of the Paigahs. It was meant for supervising the functioning of the Bashir Bagh Palace which does not exist anymore. Later, it was concerned with the administration of royal palaces. Before the structure was used for the Gandhi Medical College in 1954, it has also been used, for a long time, as the office of the City Improvement Board. The building is listed

by the HMDA for its architectural value. Recently been restored by a team of professionals the heritage structure is painted in pink and white colour, displays the influence of Mughal architecture style very beautifully. The corners of the structure have been adorned by small *chatris* at both levels of the parapet. The multi-cusped arches on the façade of the structure, the coupled column with lotus capital and the brackets supporting the *chajja* do not fail to capture the visitor's eye. The *jaali* made with lime have been restored now, which were covered with bricks at one point of time.

Lady Hydri Club (Ref. No. 70, Grade IIB, HMDA)

The idea of the Hyderabad Ladies' Association Club, as it was known, was mooted in 1901. The club came into the existence as a result of the combined efforts of Lady Hydri Casson Walker, Begum Khadiv Jung and Lady Glancy; it was meant to provide a forum for the English and Indian ladies to get together with mutual respect and affection. The foundation stone of the club was laid in 1929.

The building is single-storeyed; its landscape details are inspired by the Mughal architecture. It has huge halls covered with jack arched roofing and a technique similar to Madras terrace roofing. The doors are made with wooden panels. Each door is divided into three panels. The windows also follow the same pattern as the doors.

An entertainment centre is being built on the common premises of Gandhi Medical College building and Lady Hydri Club with Public-Private Partnership (PPP).

Andhra Patrika Building (Ref. No. 77, Grade IIB, HMDA)

Currently known as Loka Ayukta building, this structure stands in the busy locality of Bashir Bagh. Adjacent to Farhat Function Hall, on the right side of the road[42] one finds this structure. It is hardly visible from the main road due to the dense green foliage in the front of the building. This was the Guest House of the Bashir Bagh Palace[43]. Bashir Bagh Palace, one of the magnificent palaces of Hyderabad, was built by Sir Asman Jah Paigah (also known as Nawab Basher-ud-Daula) in 1868.

The guest house building was renovated by the City Improvement Board in 1930s[44]. The building was used as the Jagir Administrator office and for some time as Andhra Patrika Office; now it has in it the Loka Ayukta Institution. A new block is built at the back of the heritage structure as the extension of the office in early 1990s. Special permission is needed in order to visit this structure.

The structure is constructed on a simple, symmetrical plan with a few rectangular rooms. The ceiling is jack arched. This small and beautiful structure with a pediment standing on tall columns forming a portico with a very high ceiling, tells the story of the lost Bashir Bagh Palace complex. One can get a quick view of the heritage structure on the left from the Bashir Bagh flyover while coming from the south of the city.

Clock Tower Fateh Maidan (Ref. No. 91, Grade III, HMDA)

The Fateh Maidan Clock Tower stands on the crossing after the Bashir Bagh

flyover ends. Nawab Zafar Yar Jung Bahadur[45] (the youngest son of Sir Khursheed Jah Bahadur), the minister for defense department in Nizam's government, laid its foundation in 1903. The *nawab* personally paid for the entire construction of the clock tower and the sixth Nizam inaugurated it on his silver jubilee. The clock tower has a Gothic pointed arch on all four sides of the last visible storey. Each pointed arch is surrounded by pilasters on either side. The next storey appears to have an opening above which there is a sunshade, but this opening is actually a part of the wall. From outside only the moulding is visible. On the next storey, there are round clocks fixed in a circular enclosure, which is ornamented by moulding all around it. Above the clocks is the topmost storey, which is capped by pointed roof that stands on semi-circular arches on octagonal base. This storey has a beautiful cast iron railing on the edges of the parapet.

Nizam College (Ref. No. 60, Grade IIB, HMDA)

The Nizam College is on the main road, beyond the Bashir Bagh flyover on the left side, opposite the Fateh Maidan Clock Tower. The small *burjis* on the parapet wall of the college can be located from the flyover itself.

The built part inside the campus fits in beautifully well with the landscape. Different blocks have pointed arches and semi-circular arches; the verandah has a huge elliptical arch, facing the Principal's office. Most of the structures on the campus are one, or two storeyed buildings, giving uniformity to the structures, and also a savouring view to the visitor.

The original flooring in the administrative block has well-maintained tiles, with geometrical patterns. The building is painted in light pink with ochre bands. The original roof is done with huge primary and secondary beams, a technique similar to Madras Terrace.

The Nizam College came into existence after the merger of two institutions, Hyderabad College and Madrassa-e-Aliya (Ref. No. 128b). The Hyderabad College owes its origin to the first English School called the Anglo-Vernacular School. This school was started in Hyderabad in 1872 during the time of Prime Minister Sir Salarjung-I. With the changes in its administration, the Nizam College changed its location as well. Finally, it moved to its present location, Asad Bagh which was once the residence of the *Paigah* noble Nawab Fakhr-ul-Mulk.

Central Cooperative Training College (Ref. No. 127, Grade III, HMDA)

The heritage structure stands next to Nizam College. It was constructed in 1930. It is a two-storeyed structure with a classical façade of four fluted columns that carry a pediment[46] with *cyma recta* cornice and dentils. At the entrance, there is a huge hall with a capacity to accommodate a thousand people. This hall has been presently re-used as an exhibition space, originally known as Maharaja Kishan Prasad Hall after the name of Hyderabad State Prime Minister.

Madrassa-E-Aliya (Ref. No. 128b, Grade III, HMDA)

Standing very close to Mehboobia Girls College, it is the first structure after the Fateh Maidan Crossing, on the west side of the road. It was founded in 1871 by Sir Salarjung-I the Prime Minister of Hyderabad. It was then called Madrasa-e-Mubarak[47]. Two years later it was renamed as Madrasa-e-Aliya. The medium of instruction was English, and the teachers were mostly English. But after the Osmania University was set up, the medium was changed to

Urdu. It is now known as Government Junior College Aliya. The structure has a stone plinth and the entrance is from a porch which has six round columns. It is a two-storey structure. The ground floor is covered with jack arches. There is a wooden staircase to go on to the first floor. The classrooms here are covered with roofing that is similar to Madras Terrace Technique. The door lintels are designed with plain segmental arch. The structure is devoid of ornamentation.

Mahboobia Girls High School & Junior College (Ref. No. 128a. Grade III, HMDA)

The Indian nightingale Mrs Sarojini Naidu, Mrs Nandy, Begum Khadiv Jung and Lady Hydri are some of the famous personalities who are credited for setting up this school. They are said to have approached Nizam sixth, Mir Mehboob Ali Khan for this purpose through Mrs Casson Walker, the wife of Sir George Cassep Walker, the then Finance Minister. In January 1907, the school was opened with four girls and was first known as the New Zenana School and later it was changed to Mehboobia Girls School. Before being moved to its present location, the school was located in Nampally.

The structure originally consisted of the central hall with three small rooms on its either side. Later came up the south wing, and then the north wing to accommodate the increasing number of students. The new block was constructed in 1960, when it became a higher secondary school. The campus has internal courtyards. The most imposing part of the school complex can be seen from the road. It is a two-storeyed lofty structure made with granite stone blocks in City Improvement Board Style. This part of the complex stands on a

high plinth and with a big Osmanian arch[48] in the centre. The arched entrance is symmetrically flanked by a minaret, on the ends. The minarets terminate into domes canopies, going higher than the parapet wall of the first floor. These minarets have projecting sloped eaves/*chajja* on both the floors. The eaves are supported by the ornamental brackets.

The view of the heritage structure is different inside the campus. From the centre of the courtyard, one sees beautiful two-storeyed pavilion, approached by a two-way stairway. It is topped with six domed kiosks, four at the lower level and two at the upper level, symmetrically designed on either side of the *bangladar* roof pavilion.

Gunfoundry (Ref. No. S-6, Protected by the State Archaeology)

This is the structure due to which the locality around it was named as Gunfoundry or *Toph ka Sancha*. It is located in a lane opposite Mehboobia Girls College, just before the Lepakshi Handicrafts building. Gunfoundry was built in 1795 as a cannon manufacturing factory by Monsieur Raymond (fondly called as Musa Ram amongst his army). Today, it remains as a few massive brick walls and cubicles supported by brick and

mortar arches at ground level, and have brick kiln-like spaces underneath. Currently, it is a part of the densely populated locality, standing among residential structures and shops. The arches are lying almost buried in the earth at the level of the existing road. The site is protected by the Department of State Archaeology and Museums[49].

St. Joseph's Cathedral[50] (Ref. No. 85, Grade III, HMDA)

On 18 December 1869, at the Bishop's behest, Rev. A.Tagliabue bought an extensive plot of ground at Kotha Basti near Gunfoundry and built a church, a school and a convent for the growing catholic community of the city.

The approach to the church is from a lane just ahead of the CHERMAS' Readymade Store. A long flight of steps, beginning from the street, leads to a wide platform on which the church stands. St. Joseph's Cathedral displays a symmetrical front elevation. The massive towers with a square plan rise from the platform and are topped with <u>ribbed dome</u>[51]. The left tower has big old bells at the top. On 19 March1870, the first stone was laid by Vicar General Msgr.

Peter Coprotti. His father L. Malborti was entrusted with the execution of the church. In 1891[52] the façade and both the towers were completed and bells were installed. The church has pointed arches, semi-circular arches and Corinthian pilasters. The Nizam VII presented the clock (on the left tower) and a beautiful oil painting of Madonna and Child by Bartolome Morilio on 17 February 1953.

St. George's Church (Ref. No. 31, Grade IIA, HMDA, INTACH Awards 2008)

This church is a major landmark of Abids. Immediately after CHERMAS' Readymade Store, on the same road one finds a huge structure on the left, quite impressive in spite of its rustic, aged appearance. The church has the capacity to seat five hundred people. The construction of this structure was started in 1865, in the period of the British Resident Sir George Glue. This was the first religious congregational space for the Christian community of this area (known as Chaderghaut at that time). The British Residency officials collected liberal donations for the construction of this church. Then the members from the Church of England also subscribed to collect more money for the construction. The structure was completed in 1867 and received a good allowance from both, the Resident and the Nizam's Government.

St. Georges School Complex (Ref. No. N-1, Grade I, HMDA) *See Picture above*

The only European School in Nizam's Dominions[53], it dates back to 1814 and was built under the patronage of both the Nizam's Government and the Government of India.

Standing next to St. George's Church, the present school structure displays a date 1834 inscribed on the top. Originally the school was started in 1814 in a different building in Chaderghat. In 1860, the school was divided into two branches, one for the boys and the other for the girls. This time its name changed from Hyderabad Residency School to Chaderghat Protestant School. The school was renamed again in 1870s as St. Georges Grammer School; girls and boys received instructions separately.

Modern structures have come up around the older building of the school facing the main road; the heritage structure stands and still in its same original use. The school complex comprises a Girls' School, a Boys' School and a Preparatory School for the smaller kids. The school building is a two-storeyed structure, standing on stone plinth. The ground floor has a big semi-circular arch, flanked symmetrically, by six smaller semi- circular arches.

Opposite the school, on the main road, there is another small and interesting structure to the west of the Taj Mahal Hotel (on Abids Road) known as Punjab Crockery House, owned by a Sikh gentleman migrated from Pakistan. The metal work and the dome of the structure are uniquely done.

Taj Mahal Hotel (Old Block) (Ref. No. 123, Grade III, HMDA)

On the King Koti Road, adjacent to the Methodist School is the Taj Mahal Hotel, a heritage structure with its new block. The building is about seventy-five years old, previously a residence of a Parsi gentleman, and now beautifully re-used as a Hotel. The entrance to the heritage structure is through a lofty porch with a big semi-circular arch in front and two on the either sides. After climbing a few steps one enters the first hall where the reception desk is kept. Some interior elements that have been added to heritage structure enhance the beauty of the re-use. It consists of a big portico and over the portico there is an open roof. In the rear part there is a central hall and two halls in the side.

One can take the same road (on which the hotel stands), go in the east and reach King Koti.

Devdi Imaad Jung Bahadur (Ref. No. 116, Grade III, HMDA)

This *devdi* is standing near the Sher Gate locality of the King Koti-Gunfoundry area, and next to the SLATE School. It was the house of Imaad Jung, brother of Sir Nizamat Jung Bahadur, and was built during 1890-95. It had the Fine Arts College in it for some time. The lower level is made in rough finished stone. The upper level has four round columns supporting the pediment. The pediment once had stucco in lime; now only some impressions of it remain. The *devdi* stands on a high podium and is approached by a flight of steps from the side. It is in a poor state of repair and upkeep[54]. *Refer to the picture on the next page.*

One needs to come back on the road to Bogulkunta (to the south) and at a distance of a few hundred metres to the left one finds King Koti Complex.

King Koti Complex (Ref. No. 48, Grade IIB, HMDA)
 a) **Hospital (old)**
 b) **Usman Mansion:** It was a part of the palace complex but now demolished
 c) **Nazri Bagh**

Seventh Nizam acquired the complex before ascending the throne from a noble, Kamal Khan. Kamal Khan had his initials KK written all over the palace, these initials later represented King Kothi[55] when the Nizam acquired the palace. The area around this palace got its name King Koti or Kothi from the name of this palace.

The King Koti Palace complex stands parallel to the Narayanaguda–Abids Road, in the south. The courtyard and a compound wall facing the road is a later addition. Presently, the Administration Office of the King Koti General Hospital is located in the front rooms of this part of the palace. Beautiful floor tiles, with geometric pattern welcome the visitor to the porch (refer to Chapter 4). On entering the hall from the porch, one finds a beautiful pattern on the wooden *jaalis* in arched form, at a considerable height with the gilded ceiling. At the back of administrative office there is the Children's Ward of the hospital, in a beautiful hall that has about eighteen feet high ceiling. The hall has tall columns and pilasters with remarkable capitals.

Next to the old part of the hospital stands the new hospital. There used to be another part of the Palace complex here, known as Usman Mansion. The ramps of this new hospital block give a good view of the eastern side of the Nazri Bagh Palace which has a clock tower on its entrance gate. Frozen in time, it stands silent in the midst of the city's busy locality. In the north, facing the road, there is the main entrance to this palace– through a beautiful gate called Purda[56] Gate.

It is still draped in a huge canvas curtain. Prince Mukarram Jah the grandson of the seventh Nizam formed a trust in 2006 to protect the Nazri Bagh Palace.

Constructed with an amalgam of various architectural styles, the palace displays different types of roofs, such as flat roof, gabled roof, Mansard (or gambrel) roof. The palace has parapet walls and arches of different types: Gothic, semi-circular, segmental arches; it also has different types of doors, windows and ventilators. The Nazri Bagh Palace is closed at present. Also known as Mubarak Mansion, Nazri Bagh is the only surviving palace of the Nizam's King Koti Palace Complex.

Directorate of Industries (Ref. No. 63, Grade IIB, HMDA)
Located in Chirag Ali Lane, the structure was once used as the palace of Nawab Muqarrab Jung. The lane in which it is situated is named after the nawab as 'Kooche Muqarrab Jung'. Waheed Munawwar Khan entitled Muqarrab Jung was one of the famous men of Hyderabad. He officially worked in different capacities as *Subedar*[57] of Aurangabad in 1873 and as an Accountant General in 1887 and so on and died in 1890.

The building is now used as the office of the Director of Industries (also Commissioner of Industries). It is a typical *devdi* of late nineteenth century. It has got a central courtyard with a fountain (still functioning) in its centre, and all around it has rooms, arranged in a symmetrical manner. There is a large flight of steps at the main entrance. Its plinth is high but significantly less than in the past. The main façade of the structure has a hexa-style[58] pediment. The columns used in the front have circular shaft and resemble with Tuscan Columns. Other pilasters in the hall resemble Doric order. The building has another fountain in the right side of the main entrance. The railing used on the high entrance podium and the two projected windows on either side of the podium are remarkable for their beauty.

Golden Threshold (Ref. No. 23, Grade I, HMDA)

The residence of the India's Nightingale Smt. Sarojini Naidu, known as Golden Threshold, is located on crossing of Chirag Ali Lane and Nampally Station Road (opposite petrol pump) at a distance of 50 m in south of St. Lukes' Church. It is a small delightful place different from the huge grand *devdis* of the *nawabs* of Hyderabad. Mrs Naidu named the house after the collection of her English poems entitled Golden Threshold. In 1975, the house was taken over by the Central University of Hyderabad. The house has got a simple symmetrical plan with a façade of pointed Gothic arches.

There is St. Lukes' Church, another 120 years old a modest structure in the east

Golden Threshold

of Golden threshold. Standing on the east of the Station Road, this church is also known as Hindustani Church. It is the first church, which was started for the Hindustani community of this locality who converted to Christianity.

From this site one can walk on Nampalli Station Road to see the Land Administration Office, another attractive *devdi* and come back to Abids Junction. The next structure, Reddy Hostel stays on the main road in Hanuman Tekri, at a short distance from Abids (GPO) Junction.

Reddy Hostel (Ref. No. 129, Grade III, HMDA)

This structure displays the elements of the Buddhist architecture and stands out from rest of the buildings of the Hanuman Tekri. The Reddy Hostel was patronised by Raja Bahadur Venkat Ram Reddy, a prominent social worker of Hyderabad. Despite his busy schedule as Police Commissioner of Hyderabad he managed to work for the society. The credit for starting the Reddy's Hostel rests with him. The hostel was established in 1920 in the city. In the later years it could accommodate150 students. The structure also has a good library for the students. The structure resembles a temple, with its Buddhist Chaitya arches all over in the façade. The Reddy's Hostel building, as a whole, does not conform to any particular style existing in the heritage structures of the city.

One can come back on Jawahar Lal Nehru Road (JN Road) and to start with the next trip. Starting from GPO Crossing, walking on the same road for one kilometre one can reach the Mozam Jahi Market crossing. JN Road is the famous shopping street of the city, with the shops lined up from the Lepakshi Handicraft Showroom to MPM Mall (right at the GPO Crossing).

III) MOAZZAM JAHI MARKET

The area of the Moazzam Jahi Market (also MJ Market) was earlier a residential locality. A triangular piece of land was selected for the market site. To begin with the market mostly dealt with the food grains and general merchandise. Presently, it is one of the biggest and most famous markets of Hyderabad. Moazzam Jahi Market stands as a Traffic Island joined by several roads meeting from different directions. The road to the south goes to Afzalgunj. The one in north-east known as Jawahar Lal Nehru Road leads to Abids. The road known as Mukarram Jahi Road goes to Nampalli and the road to the east is known as Jambagh Road. Moazzam Jahi Market trip with heritage structures of commercial and residential uses can be planned at any point of time from morning till evening, if the visitor does not mind walking on the busy streets past vendors selling their wares at different locations.

Moazzam Jahi Market Building (Ref. No. 71, Grade IIB, HMDA, INTACH Awards 1996)

The Moazzam Jahi Market (MJ Market) structure was built by the City Improvement Board between 1933 and 1935. A clock tower facing the main crossing of the market was installed in one of the *minars* in 1935; the market was named after the younger son[59] of the seventh Nizam, Prince Moazzam Jah Bahadur (Shujaat Ali Khan). The material used for construction is granite stone, with jack arches roofing technique. The market has a flat terrace accessed by the spiral staircases; its interior courtyards form an integral part of the building designed with the city's climate in mind. There are a number of shops lined up on the roadside selling items ranging between fruits, dry fruits, vegetables, betel leaves, perfumery, metal workers and ice-cream. The FAMOUS ICE-CREAM Shop in the market is the visitor's delight; it serves a variety of handmade ice-cream to the people in all seasons. As one walk inside the courtyard along with the Osmanian arched verandah, one can see huge flocks of pigeon co-existing harmoniously with the shopkeepers. The market structure owes its triangular form to the shape of the site on which it was to be built. It is a centre of attraction for both, the local people as well as the outsider.

Opposite MJ Market stands the Karachi Bakery set up by a Sindhi family, who migrated from Pakistan. The fruit biscuits sold here are quite famous and have a unique flavour. Karachi Bakery is another major landmark opposite MJ Market structure.

Façade Baitul Ghouse (Ref. No. 102, Grade III, HMDA)

This heritage component is located at a distance of about a hundred metres from the MJ Market in the north and can be seen from the JN Road. Its façade has three similarly projected verandahs. The structure is about hundred years old. Its parapet is topped with big vases standing on the pedestals as a part of the parapet wall. In the centre of the front elevation there is an element similar to broken pediment made with lime mortar and bricks. The pattern of the parapet wall is different for the central part, in the form of a *jaali*. In the cantilevered part of the first floor, jack-arched roofing can be seen. The ground floor of the building has a commercial establishment.

Mahal Wanaparthy (Ref. No. 130, Grade III, HMDA)

The original name for this structure is Mahabhoopal[60] Manzil. It was constructed by Raja Rameshwar Rao II[61]. The family of the Raja came from Wanaparthy Samasthana (currently in Mehboob Nagar district) to the city of Hyderabad and made his permanent residence here in 1910. This structure stands on Jambagh Road, behind Vikranti Theatre.

Entrance gate to the Palace was on Jambagh Road with a beautiful garden and a water fountain in the centre. On the main entrance (south) there was a lofty porch[62] with a flight of steps, which further led to a voluminous verandah. Verandah leads to the central hall, which has three entrance doors. This hall was known as *Durbar* hall. The central hall opens into another rectangular hall with two huge elliptical arches on eastern and western sides. The main access to this rectangular hall was from the northern verandah. On both the storeys each verandah is attached to a set of one hall and two to four rooms.

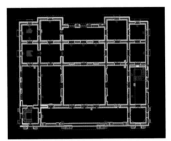

Planning of the building is done in a simple and symmetrical manner. The main entrance to the palace was from the south side. It is a double-storeyed structure, where the first floor came up little later than the ground floor. The central axis of the built mass passes through the Durbar Hall. The roof of this hall is higher than the first floor roof.

The domes on the south face are constructed with lime and terracotta tiles. The building is constructed with stone, brick, steel and lime, mainly. The interior surfaces, walls and ceilings are of smooth lime finish. The flooring on the entrance of both the floors is done in beautiful coloured tiles. Flooring of the other spaces is done with local stone in the checker board pattern. The wooden built-in cabinets are very much part of all the four halls on both the floors. The rainwater pipe on the top terrace has an engraving, which proves it to be imported from England.

Façade Hifazath Hussain (Ref no. 103, Grade III, HMDA)
The building is situated on the opposite side of the market, on the Moazzam Jahi Road, almost two hundred metres away from it. The structure is occupied by the shops that sell hardware and plywood. The building is about hundred years old. The entrance to the upper storey is through a pointed arch-shaped door. The structure forms a part of the city's vernacular architecture.

Goshamahal Baradari (Ref. No. 104, Grade III, HMDA)
Baradari refers to a residential structure with twelve doors. The Goshamahal Baradari was originally built by Sultan Abdullah and finally completed by Abul Hassan Tana Shah, the last

ruler of the Qutb Shahi dynasty; it was meant to serve as a pleasure garden for the royal ladies. The palace is supposed to have been connected with Golconda Fort by an underground passage. Later, Nizam's regular troops: an infantry regiment and an infantry of artillery worked from this place.

The structure displays the features of the Qutb Shahi architecture. The pointed Qutb Shahi arches are enframed by multi-cusped arches in interiors. The exteriors are dominated by intricate *jaalis* designed for the arched and rectangular openings.

Currently, the structure is being used by the local shopkeepers on the ground floor level (accessed from the road side). From the main entrance the Freemasons Lodge of Deccan can be accessed. *Baradari* is a beautiful specimen of historic architecture existing in the centre of the city and deserves proper attention and care. The area around it gets the name Goshamahal Baradari after this heritage structure.

IV) PUBLIC GARDENS

It is one of the largest city gardens in India, was also known as Bagh-e-Aam. It is located on the south of the Hussain Sagar Lake, close to the Fateh Maidan and has many small and big structures.

State Legislative Assembly

Originally it was built as a palace for presentation to Nizam VI, since he died before its completion, it was converted into Town Hall. It is one of the very

attractive historic structures of the city. This structure is not included in any of the lists published so far. While coming from north of the city, along with Hussain Sagar Lake, about one kilometre later, one begins to see some domes and minarets on the left. The exterior of the complex give the impression of a palace; which it is not; it is the State Assembly, old block. In front of the heritage structure there is a big black statue of Mahatma Gandhi, which is a recent addition. The new block next to it has the similar elements as the old structure. The soaring white domes and canopies of different sizes fill the sky. The combination of domes (an element of Qutb Shahi architecture) with multi-cusped arches and *jharokha* windows (originally an element of the Rajasthani architecture) define the Indo-Saracenic architecture designed by architect Vincent Esch.

Visitors require special permission to visit the premises.

The library of the Assembly stands at the end of the old block. This is another historic structure of interest which generally goes unnoticed. An attractive double-storeyed structure with a central hall twice as high, adds to the beauty of the Assembly structure. The library was built at the same time as the old block of secretariat. The beautiful lime ornamentation in the exteriors and interior is reminiscent of the architectural practices of later Asaf Jahi period. In the premises of Public Gardens, there are two more structures of academic interest: the Abul Kalam Research Library and the Osmania Mosque.

Jubilee Hall (Ref. No. 66, Grade IIB, HMDA, INTACH Awards 2001)

The Jubilee Hall is another very famous structure from the period of the Seventh Nizam. It was built in 1936 to commemorate the Silver Jubilee of the then Nizam Mir Osman Ali Khan. It is currently being used as the meeting place of state dignitaries, with a facility for conference and dining.

The discussion of the Jubilee Hall shall be incomplete without a reference to its lawns. The lawns in front of the Jubilee Hall are used for the regular flower shows, organised by the State Horticulture Department. The internal lawns provide a picturesque setting to the heritage structure. There is a small marble pavilion, where the Nizam held *durbars* and received *nazar* (cash offerings) and homage from his subjects. Jubilee Hall structure has rich interiors. There are original oil paintings of the last two Nizams. The surface of the walls has been treated with panels of arabesque, made in lime, in golden colour. Some organic/floral patterns are designed around the Osman Shahi arches. The column capitals exhibit the influence of the Egyptian architecture. The seventh Nizam is remembered, among others for the architecture of the Jubilee Hall and the surrounding structures in Public Gardens.

Jawahar Bal Bhavan (Ref. No. 105, Grade III, HMDA)

Standing in the green and cool surroundings of public gardens the Jawahar Bal Bhawan is a centre for children's activities and entertainment. The structure has educational value for the local citizens. It has a library, an aviary, swimming pool, a lot of toys and educative objects for children. The royal insignia of Nizam's Government is designed on the top of the entrance arch. Opposite to the Bal Bhavan is the Health Museum, the mirror image of Jawahar Bal Bhawan.

The architecture of Jubilee Hall, Health Museum and Jawahar Bal Bhavan dates back to the late Asaf Jahi Period and displays a judicious mix of a number of architectural styles, predominantly Islamic, in the ornamentation of interiors. The main features here are the *jaali* panels in the arches, the simple stucco work and the round column with the papyrus capital. The ceiling is two storeys high in the big hall. There are big pointed arched panels divided symmetrically in to three smaller archways. The arches of the archway rise from the base of coupled columns. Outline of the arches and their rectangular panel has been treated with decorative bands in lime, golden in colour.

Mini Bal Bhavan (Ref. No. 121, Grade III, HMDA)

The Public Gardens was the hunting grounds for the Nizams until the sixth Nizam converted it into a public use in 1872. In the same year an iron bungalow was shifted to the Public Gardens, from Farahat Mahal–a palace of the Nizam. It is a small structure consisting of deep verandahs on all four sides and wonderful cast iron work of *jaali* and a metal roof. It conforms to a western architectural style called 'Jugendstil'. Currently, it is being used as the Office of Horticulture.

State Archaeological Museum[63] (Ref. No. 69, Grade IIB, HMDA, INTACH Awards 2004)

The Museum is located in Public Gardens and is known for its Islamic architecture. It came into being in 1930 and has a well-equipped section of prehistoric implements, sculptures, paintings and other museum artifacts. The structure of the museum relates it to the group of Indo-Saracenic style buildings in Hyderabad. Standing next to the Andhra Pradesh Legislative Assembly structure, it has entrance through a gate close to the entry gate of the Assembly. The gateways of the Public Gardens, too, are remarkable for their architecture. These gateways display the features of a Gothic castle. A massive structure stands with a pointed arched entrance with a bastion on its either side. The crenellated parapet of the gateway lends it an interesting and mysterious look.

Ali Manzil (Ref. No. 122, Grade III, HMDA)

Situated in the street opposite Public Gardens, next to 'Westside' Showroom is the Ali Manzil. This residential structure is named after Ali Mohammed, the Murshid (the spiritual leader) of Sulaimani community. It is said to be 90-100 years old. It has beautiful sunshades over the windows and the sloped roof with ornamental brackets over the verandahs. The cast iron railing found on the ground and first floor is similar to the one used in Mahal Wanaparthy at Jambagh Road.

Kalanjali Showroom is located on the road, which is on the northern limits of the LB Stadium. Some of the hand-made souvenirs could be collected on the way to next heritage components.

Nizam Club (Ref no. 80, Grade IIB, HMDA, INTACH Awards 2006)

The Nizam Club is located in Saifabad, right opposite the State Legislative Assembly building. It is said to have been founded by Sir Nizamat Jung in 1888. He was the *Subedar* of Warrangal.

The entrance to the club is from a porch with a big semi-circular arch in the front and a set of two (one big, and one small) arches on its either side. The porch is made of stone, giving bold and rustic look to the structure, while the rest of the structure has a delicate look with lime finish and multi-cusped arches. The porch has a sloping *chajja*, supported on a series of small brackets—a distinct feature of the Mughal architecture. There is a reception desk just after the porch. A grand staircase behind the reception desk leads to the office room of the club on the first floor.

The arcaded verandah on this floor is attached to the banquet hall. The hall has jack arched ceiling, higher than the verandah, providing clerestory windows to the hall. The pilasters inside the hall are ornamented with flower and vegetal capital (similar to the Corinthian capital) and a fluted shaft. Various additions and alterations have been made to the original structure and site, over a period of time.

Roshan Manzil (Ref. No. 126, Grade III, HMDA)

Roshan Manzil is situated right opposite to Rabindra Bharathi[64]. It was built in 1915. There is an open yard in front of the house. The building has beautiful architectural features such as double staircase leading to the first floor, a side portion with wooden louvered doors and windows with beautiful traceries in their panels. The structure is continued to be used for a residence, and one needs owner's permission before visiting it.

Ritz Hotel (Hill Fort) (Ref. No. 94, Grade III, HMDA)

This extraordinary palace of Hyderabad was once the house of Sir Nizamat Jung, the Minister of Political Affairs in the Executive Council of Hyderabad State, during the rule of the seventh Nizam Mir Osman Ali Khan. Sir Nizamat Jung (refer to Nizam Club) was a great poet and a literary figure of his time. He was the founder of the Nizam Club. Sir Nizamat Jung built his house on the hillock adjoining the Kala Pahad rock. Later, it became the palace of Mir Moazzam Jah Bahadur, the second son of Nizam VII. The building once known as 'Hill Fort' is constructed in the form of a Gothic Castle. In 1950s the palace was put to reuse as Ritz Hotel. The hotel had to be closed down for a few years because of some dispute. It is currently being renovated; this is the part of the effort to restore its former glory.

Picture courtesy: Ar. Divay Gupta

V) NAMPALLI MALEPALLY AGHAPURA

In the east of Hyderabad Railway Station is the Aghapura locality. It was named after Hazrat Agha Dawood. Nampalli (Nampally) area is full of religious structures: mostly the *dargahs* and the mosques. There are many gateways to these *dargahs*, contributing to the historic fabric of the area. This trip starts at Nampalli Sarai and ends at Sitaram Bagh Temple.

Nampalli Sarai (Ref. No. N-12, Grade I, HMDA)

Nampalli Sarai stands on the entrance road to the Nampalli Railway Station. It was constructed by the seventh Nizam Mir Osma Ali Khan, and the foundation stone was laid by Sir Imam Ali, President of the then Executive Council. The *sarai* was planned with a big central courtyard. It is a two-storeyed structure entered through a monumental arched gateway. The ground floor has pointed arches and the first floor has multi-cusped arches. The structure was once used as the rest house of the Municipal Corporation.

Coming back from Nampalli Sarai, one has to go to Dar-us-Salam Road, near Ek-Minar Mosque. There are several heritage components here, mainly the entrance gateways to different religious structures that have come up over a period of time. One of these is the Dargah Yousufain.

Dargah Yousufain (Ref. No. 36, Grade IIB, HMDA)

The Yousufain Dargah in Nampalli is the sanctum sanctorium of the Hazrat Yousuf Sahib and Hazrat Sharif Saheb Quibla. Originally, Yousuf Saheb was from Egypt and Sharif Saheb from Syria. During their pilgrimage, they met the Indian saint, Hazrat Kalimulla Shah Jahan Abadi and under his influence they migrated to Delhi in India. Here, they joined the Aurangazeb's army. When this army reached Hyderabad, the saints were overwhelmed by the cruelty and killings of the war. They chose to spend the rest of their lives in the remembrance of God.

The *Urs* is performed every year at the dargah and the devotees flock here from different parts of the world.

The huge yellow dome of the dargah can be easily noticed in the Nampalli locality which is rich in the religious and cultural heritage.

Gate Portion Dargah Nooruddin Shah (Ref. No. 13a, Grade I, HMDA)

Dargah Nooruddin Shah is situated on Dar-us-Salam Road. Behind the gate is a high graveyard. This locality came into existence during the period of the sixth Nizam Mir Mehbub Ali Khan. If one comes from Old Malepalli, on the Darussalam Road, one passes through the entrance gateway to the Dargah Nooruddin Shah on the left (north). This gate, which represents the cultural heritage and religious wealth of the locality, is, sadly, not in a very good condition.

While coming from Dar-us-Salam Road, passing a number of monumental gateways on both sides

A monumental gateway in Nampally

of the road one reaches the Goshamahal Crossing. Apart from the main road these are standing in another street of Aghapura also. Across the road is Panmandi a market for the fresh betel leaves, locally known as *paan*.

Dhanrajgirji Complex (Ref. No. 59, Grade IIB, HMDA)

This is the largest of the palace structures that exists today almost intact in form and function. The entrance of the structure is from Pan Mandi Road (Aghapura to Dhoolpet). A number of shops selling betel leaves are lined right up to the entrance of the complex. Raj Dhanrajgir Ji was one of the famous people of Hyderabad, belonging to the family of Dasnam Gosais, the followers of Sri Shankaracharya. He was well-educated and renowned for his philanthropy. His family maintains this 160 years old[65] palace complex.

Walking through a long shaded pathway, ascending a few steps, one finds a grand verandah on the left and a beautiful water channel with fountains on the right. The double-height verandah reveals the scale of the grand palace. The entrance to the structure is from this verandah. A number of statues methodically placed in the complex give it a look of a European Mansion (house). The complex is planned symmetrically and a statue of *David* stands at the focal point of the huge central courtyard. The two blocks on the left and right are attached through bridges to the central block. The exteriors as well as the interiors of the palace are really admirable. The big central hall still stands with its grandeur. The gilded ceiling, the fan-shaped brackets, the rich upholstery, huge pictures, the marble seats, outdoor lamps combining all of them one is overwhelmed by the wealth of this palace.

Permission of the owner is required for visiting the palace.

Ghode ki Kabr [66] (Ref. No. N-14, Grade I, HMDA)

It is believed that this is the resting place of a well-bred horse which was remarkable for its speed and alacrity. It is said that one day, when its master (a soldier from Nizam's army) was riding it, the faithful horse suddenly fell and died. The grave has a small statue of the faithful horse and the area around the grave is known as Ghode ki Kabr. No authentic source could be found out to know the correct date of the construction of this heritage component.

After visiting the two structures here, one may return to the crossing and continue to go on the road to the west towards Malepally (Malepalli).

Bhoiguda Kaman (Ref. No. N-9, Grade I, HMDA)

This arched gateway known as Bhoiguda Kaman leads to a series of the gateways on the road it stands. On the west side of this road are some more gateways leading to the famous dargahs of the Nampalli locality. The gate has a big Qutb Shahi arch topped with small minarets on both the ends of gate. Condition of the gate is reasonably good. The development on this road is more or less low-rise; because of this the original character of the religious site remains intact, to an extent, and the visitor can get a better view of the gateway.

Puranmal Samadhi (Ref. No. 84, Grade III, HMDA)

It is situated near Sitaram Bagh on the Asif Nagar Road. Seth Puranmalji, a Marwari businessman was the contemporary to Maharaj Chandulal, the Prime Minister of the Nizam IV. He made a beautiful garden in Asif Nagar in 1850. The compound wall of the garden and the two melon-shaped canopies inside can be seen from the road. The canopies are built on the *samadhis* of the members of the Seth's family. A canopy stands on twelve pillars with brackets; they can be can be accessed by an open staircase.

Sitaram Bagh Temple (Ref. No. 28, Grade IIA, HMDA, INTACH Awards 2000)

This temple was built some two hundred years ago, either during the reign of Nizam III, or IV. This structure is a unique typology in the list of all heritage components of Hyderabad. It is a walled temple complex, with different types of structures to serve different functions. The complex contains huge gateways, two temples, *gaushala* (cow shed), a *vedic pathshala, samadhis, baolis.* There are a few houses inside the complex – for the owner of the complex (a descendant of the founder, Sri Puranmal Generiwal) and for a few brahmin families. The lofty wall of the temple looks like a fort wall. The ambience inside the temple, the ages-old statues, the sculptures in the complex transport the visitor to the world of spirituality.

For its upkeep and maintenance, the temple received two villages in Berar from the Nizam and later in 1814, some land in Aurangabad district from Maharaja Chandulal, the Prime Minister of Hyderabad (between1832-1843). The statues of Sitaram Swami and Varadhrajaswami, to whom the temples are dedicated, are made of marble stone and brought  from Jaipur in Rajasthan. A trust has been set up by the Generiwal family to look after the temple affairs. The open green space near the temple entrance is being used commercially for functions. Due to the disrupted network of water bodies of the city, the old baolis of the temple complex are not clean anymore.

From Circle II we move on to the heritage components of the Circle III the Masab Tank and Mehdipatnam.

CIRCLE III

MASAB TANK AND MEHDIPATNAM

MASAB TANK: The term 'Ma Saheba' refers to Hayat Bakshi Begum (refer to Circle VI-Hayat Bakhshi Mosque and Serai), the Queen Mother. She is a famous name in the history of the Qutb Shahi lineage, the only daughter of Mohammed Quli Qutb Shah. A tank, named after her, as Ma - Saheb Talab, once existed, where Chacha Nehru Park stands today. The heritage structures discussed below are presently hidden by the surrounding buildings. The access to the heritage component is not difficult, but the fact is that most of them do not exist in their original form and in good condition; nonetheless, they are worth visiting as they are an important part of city's architectural, cultural and religious mosaic. A trip to this area is useful in rediscovering various architectural and natural typologies that were a significant part of the era gone by. The trip could be started from Chacha Nehru Park. After visiting the park one can go to the Vijay Marie Church.

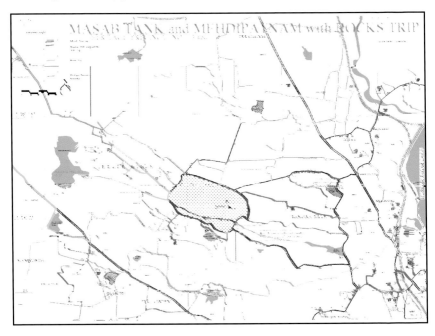

Vijay Marie Church (Ref. No. 83, Grade III, HMDA)

The church, variously referred as Arogya Mata, Our Lady of Health and Our Lady of Khairatabad is the first ever octagonal church of India. It is situated in Chintal Basti near Mahavir Jain Hospital and Saifabad Barracks. The church is said to have been built by Mir Osman Ali Khan (the last Nizam) in 1959. The construction of the existing structure—originally a smaller one built in 1905—was necessitated by the growing number of devotees each year.

The altar of the church is remarkable for its octagonal shape and visible to all the devotees from all sides.

Khusroo Manzil (Ref. No. 111, Grade III, HMDA)

Nawab Major Khusro Jung Bahadur, was the son of the Major General Nawab Sir Afsar-ul-Mulk Bahadur, the Chief Commander of the Regular Forces, at the time of Nizam VI. Nawab Khusro's father died in 1930. Khusroo Manzil is situated on a hillock between Lakdi-ka-Pul and Masab Tank. It was built in 1920.

It has a strange façade, with unique architectural vocabulary that is reflected in the components of the building. The six long and round columns in the front elevation has <u>papyrus capital</u>. The structure is approached by a long flight of steps which turns to the left and then to the right. At the end of the first flight of stairs there are lamp posts on either sides. There were four of them earlier; only three remain at present. The last part of the staircase provides access to the main floor from two sides. The front part of the structure has a verandah with five tall

semi-circular arches. On top of the central arch there is an element made in lime which seems to be a royal insignia.

The structure has jack-arched roof with iron joists. It was previously used by the Census Department; its present use (a warehouse) is harming the heritage structure.

Asman Mahal (Ref. No. 113, Grade III, HMDA)

The name Asman Mahal to this structure is given by the public after a movie called Asman Mahal a couple of decades ago. The actual name of the heritage structure is Mumtaz Mansion. It was built in 1911 by Mumtaz-ud-Daula, the son-in-law of Nawab Afsar-ul-Mulk. In 1980s the building was purchased by the Mukarram Jah Trust. At present, it is functioning as a students' hostel owned by the same trust, and partly as the Wardon's Lodge. The structure stands on a small hillock in the Masab Tank locality and can be seen from the Lakdi ka Pul-Masab Tank Road, on the right (north) side of the road in a street, next to the petrol pump.

The entrance to the structure is from a mighty porch through a semi-circular arch. The main elevation of the structure is quite impressive. The lower two storeys of the structure are made with rough finished stone. On the first floor there are semi-circular arches contained within the pointed arches, overlooking the street. The most interesting feature of this structure is the conically capped circular tower, with hexagonal openings which goes beyond the height of parapet wall of the last floor. This element originated in the Early Christian architecture was used mainly in the defense structures.

Baitul Ashraf (Ref. No. 114, Grade III, HMDA)

This is approximately a hundred year old heritage structure, once the home of the poet Dr Ashraf. It is presently known as Saba Function Hall. A few additions have been made to meet the needs of the reuse of the structure.

The building stands on an elevated plinth and is treated with rough finish stone. The four tall fluted columns with ornamental capitals hold a pediment. This central part of the building is projected outwards. The central verandah is flanked by two rectangular balconies on either sides on upper floor, and sit-outs on the lower floor. Different elements of the structures seem to be influenced by the European architecture. The front doors of the ground floor have fanlights on top.

Tipu's Lookout, Lakdi-ka-Pul

This structure is associated with Tipu Khan. He was a noble of Nizam, who constructed a culvert near Golconda.

Tipu's Lookout is a defense structure. There is a stone staircase constructed on three ascending arches. At the end of the staircase there is an enclosure on the Hillock. From here one gets a good view of Khairatabad. It could have been a watch tower that was in use during the siege of Golconda by the Mughals. Later on, this structure became a part of the house of Liyaqat Jung. Son of Liyaquat Jung worked for the Nizam's army and served as a chief of his guard after the merger of Hyderabad State with Indian Union in 1948. This structure exists due to the efforts of the local citizens.

Khairti Begum's Tomb and Mosque (Ref. No. S-17, Protected by State Archaeology Department)

This heritage site is located on the road behind Dwarka Hotel, in Lakdi-ka-Pul locality. It was built by Kairat-un-Nisa[67], daughter of Sultan Mohammed Qutb Shah (1612-1626), for her tutor Akhund Mulla Abdul Malik.

The mosque has a façade of three arches and two tall minarets. These Qutb Shahi arches have medallions in their spandrels, the apex of the arch hold a fruit-like object, with a bewildering design of entwining creepers[68] spreading both sides of the apex of the arch. Due to addition of a verandah in front of the mosque, it is difficult to see the original elevation, yet one can appreciate the scale and the ornamentation of the mosque in the rear view. In the rear elevation the central part of the structure projects out. The ornamentation in the exterior surface of the structure starts at the level where the walls and roof meet; a row of double beads with another row of petals in lime run all over the mosque. This row becomes a base for the arched alcoves. On these alcoves sits the *chajja*, supported by brackets. Above the *chajja*, there start another level of arches, with a perforated screen at the back. The top of this level is kept quite delicate, with the repeated crossing of a diamond shape pattern, made in lime. The minarets display an ornamental honeycombing pattern on their surface. There are three multi-tiered arches in the interiors of the mosque.

The tomb of Akhund is built with a square plan. It stands on high plinth with a façade of three blind pointed arches on all four sides. The arches are decorated with cut lime plaster and the floral-shaped medallions. The entrance side has a few steps up to entrance door, which is enframed by the central arch. The structure is covered with a huge dome surrounded by four smaller minarets. The tomb[69] remained vacant as the tutor died in Mecca.

The surroundings of this heritage site needs to be cleaned and maintained on regular basis.

Visiting the mosque the visitor can plan to go to PRASADS, an attractive modern structure and quite favourite among city's youth. One has to go in the eastern direction to reach this Multiplex; at PRASADS one can watch some good movies and shop also.

BANJARA HILLS AND JUBILEE HILLS

Banjara Hills derives its name from the nomadic tribe, the Banjaras, who once inhabited this rocky area. Nawab Mehdi Nawaz Jung was the first civil servant, from Asaf Jahi court who planned to settle here. Slowly, this sparse residential development gave birth to rapid urbanisation.

Development of another rocky terrain is associated with the Silver Jubilee celebrations of Mir Osman Ali Khan's coronation. This is Jubilee Hills, today's posh locality of Hyderabad.

The trip to Banjara Hills and Jubilee Hills is a treat to the lovers of natural heritage. The built heritage of this trip is unique as it merges very well with the natural heritage components[70] of the site. This trip[71] is divided into two sections. The trip can be started from Errum Manzil[72], standing on the main road, close to Punjagutta Crossing. The other part of the trip is devoted to the invaluable rock heritage of the city.

Some sites in this trip are declared as Heritage Precincts by the HMDA. These are marked in the map.

Erram Manzil[73] (Ref. No. 47, Grade IIB, HMDA)

Hyderabad heritage has a different building typology amongst the big palace structures. It is a palace standing on a hillock and guarding the locality at the lower level. Falaknuma and Erram Manzil are the examples for this typology.

Nawab Fakhr-ul-Mulk, an aristocrat of the Nizam's court built this palace for himself in 1904, on a hillock beyond Khairatabad locality. The nawab stayed in the palace for quite some time. The interior and exterior finishes of the palace complex are done quite lavishly. To maintain the grandeur of the palace Fakhr-ul-Mulk appointed an army of attendants and to attend to him[74]. These people were given free quarters inside the palace compound.

A long and majestic flight of steps from the east side ends at the main entrance of the building. The plan of the palace is huge measuring around 400'x500' approximately. Clustered arrangement of the quarters around different courtyards can be experienced as one visits the vast palace. In the front elevation the palace looks to be planned in a symmetrical manner, but it is not completely symmetrical. The designer attempted not to disturb the natural beauty of the site while placing different blocks of the palace complex. The architecture of the palace is a mix of different styles such as the European, Mughal, Rajasthani.

After 1948, the palace was put to re-use. More than two decades back the Central Record office was situated here. Currently, the Chief Engineer's office of PWD, the Roads and Buildings Department and State Architect's office are functioning from this heritage structure, and permission from the concerned authority is required to visit the place.

J Vengala Rao Park (HMDA List- Heritage Precinct No. 14)

Situated opposite Metropolis Bakery on Road No.1 Banjara Hills, this park was started in 2002. The entrance of the park is designed with steel members. Three arches at the entrance gate greet the visitor. It is made around a lake[75]. Stones are arranged around the pond. The park has a play area designed for the children and arcade games and cafeteria for all age groups.

Devdi Mehdi Nawaz Jung[76], Road No. 4, Banjara Hills (Ref. No. 21, Grade I, HMDA)

Nawab Mehdi Nawaz Jung (1894-1967) was greatly impressed by the landscape and natural terrain of Banjara Hills. He decided to develop it as residential area along with his friends, and built the first house in Banjara Hills, for himself. His love for the rocks has become a family tradition. They do not destroy rocks but build house with them inside.

This structure is a modern residential unit, built in 1930, appreciated for the uncommon interiors and exteriors. Two huge rocks go through the living room, washroom and finally spill into the garden, making people feel like living with nature. The house is actually a part of the list of the built heritage components, yet it embraces the natural heritage, too. This uniquely constructed house gives different views when seen from different angles.

Mehdi Nawaz Jung was appointed as Municipal Commissioner of Hyderabad in 1937. He received Padma Vibhushan in 1965.

Kasu Brahmananda Reddy Park, Jubilee Hills (HMDA List, Heritage Precinct No. 13[77], INTACH Awards 1999)

Located in Jubilee Hills the park sprawls over seven hundred acres. The park represents some special features displaying a beautiful combination of natural and built heritage. These components are the natural rock formations, the flora and fauna, the lake and the residence of the Prince Mukarram Jah known as Chiran Palace. It also has a mosque close to the south-east entrance of the park, made on the lines of modern architecture, from the remains (stone *jaalis* mainly) of the older structures by architect Mariott. It is a simple but an outstanding structure.

Lotus Pond, Jubilee Hills (INTACH Awards 2003)

Located in the Jubilee Hills area inside MLA Colony, it is part of the Qutb Shahi water management system. The idea of this park was conceived as an eco-conservation project, where an effort has been made to bring the natural elements together into a manmade-cum-natural space. The park is designed around a small water body.

The pathway created in the park is 1.2 kilometres. Completed in the year 2001, this park is a home to different species of birds. It is maintained by the GHMC.

Hakim's Tombs (Ref. No. S-14, Protected by State Archaeology Department)

INTACH Awards 2001, commendation

The Hakim's Tomb complex is situated at the south western end of the Jubilee Hills, on Road Number 86, towards east, could be accessed driving past Apollo Hospital. The site is locally known as Dargah Hakim Nizamuddin Geelani Quadri. It contains grave (dated 1649) of a Hakim of the reign of Abdullah Qutb Shah (1626–72). There is a mosque and a *Khanquah*[78] (hospice) attached to it. This novel structure, in the shape of a vault, is open from all four sides. From the rear deck one can enjoy a panoramic view of the Qutb Shahi Tomb, fort of Golconda (about 5 kilometres in south-west) and a wonderful sunset, too.

The design of the structures is simple and has minimum ornamentation. Climbing a few steps, one enters the tomb. The entry to this structure is from a Qutb Shahi arch, with two blind arches on either side. The tomb stands on a square plan with a huge dome in the centre. The dome rises from the first storey of the tomb. On the corners the tiny minarets rise just till the parapet level of the dome. It makes the overall composition simple and balanced. The mosque has a simple façade of three arches, with *minars* at both the ends. The roof of the mosque is made with three shallow domes, standing with the help of squinches.

The mosque stands at the end of a courtyard which provided accommodation for the students and travellers at one time. A part of this courtyard, in front of the mosque is covered with the RCC verandah, added at a couple of years back. The other part of the courtyard has the rooms and a cistern in centre. These rooms are habited at present.

THE ROCKS OF HYDERABAD

Tortoise Rock

Monster Rock (No. 6- HMDA list, Heritage Precinct- Rocks No. 6)
It is situated between Jubilee Hills Society's Road No. 71 and Road No. 70 (near Film Nagar) in Journalist Colony. It can be seen from the road after Jubilee Hills Public School.

Obelisk (No. 9- HMDA list, Heritage Precinct- Rocks No. 9)

Obelisk is located on Road No. 66 in Jubilee Hills Society, in front of a residence next to the office of Society to Save Rocks. Sristi Art Gallery is close to this site. It is a piled-up rock formation on the side-walk.

Tortoise Rock (No.7- HMDA list, Heritage Precinct- Rocks No 7)

In the south of Jubilee Hills Road No. 52, stands the Tortoise Rock, within limits of BN Reddy Hills. It is restored in good shape.

Cliff Rock (No. 5- HMDA list, Heritage Precinct Rocks No. 5)

It is situated opposite Prija Rajyam Party Office, between Road No. 46 and 45 in Jubilee Hills, near Dr Ambedkar Open University.

Toad Stool (No. 8- HMDA list, Heritage Precinct- Rocks No. 8)

Toad Stool rock can be accessed from the Road No. 35, Jubilee Hills and is located at a distance of half a kilometre in the south-west of Dr M Chenna Reddy HRD Institute. This site belongs to Blue Cross Hospital. One can get a good view of this rock while standing in front of the Hospital entrance. It is a single formation in rocks overlooking Kaveri Hills.

Bear's Nose (No. 3, HMDA list, Heritage Precinct- Rocks No. 3)

This beautiful rock is situated very close to Shilparamam, behind Cyber Towers, right side of the road to Baan Info Systems.

Shilparamam is another favourite site of the tourists. Designed by Architect Sri G Shankar Narayan, this is an Arts and Crafts Village, located on Hi-Tech City Crossing. The site has a lake and a Rock Gallery, too. Artists from different parts of India and world come here and display their talents ranging from arts, crafts, dance, drama, etc. All Indian festivals are celebrated here with full zeal.

Mushroom Rock (No. 4, HMDA list, Heritage Precinct- Rocks No. 4)

Mushroom Rock is located in the south-eastern part of campus of Central University of Hyderabad, Gachibaoli, ten kilometres west of the city. Central University second gate is a right way to reach the rock site, which is a single rock formation.

Hillocks around Durgam Cheruvu (No. 1, HMDA list, Heritage Precinct- Rocks No. 1)

These hillocks are also known as Shore Hillocks. The lake Durgam Cheruvu is surrounded by rocks on one side and encroached by new settlements on the other side. The lake's existence was kept a secret to prevent sabotage during the time of war. It was the source of water supply for the Golconda Fort, for centuries together. It is located at a level higher than the highest palace of fort. It provided piped water to the people living in Golconda Fort. It is the best example of the engineering fete of Qutb Shahi rulers in Hyderabad.

The entrance to Durgam Cheruvu is next to Ambedkar Open University, Jubilee Hills. The lake attracts the visitors with boating, trekking and other outdoor activities. It is quite popular among couples. In the north-west of this site stands the State Gallery of Fine Arts.

Kothaguda Reserved Forest

Previously been in the outskirts, now it is very much part of the modern Hyderabad, the Hi-tech City. It is located at a distance of two and a half kilometre from Shilparamam, in east, near Forest Department Colony. This is the first Botanical Garden of Andhra Pradesh and coming up in stages in Kothaguda Reserved forest. The site area of this reserved forest is 120 acres and contains hundreds of varieties of plants. This place attracts all age-group visitors and astonishes them with a mega-size tortoise-shaped structure, housing a hundred varieties of Cactus.

The park has natural forests, the rock formation, a water body, slides, rich grassland and green meadows.

Rock Park (No. 2, HMDA list, Heritage Precinct Rocks No. 2)

This site is easily visible while coming back from the earlier site. The Gachibaoli Mehdipatnam Road meets the Old Bombay Road, it goes to the city.

Rock Park is situated near Khajaguda Village, after Prashanti Hills, off Old Bombay Road. Close to the Rock Park is located the Hussain Shah Wali Dargah. It is a long rocky ridge with many massive impressive formations. It is an ideal location for the adventure park[79], but not yet landscaped in the form of a park. One can experience a beautiful view of the ridge while driving on this road.

There is a two hundred year old Temple Complex on Old Bombay Road known as Laxman Bagh. It received INTACH Award in the year 1999. It is owned by the Pitti family of Hyderabad.

The next Circle for the discussion is Circle IV – The Golconda and Karvan.

CIRCLE IV–MEHDIPATNAM, GOLCONDA AND KARVAN

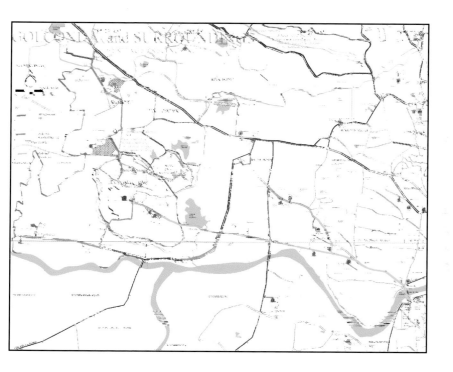

MEHDIPATNAM

Mehdipatnam, one of the busy areas, is located in the western side of the city. It connects the Golconda fort (via Reti Baoli) with the rest of the city. On the eastern limits of Mehdipatnam is the Old Bombay Road. The geographical terrain of this area offers commanding views to the historic structures standing here.

The trips to Mehdipatnam and Masab Tank can be clubbed together as both the localities are close to each other. From Mehdipatnam, the trip can be extended to the Golconda Fort. The trip to the Golconda Fort is also possible via the historic trade route Karvan. The first of the heritage structures in Mehdipatnam trip is 'Mr Krishna Reddy's Building'.

Mr Krishna Reddy's Building (Ref No. N-8, Grade III, HMDA)

This heritage structure, believed to have been the residence of a noble from Asaf Jahi court once, stands on the eastern side of Inner Ring Road, opposite the Crescent Hospital, Mehdipatnam. The two-storeyed heritage structure displays, mainly, the features of the Mughal architecture: the multi-cusped arches with fluted columns, the domed canopies with *chajja*, which is supported on miniature brackets.

The lower level of the structure is built with stone masonry. The entrance is from a rectangular porch which is designed with a set of three arched openings in front and one big arched opening on its either side. The structure is being used as a shooting locale for movies.

Yousuf Tekri (Ref No. 110, Grade III, HMDA)

The building belonged to Nawab Yousufuddin Khan, a *subedar* of Gulberga, during the reign of the sixth Nizam Mir Mehbub Ali Khan. The Yousuf Tekri so called because it stands on a *tekri* (a hillock) is more than 120 years old and is built in the form of a castle. The lower storey on the hillock is constructed with rough finished stone. The retaining walls are meant to strengthen the structure against the thrust generated by the rocks.

The most attractive feature of this structure is the treatment of corners in the exteriors, along the surface of the upper floor wall up to the parapet. These corners are ornamented by stucco in lime with Gothic features. The rectangular windows are topped with semi-circular ventilators that have lime mouldings around them. At the top of the semi-circular part of the window, the moulding is made in the profile of an Ogee[80] arch.

The Yousuf Tekri also is a favourite spot for the shooting of movies. The watchmen and caretakers look after the heritage structure.

GOLCONDA FORT (Inner Fort Protected by the Archaeological Survey of India)

The Golconda Fort is situated in the western part of Hyderabad about nine kilometres from Charminar and sixteen kilometres from the Hussain Sagar Lake. Earlier, it was a mud fort, built by the Hindu Kakatiya rulers, it was later strengthened by the Bahmani and the Qutb Shahi kings between fourteenth and seventeenth centuries. Golconda, as we know was the capital of the Qutb Shahi kings.

The outer fort wall is 4.8 kilometres long in periphery, encircling a historic settlement. The inner fort has the ruins of the palaces, the mosques, the pavilions, the gardens, etc.; its highest pavilion, known as Bala Hisar, is located at a height of 130 metres from the surroundings. Currently, the inner fort is protected by the Archaeological Survey of India, and two of the outer fort buildings, the Khazana Building and the Shamsheer Kot, are included in the list of the State Archaeology.

Golconda Fort has educational value, in addition to its historic, religious[81], architectural and archaeological values. The ruins of the heritage components inform us about the building techniques, and the use of building materials that were prevalent in the Qutb Shahi period. There is another site, on a hillock, an incomplete structure, located in the north-east of the Golconda Inner Fort, known as Naya Quila (the new fort).

A trip to Golconda Precinct thus has several historic structures of interest for the visitor. The trip can begin at the entrance of the Golconda Fort; after visiting the main fort one can proceed to the Naya Quila and other heritage structures as suggested below:

Golconda Fort Area (Ref. No. S-2, Protected by Archaeological Survey of India)

Golconda Fort is the oldest part of the city of Hyderabad and has been a focus of attraction for a large number of historians, archaeologists and the national and international tourists. Different building typologies found in Golconda Precinct[82] are – the Gateways, the fort walls, the Inner Fort with the palaces and the *baradaris*, the ramparts, the bastions, the mosques, the gardens, the tomb gardens, the tombs, the caravanserais, the *baolis* (stepped wells) and the baths (*hamam*). The Golconda heritage precinct includes the complete fort area within the outer walls, Qutb Shahi Tombs and Sheikhpet Sarai and extends right up to the south-west of Old Bombay Road. (Refer to Precinct boundry in the trip map of Circle No. 4)

Naya Quila

Naya Quila is situated in the north-east of the Golconda Fort and it was built by Abdullah Qutb Shah. This area was used as a base by Mughal Emperor Aurangazeb for his first attack on Golconda in 1656.

There are two built heritage components and one natural heritage component inside Naya Quila. The heritage components are the mosques known as Mustafa Khan's Mosque dated 1561 and Mulla Khiyali ki Mosque dated 1570. Right opposite Mulla Khiyali's mosque stands the natural heritage component Hathiyon ka Jhad, the Baobob tree. It is of African origin and more than two hundred years old. It has a hollow trunk.

Qutb Shahi Tombs (Ref. No. S-9, Protected by State Archaeology Department)

The tombs stand in the north side of Golconda Fort, approached either through Banjara Darwaza, or from the Toli Chowki Road. The site is a necropolis of the Qutb Shahi Kings, Queens and their family members. The complex includes tombs, mosques, mortuary bath, a *baoli* (step well) and a site museum (added by the State Archaeology Department).

The tombs represent the finest of the Qutb Shahi art and architecture. The site plan of this complex displays a geometrical layout based on straight lines, squares and rectangles. On the right side of the walkway there is a small mosque with three pointed arches in its front, known as Abdulla's Mosque.

At a distance from here, on the opposite side, there is an incomplete structure–the tomb of Tana Shah[83]. The tomb complex is remarkably cool even in the hottest month of summer, thanks to the numerous fruit and flower trees with good foliage. The defined pathway of the site opens into various tombs and mosques. The most magnificent tomb of the complex is the tomb of Mohammed Quli Qutb Shah. It is enclosed by a wall and stands on a high terrace amongst a well laid garden with the water channels. This tomb can easily be identified by its uncommon façade of pillar and lintel system–quite distinct from the usual façade of an odd number of Qutb Shahi arches (three, five, seven, nine).

All the tombs standing here share a few commonalities; the plan of the tombs is square, and rises from a high podium. The Qutb Shahi arches make the gallery of the tomb supporting the domed ceiling with the help of squinches. The main dome is designed symmetrically in the centre of the plan (refer to the plans of the Tombs in Chapter 4). The dome rises from one/two storeys high cuboid base. The dome has a necking of lotus petals and is complimented by the minarets at the four corners. At the front and rear entrance of tombs big urns made of stone can be noticed. Even the railing of the entrance is embellished with the lime moulding and stucco work. Small vents have been provided in the huge domed structures for the natural light and ventilation. The big *minars* have an arched gallery at different levels, creating an effect of solid and void. The *chajja* is supported by the stone brackets. The intrados (inner surface) of Qutb Shahi arch is decorated with plain or designed mouldings, and the spandrels have the round medallion.

The structures standing in the Tomb Complex includes Tomb of Abdullah Qutb Shah, Tomb of Syed Ahmed (refer to Footnote No. 3) , Tomb of Hayat Bakshi Begum, Tomb of Qutb Shah, Tombs of Premamati and Taramati, Tombs of Mohammed Qutb Shah, Sultan Qutb Shah, Ibrahim Qutb Shah, Subhan Quli, Jamshid Quli, Mirza Mohammed Amin and the mosques.

Shaikpet Mosque and Sarai (Ref. No. S-13, Protected by State Archaeology)

It is located in the Maruti Colony, Shaikpet village, to the north of the Qutb Shahi Tombs. There is a Sai Baba Temple opposite the heritage complex.

The Shaikpet Sarai was built during the period of Ibrahim Qutb Shah (1550-1580). Trade caravans from different parts of India and abroad halted at this caravanserai waiting for a clearance from the officials to enter the walled city of Golconda.

The *sarai* complex consists of a mosque, a caravanserai, stables for horses, tombs and other minor structures, currently in partial ruins. The mosque has an interesting front facade dominated by two minarets *(See the sketch at left)*. In between the mighty minarets stand three multi-tiered pointed arches with a pair of medallion on both sides of the arch apex. The terrace of the Shaikpet Mosque is accessible through a staircase. From here one can get a good view of the Qutb Shahi Tombs and the Golconda Fort.

Opposite the mosque stands the *sarai* — a two-storeyed structure composed of a number of rectangles in plan. The rectangular cells of the *sarai* were meant to be used by the travellers at night. The verandah in front of each cell was probably meant for tying the horses; the flat roof was probably meant to be used by the travellers at night. Next to the mosque there is another structure, a roofed pavilion. This has the graves inside. There are a few more tombs in the *sarai* complex.

The entrance road to Shaikpet Sarai, in Maruti Colony meets the Old Bombay Road in the east. From this junction one can go back to the street going to Hussain Shah Wali Dargah.

Hussain Shah Wali Dargah (Ref. No. S-16, Protected by State Archaeology)

Hussain Shah Wali Dargah is also the burial ground of the saint. The holy saint died in 1692. His devotees celebrate the *urs* here regularly and maintain the dargah premises. The architecture of the main shrine conforms to the Qutb Shahi style. The sanctum sanctorum is a domed structure, in which a number of arches carry the load of a massive dome at the base. A system of the netting of the arches is designed in the drum to distribute the load of the dome.

Little ahead of the dargah structure, on the opposite side there is a graveyard. A beautiful pavilion with graves, is covered with Bangladar roof attracts the visitor. This place is culturally and architecturally rich as there are quite a few elaborate structures with the graves of the saint's descendants, around the main dargah structure. There is a *naqqarkhana* also, standing opposite the dargah structure.

On the way to the dargah Complex, there is a *baradari* on the left, while coming from south-west side of the Bombay Road (as suggested in the trip). It is said that a very famous saint Syed Mir Hussaini also called Majzoob[84] stayed here, after being evicted from the fort of Golconda, at the time of Mughal seize.

Taramati Baradari (Ref. No. S-10, Protected by State Archaeology Department)

The Taramati Baradari, built around 1625, stands on a hillock, on the left side of Golconda Gandipet Road near army officers' houses. It is attributed to a famous dancer of the Qutb Shahi court during the period of Sultan Abdullah Qutb Shah and Sultan Mohammed Qutb Shah. The structure provides picturesque views of the Golconda Fort and the Premamati Baradari. The structure is basically an arched pavilion standing on a high platform of 150'x150'. There is a new Convention Centre built on the foothills of the *baradari* by the Andhra Pradesh Tourism a couple of years ago. Approached by a long flight of steps, the structure has a symmetrical plan with a façade of five Qutb Shahi arches. Inside the structure there are arches supporting the domed ceiling, with squinches. The structure is made of stone and lime mortar.

The area surrounding the *baradari* is known as Ibrahim Bagh is 2.5 kilometres from Makka Darwaza, the south-western entrance to Golconda and 3.5 kilometres from the Inner Fort entrance.

Premamati Mosque (Ref. No. S-11, Protected by State Archaeology Department)

The Premamati Mosque stands on a hillock overlooking the Taramati Baradari. It can be approached from a street to the right of Golconda-Gandipet Road. After walking a few hundred metres in the street, on the left one finds a long flight of steps, (right opposite Vasavi Engineering College). Climbing up the steps one finds the façade of the mosque with five Qutb Shahi arches and two *minars*. The *minars* are devoid of ornamentation, looks quite unusual unlike the *minars* as other Qutb Shahi Mosques. These minars do not go higher than the roof of the mosque. The roof of the mosque[85] is flat and accessible from the side of the mosque in the front side. From the roof of the mosque one can see the Taramati Baradari complex with the newly added structures on the foothills.

The mosque has two bays and five aisles. The arches hold ten shallow domes rising from an octagonal plan, at the level where the arches intersect. The interior as well as exterior surfaces of the mosque unlike Taramati Baradari, are not plastered.

KARVAN

The term *Karvan* means a group of people travelling together with vehicles and/or animals. This locality between Puranapul and Golconda Fort came up during the Qutb Shahi period. It defines the famous trade route from Golconda to Charminar (via Puranapul). It adds up to a vast area that includes Karvan Sahu[86], Mustaidpura, Subzi Mandi, Kulsumpura and Rangrezpura[87], etc. During the rule of Ibrahim Qutb Shah, Karvan became a famous trading centre and the merchants used to camp here.

This trip introduces the visitor to most of the Qutb Shahi architectural and natural heritage component built on this historic trade route. This stretch is nine kilometres long and different building typologies found here, are: the gateways, the mosques, famous water body–the Langar[88] Houz. The trip can begin at the Bala Hisar Gate, Golconda Fort. Habshi Kaman is the first structure on the trip facing the entrance of Golconda. After the Jama Masjid, Khazana Building, Shamsheer Kotha and Chota Bazaar Street, one reaches the Fateh Darwaza. This road leads straight to the Puranapul. Langar Houz is located on the eastern side of this road.

BALA HISAR GATE

Bala Hisar Gate in the centre of the fort, leads to the second line of fortification. The gate is not visible from outside and is approached through a pointed arch. The surface of the exterior wall of the Bala Hisar Gate is ornamented with the animal figures.

HABSI KAMAN

Habsi Kaman is located right opposite the Bala Hisar Gate. There are two large structures symmetrically placed on either sides of the entrance axis; the Abyssinian (*Habshi*) guards of the Qutb Shahi kings lived here. These structures have a domed ceiling, and display interesting stucco work in lime on the external walls.

JAMA MASJID[89]

Entrance to this oldest mosque of Golconda is from the lane which is located on the left of the Bada Bazaar Street, immediately behind the Habsi Kaman. The Jama Masjid, also known as Masjid-e-Safa, was built by Sultan Quli in 1518; twenty-five years later, Sultan Quli is said to have been killed here while he was praying.

At the mosque entrance, there is a domed gateway, its big pointed arch is flanked by blind arches. The dome of the gateway and arches bear no resemblance to the Qutb Shahi domes and arches. The architectural features of this first mosque of the Qutb Shahi period are noticeably based on the Bahmani architecture. Two rooms, with domed ceiling, flank the central dome. The front façade of the main mosque structure is covered with aluminum sections and tinted glasses. A set of four arches and the squinches hold the dome. While the apex of the squinch is ornamented with a small floral component, and the apex of arch has a larger ornamental component. The mosque has three bays and five aisles.

Khazana Building (Ref. No. S-7, Protected by State Archaeology Department)

Khazana building stands inside the walls of Golconda outer fort, along the right side of the main road of the Bada Bazaar; this is the same road that links the inner fort's main entrance with the Fateh Darwaza.

Bada Bazaar and Chhota Bazaar are historic markets of Golconda.

Khazana Building was built by the Ibrahim Qutb Shah (1550-1580), during the expansion and the strengthening of the fort. As the name suggests it housed the Shahi Khazana (the royal treasury). The complex has a large courtyard surrounded by structures with arched galleries. It is at present being used as the State Archaeology Museum, generally known as KB Museum.

Shamsheer Kotha (Ref. No. S-8, Protected by State Archaeology Department)

The structure stands right next to the Khazana Building. It was built during the period of Ibrahim Qutb Shah (1550-1580) and used to store weapons. The complex has two courtyards and one Ashurkhana. Except for a part of it, which serves as a *dargah* and is accessed from the roadside, the rest of this heritage component remains closed at present. The heritage site is a fit candidate for re-use as a Photo Museum of items that represent the history of this remarkable city that is Hyderabad.

Fateh Darwaza

At one time, there were eight gateways to enter the fort of Golconda: the Fateh and Bahmani Darwaza in the south, the Mecca and Bodli Darwaza in the west, the Patancheru and Banjara Darwaza in the north, and Jamali and Moti Darwaza in the east. Only the Fateh, Mecca, Bajara and Moti Darwazas are open now, rest four gateways have been blocked. Fateh Darwaza is the gateway from where the Mughal army entered and plundered the Qutb Shahi fort. This gateway has two huge wooden doors and there is an open court between both the doors. The door panels are made with heavy teak; they are studded with sharp iron spikes.

There is another gateway (the internal one) that connects the Naya Quila to the main fort.

Langar Houz

A number of tanks were constructed in Qutb Shahi period of history: Ibrahim Tank, Langar Houz, Shah Hatim Tank, Ma- Saheba Talab, Hussain Sagar, other than Durgam Cheruvu, to name a few of them. Langar Houz located on the left side of the road, supplied water to Naya Quila.

On the left (north) of Langar Houz Road, one finds a huge mosque, displaying Qutb Shahi features. It is locally known as the Qutb Shahi Mosque. The main elevation of the mosque cannot be seen clearly from the road due to the extension of the front verandah.

To the south of the Langar Houz on the State Highway No. 4 is located the Bapu Ghat— a site that has associational and national value. There is a memorial of Mahatma Gandhi and a stepped well of heritage value, along the Musi River.

Continuing on the same road one comes to the inner ring road junction; a right-turn from here, about two kilometres in the south leads to the Mushk Mahal. There is a mosque in the same vicinity; it belongs to the same period as Mushk Mahal.

Mushk Mahal (Ref. No. 19, Grade I HMDA)

The Mushk Mahal at Attapur near Karwan is one of the surviving architectural monuments built during the reign of Abul Hassan Tana Shah (1672–1687), the last ruler of the Golconda kingdom. Mia Mishk (or Mia Mushk, see Mia Mishk Mosque) was the *Sar Lashkar* of the Karnataka forces before he moved to Golconda during the reign of Abul Hassan Tana Shah. He built this *mahal* at Attapur, It was meant to be a garden pavilion befitting a well-to-do gentleman of the late Qutb Shahi period.

The Mushk Mahal was built in the middle of a vast land enclosed by a high wall all round with two gateways[90] one facing north and the other facing south. The *mahal* is a two-storeyed structure, the lower storey consisting of a large hall with arched partitions and a staircase leading to the upper storey. The upper storey was perhaps meant for *zenana*; it was enclosed by a seven feet high wall. There is another staircase that leads to the open roof that is enclosed by a low height wall, which was probably meant for the summer season night sleep.

There is a small platform on the upper storey, from here one gets a fine view of the Golconda Fort, the Qutb Shahi Tombs and the city of Hyderabad. The front façade of the building has a double-storeyed oriel window, with rectangular openings on the upper storey well proportionate pointed arched openings, on the lower storey. The façade on the other side has the pillar and lintel system with small Gujrati brackets. The structure is built from stone and lime. Today, it lies uncared for.

To return to the Inner Ring Road Crossing, one needs to take a U-turn from the Mushk Mahal; from here a right turn at the Ring Road Crossing leads to the Karvan Road (an extension of the same Langar Houz Road).

Toli Masjid (Ref. No. S-5, Protected by State Archaeology, INTACH Award 2005)

Toli Masjid stands on the Karwan Road connecting the Puranapul to Golconda Fort. It was built by Musa Khan Mahaldar during the reign of Abdullah Qutb Shah (1627-72); the Musa Burj in Golconda is also said to have been planned by him. The mosque is remarkable for its Qutb Shahi architecture that blends with it certain features of Hindu temple architecture. It stands on a huge platform with a tank in front of it. The tank and mosque is planned in such a way that when one stands next to the tank he can see the whole mosque reflected in the tank. There are two large *minars* in the front façade of the mosque; they seem to rise from a round-shaped element similar to the *kumbha* – the pitcher of the Hindu temple architecture. In between these two *minars* are five multi-tiered pointed arches with round medallions in their spandrels. The arch in the centre of the front façade is a pointed arch with a multi-cusped arch in it. A row of black basalt pots (*surahi*) is used in the exterior and interior of the mosque. This feature is observed in a few other Qutb Shahi structures, contemporary to Toli Masjid and later. There are six polygonal slender columns that seem to be dropping downward in pairs from the roof brackets of the ground floor to enframe the arches and end at the springing points of the multi-tiered Qutb Shahi arches. At the first floor level there are brackets shaped like elephant tusks, to support the *chajja*.

The mosque has two aisles: one is covered with flat ceiling and the other with domed ceiling, made of stone and lime. A few niches are designed displaying the pillar and lintel style[91] of Hindu temple architecture on the wall parallel to the main entrance wall. The walls of the mosque are well covered with unmatched ornamental lime stucco, including a unique mural. This mural displays façade of a mosque with two *minars* and three arches. The flat ceiling in the first aisle is full of lime stucco; it starts from the apex of the arch and ends at the ceiling, covering the joint of wall and the ceiling. The second aisle has a shallow domed roof. The domes stand on the squinches designed with the intersection of smaller arches. The plan of the mosque is symmetrical along the central axis of the entrance arch. With its marvellous proportion, monumental scale, magnificent exteriors and skilful interiors (with mural and

stucco), this exceptional mosque carry significant architectural and artistic value, apart from the historic value.

Kulsum Begum Mosque (Ref. No. S-39, Protected by the State Archaeology)

This mosque stands beyond the Police Station in Kulsumpura locality, five hundred metres to the east of the Toli Masjid. It was built by Kulsum Begum, the daughter of Sultan Mohammed Qutb Shah (1612-1626). The mosque has a caravanserai all around it. The entrance to the mosque is from a gateway with a big Qutb Shahi arch, symmetrically flanked by two blind arches (they are currently covered by the surrounding structures on the road). The main central arch has another smaller arch within it. The apex of the arch opens into beautiful lime stucco work, with a fruit-like object in the centre–a typical feature of Qutb Shahi ornamentation. There are medallions with a concentric flower pattern on either side of the big arch facing the road. There are arched niches, above the level of the arch apex on the surface of the gateway wall from both the sides. The gate once served as an entrance to the caravanserai.

The mosque has a façade of three arches (visible in parts due to the recent addition of a pavilion in 2008). Two big *minars*[92] looks quite imposing in the front elevation of the mosque, with a well ornamented roof level band and parapet wall. Each of these big *minars* rises from the base of the mosque. The shaft of the minaret has a wavy pattern on all its sides. Above the apex of the entrance arch, a row of small pot-shaped member-the *surahi* has been inserted in the exterior surface of the mosque. The parapet is designed with an even number of arches in each façade. The elephant trunk-shaped bracket (similar to the one in Toli Masjid) rises from the springing point of these aches support the projected cornice (*chajja*). The miniature minars above this level rise from the ends of the second parapet. Many elements of this mosque are similar to the ones in Toli Masjid.

Gate Portion – Devdi Akram Ali Khan (Ref. No. 12, Grade I HMDA)

On the way to Toli Masjid from Mustaidpura, past the Subzi Mandi locality on the Main Road, stands this heritage component. It is the part of the entrance gateway to the Devdi Akram Ali Khan. In the front portion of the gateway, over the arched entrance, there is a balcony made of wooden members. Mixed features of Mughal and European architecture are reflected in this component.

The *devdi* does not exist anymore; on entering this gate one finds the residential locality instead. The shops of other informal commercial sector are lined up on the either side of the *devdi*.

In order to visit some more built and natural heritage components in the Karvan locality, one can take the first left turn (to the north), at the Police Station, going towards Gudi Malkapur, visit the sites and come back. This part of the trip covers two kilometres from the Police Station.

Pavilion in Bhagawandas Garden (Ref. No. 16, Grade I HMDA, INTACH Awards 1997)

The street next to Andhra Bank ATM kiosk, to the left side of the road from Kulsum Begum Mosque, leads to this site. The ancestors of Raja Bhagwandas Hari Das (refer to Raja Bhagwandas Building in Circle II), the natives of Morera, Gujarat, migrated to Delhi during the period of the Mughals. They set up their business in jewelry and banking under royal patronage. In 1729, Raj Hari Das and a few other members of this family chose to accompany the Nizam-ul-Mulk Asaf Jah I to Hyderabad. This two-storeyed structure is said to be more than two hundred years old, is carved in wood, it is a unique sample of that century.

Seth Kishen Das, uncle of Raja Bhagwandas, was the first one to live in this house. The structure appears to be a part of the bigger complex presently stands at the end of a lawn, which is surrounded by mature trees. A big rectangular opening surrounded by a tall multi-cusped arch on its either side, constitute the front façade of the structure. The wooden columns with their capitals turning in to a shape of peacock are forming a part of the paired multi-cusped arches. The rectangular opening makes a part of the two-storeyed high front hall. There are rooms and verandah on all three sides of the hall. The intimacy of the scale reminds us the rural architecture of north India; small windows and doors, beautiful *jharokhas*, low height ceiling (except the central hall) captures the visitor's imagination. The niches in the wall also have multi-cusped arches. The traces of ornamental painting can be seen on the wooden beams. The interiors of the structure look quite similar to the Tipu's Palace at Bengaluru (under the State Archaeology Department, Karnataka). The efforts of the family to maintain the heritage components are really commendable. The permission of the owner is needed before visiting the structure.

Returning to the main road, moving a little distance, one finds a beautiful rocky ridge on the right side of the road. After a few hundred metres down the road, to the left, there is Jhamsingh Temple.

Jhamsingh Temple Gate Portion (Ref. No. 29, Grade IIA HMDA)

Because of this temple a common man is registered in the annals of history. In the early nineteenth century a soldier named Jham Singh was given some money by the then Nizam to buy horses. On the way, at Gudi Malkapur, he dreamed in his sleep that God wanted him to build a temple at the place where a black stone stood. As per his dream, Jham Singh spent all the money on building this temple. He was imprisoned for this but later released. The temple can be approached from the side entrance on the road, adjacent to the recently built Sri Krishna Venkateshwara Apartments.

The architecture of the temple complex does not conform to any particular contemporary building style in the city except for some elements that distinctly exhibit the influence of the temple architecture of south India. The entrance gate to the temple displays an unusual combination of the Rajasthani and South Indian temple architecture. The rectangular entrance gateway is topped with a tower-like structure giving it the look of a *gopuram* (the entrance gateway in South Indian temples). This opening is flanked by oriel/*jharokha* windows in Rajasthani style, symmetrically designed one on either side. There is another structure opposite the temple gateway; it has multi-cusped arches and oriel windows, probably a *naqqarkhana*, a place for drum beaters.

Mosque near Jhamsingh Temple (Ref. No.30, Grade IIA HMDA)

Close to the Jhamsingh temple on the opposite side of the road (towards the east) stands an old mosque, built in early Asaf Jahi Period. The mosque exhibits the features Qutb Shahi architecture slightly modified, simpler in form termed as neo-Qutb Shahi architecture. The verandah in front of the main mosque is a recent addition; it has affected the original front facade of the mosque.

Mia Mishk's Mosque (Ref. No. S-15, Protected by the State Archaeology)

This mosque was built by Mian Mishk[93]-the Abyssinian slave of Abul Hassan Tana Shah in 1676. Before his death in 1680, Mian Mishk held important positions of the Secretary, the Commander and the Keeper of the royal keys. This mosque can easily be identified from the Puranapul (while walking from south to north); its two bold minarets with miniature galleries can be noticed. The mosque has a symmetrical façade of three arches and two big minars in front (visible in parts due to new addition). The mosque has less ornamentation compared to that of the Toli Masjid and Kulsumpura Mosque–structures built in the same period in the Karvan locality. The polygonal minarets are simple yet elegant; their balconies have rectangular openings that have the *jaali* panels fitted in them. The parapet also has rectangular openings–rather than arched-openings; this is a feature rarely seen in other Qutb Shahi mosques (not repeated in the structures discussed in this book). The smaller minarets lend variety to the parapet with a zig-zag (cheveron) pattern on all the sides of their shaft.

In the interiors of mosque, there are two bays; the first bay has a flat ceiling and the second one has a domed ceiling with the domes rising from the squinches.

Next to the mosque there exists a mortuary chamber of Mia Mishk that has a verandah in pillar and lintel style-on its four sides. This verandah is similar to the pavilion at Shaikpet Sarai complex and Dargah Shah Raju Kattal (Ref. No. S-13 and S-16). A big old stone urn in verandah is quite conspicuous. There is a *hamam* in the complex. There is a *madrassa* structure, neighbouring the mosque. The fifty enclosures surrounding the mosque have the arched openings; they were probably meant for the travellers to stay.

Ancient Gateway Puranapul (Ref. No. S-38, Protected by the State Archaeology)

Puranapul gateway is located in south of Musi River, opposite the Puranapul. It is said to have been built in 1578 along with the bridge to serve as the entrance to the north-western corner of the city, later, it was made a part of the city walls built between 1724 and 1740. One can climb a few steps of this heritage component to get a view of the Puranapul and also to get some idea of the defense system of the Qutb Shahi and Asaf Jahi Hyderabad.

Puranapul Bridge (Ref. No. 11, Grade I HMDA)

This bridge was built in 1578, thirteen years before the Hyderabad City came into being (1591). It was the first link between Golconda via the Karvan route and the new city of Hyderabad. Built by Ibrahim Qutb Shah, the bridge provided tradesmen an easy access to the Trunk Road and facilitated their trade on the Golconda – east coast route. Thus, the bridge has a functional as well as historical value.

Made from stone masonry with lime, the bridge has twenty-two semi-circular arches. It is 608 feet long, 36 feet wide and stands 42 feet above the river bed. At present the   Puranapul functions as a vegetable market. Because of the structural condition of the bridge, heavy traffic movement on it has been restricted; it is however open to the pedestrian movement. A new bridge has been built parallel to it.

The Puranapul provides a clear view of the north of the city that has a remarkable mix of built and natural heritage: the minarets of the Mian Mishk mosque in the foreground and the beautiful hillocks of the Sitarambagh – Asifnagar locality in the background. The only unpleasant part of this site is the condition of the Musi River. Sewage treatment plants have been set up recently on the banks of the river. The Puranapul Bridge, too, needs immediate attention; the vegetation growth at several places in the bridge is a serious threat to its structural condition.

From here we move to the next circle Charminar—the walled city and surroundings.

CIRCLE V- CHARMINAR

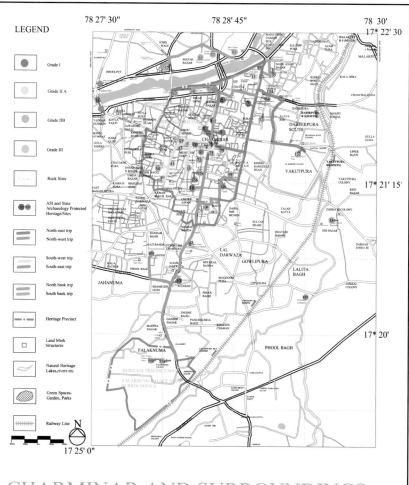

CHARMINAR AND SURROUNDINGS

HERITAGE PRECINCT NO.12 and 14

Mosque atop Charminar

The Charminar locality, with its many historic settlements and structures, is a part of the living heritage of Hyderabad. Most building typologies of this area were meant to suit the needs of an Islamic city. Different communities from all over India and abroad came here to serve the city's various dynasties to begin with, but later chose to stay on. The cultural diversity of the various ethnic groups settled here over a period of time is abundantly reflected in the planning of the walled city and the architectural features of its heritage components. The city of Hyderabad became the land of the *dargahs*, mosques, the minars and *ashurkhanas*.

Today's Hyderabad has its origin in a Garden City[94] of four centuries ago, planned by Mir Momin Astrabadi, a Qutb Shahi prime minister. The focal point of the city is the Charminar, situated at the intersection of two main streets: the historic trade route, from east (Golconda) to west (Machlipatnam), and the road that lies between the river Musi in the north and the Koh-e-tur (the hillock on which the Falaknuma Palace stands) in the south. The famous Charkaman to the north was designed along with the Charminar; they together formed a Latin Cross (a double Cross) in the site plan.

The cultural heritage of Hyderabad is no less unique than its built and natural heritage the culturally significant objects sold here—the wedding wears, the *itars*, the *Janamaaz*, the holy books, the walking sticks (locally known as Chhadi), the pearls and the semi-precious stones—famous throughout the world. The aroma of *naan, shermaal, kebabs, halim, biryani, Irani chai, Osmania biscuits, khova*, etc., lends identity to the city's different streets. It is the combination of the cultural, natural and built heritage of Hyderabad that gives the city its unique character.

A discussion of the Charminar and the Charkaman is necessary before we move on to the different parts of the walled-city.

Charminar

The Charminar has been the identity of the city ever since it was built by Mohammed Quli Qutb Shah in 1591. The structure is made from granite and has four arches, one in each of the four directions. These arches support two floors of rooms and the gallery of the archways. At each corner of the square plan there is a 24 metres high minaret; this gives the structure its fifty-four metres height.

It is said that the first floor of Charminar was used as a *madrassaa* —school for studying Islam—during the Qutb Shahi period. The second floor has a mosque on the western side; its fluted dome is visible from the road when seen a few feet away from the base of the Charminar. The Qutb Shahi ornamentation skills are at their best here.

Prayer niche in the mosque atop Charminar

The view of the city from the first floor galleries of the Charminar give some idea of how the Qutb Shahi Hyderabad was originally planned. The first Cross on the south side starts from the Charminar and the second one is at Charkaman, with Gulzar Houz at its centre. A view of the south shows the city's architectural history in its different layers: the Charminar and Jama Masjid belong to Qutb Shahi period, the Mecca Masjid to the transitional phase of the Qutb Shahi and the Mughal, and the Unani Hospital, with its Indo - Saracenic architecture, to the Asaf Jahi period.

From the top of the Charminar (at the level of its galleries), one can see the four streets moving away in the four directions. On the street to the east are the Jama Masjid, the Sardar Mahal (the mansard roof of the palace is visible in the skyline) and, at a little distance from here, the Purani Haveli. On the street to the west are the Laad Bazaar, the Jilu Khana, Chowmahalla and the Mehbub

Chowk (the clock tower of Mehboob Chowk contributes to the skyline). On the street to the north, one can see the Jama Masjid (to the north-east), Badshahi Ashurkhana, the soaring domes of the High Court and the hoards of buyers/visitors of the Patharghatti Market. On the street to the south there is the famous Mecca Masjid with its huge courtyard and a magnificent entrance gate; down the road, there is the most beautiful palace of Hyderabad, the Falaknuma Palace.

The four Qutb Shahi gateways stand at a walking distance from Charminar.

The heritage structure Charminar is protected by the Archaeological Survey of India. Few years back, the HMDA declared the Charminar area a heritage zone; now the government agencies and the city's NGOs jointly endevour to preserve the three-dimensional panoramic view of the area.

The four Qutb Shahi gateways stand at a walking distance from Charminar.

Charkaman, Machlikaman, Kalikaman, Sher-e-Batil-ki-Kaman (Ref. No. 8a, b, c, d, HMDA Grade I)

These four imposing gateways (Kamans[95]) were built after the completion of Charminar, in 1592[96]; they were later renovated by Mir Mehboob Ali Khan, the sixth Nizam of Hyderabad. Facing the four cardinal directions, they once served as gateways to both the royal Qutb Shahi palaces, which stood beyond them, and the heart of the city. The northern arch, through which most visitors enter the Charminar area (when coming from Afzalganj), is known as Machhli

Sehr-e-Batil ki Kaman

Kaman (Fish Arch). The eastern arch, originally called the Nagarkhana-e-Shahi (Houses of the royal drums), is now known as Kali Kaman. The western arch is known as Kaman Sher Dil or Sehr-e-Batil ki Kaman (arch of lion hearted or Magic breaker). This was originally called the Daulatkhana-e-Aali (the gateway to the royal residence), and was at one time decorated with a huge tapestry of gold. The southern gateway close to the Charminar was called the Charminar Kaman and is now known as the Mewewalon ki Kaman (fruit vendors' arch). Charkaman frames the Charminar beautifully, when seen from a distance.

The walled city was planned with different localities divided by principal streets passing through the Charminar. The city had four sectors north-east, north-west, south-east and south-west. A trip to Charminar is also divided with the same system. It has been done so to keep every part trip short and easy; this system will also explain the character of each quadrant/cultural zones, which are comprised of different ethnic groups.

THE NORTH-EASTERN QUARTER

The first trip can be planned from the eastern side of the Charminar. The north-eastern quadrant of the walled city was known as the commoners' quadrant. The first structure on this trip is the Jama Masjid, approached by a narrow lane from the north-east of the Charminar, as the original entrance is now encroached upon.

Jama Masjid (Ref. No. 32, Grade IIA, HMDA)

This is the earliest mosque of the city of Hyderabad and was built in 1598, during the reign of Mohammed Quli Qutb Shah, but not before the mosque atop Charminar had been built. There are seven arches and two minarets in the front façade of the mosque. The central one is a Qutb Shahi pointed arch and the other six are multi-cusped arches[97]. Each multi-cusped arch frames a multi-tiered Qutb Shahi pointed arch in it. This composition of two different types of arches in the front façade of the Jama Masjid is quite uncommon in rest of the city's other contemporary mosques. Some ornamental niches can be seen above the apex of the multi-cusped arches, formed by the projected cornice and brackets. The structure is laced by a parapet of crossing pointed arches. This mosque is an example of the early Qutb Shahi architecture in Hyderabad. The extended verandah in front—a subsequent construction in RCC—obstructs the view somewhat.

There used to be a school, a *Khanquah* and a Turkish bath in the mosque complex; they do not exist anymore. An arched gateway[98] to the mosque does exist in the east but in a dilapidated condition; it needs to be restored.

After visiting the Jama Masjid, one can return to the eastern road—the Maidan Chowk Road—from where one can move on to more heritage components. One can see on this road several shops of dentists and bone setters along the wall of the Unani Hospital. They are more than a hundred years old. Beyond these shops, at a distance of one hundred and fifty metres from Charminar on the right hand side stands the   Sardar Mahal.

Sardar Mahal (Ref No. 79, Grade IIB, HMDA)*

Sardar Mahal was built in 1900 and was named after Sardari Begum, the wife of the sixth Nizam of Hyderabad. Its main entrance is from the Maidan Chowk Road. The palace complex is presently occupied by the south zone office of the Greater Hyderabad Municipal Corporation (GHMC).

The elliptical arched entrance of the Sardar Mahal opens on a large courtyard. To the left, there is a big porch with elliptical arches. The plinth of the structure has rough stone finish. The elliptical and semi-circular arches, the heavy lime mouldings, the louvered and panelled doors, and the Corinthian pilasters of the structure conform to the European architecture; yet, its planning is indigenous. The interior courtyards of the *mahal*, with their fountains and green, shady trees, have been designed to serve dual purposes: the aesthetic and the functional: in addition to separating the *zenana* from the *mardana* quarters, they are meant to provide the ever-so-welcome cool breeze to the inmates.

This palace has a history of re-uses: it was initially rented out to the Unani Hospital; then, for some time, it was occupied by the City High Court, and finally, it is with the Municipal Corporation of Hyderabad (known as GHMC at present).

The site presently is in a bad shape owing to the lack of proper maintenance; this notwithstanding, it is a suitable location for a heritage museum. To the right of the main entrance of Sardar Mahal stands a simple yet interesting small mosque, initially a part of the Mahal.

Another one hundred and fifty metres from Sardar Mahal on the same side of the Maidan Chowk Road used to stand Malwala Palace[99] (see picture of the gateway).

Further down the Maidan Chowk Road there is a crossing, known as Ali Jah Kotla[100]. The Itebar Chowk[101] Road on the left of this crossing—one of the few original Qutb Shahi roads—leads to the Purani Haveli.

Purani Haveli Complex (Ref. No. 52, Grade III, HMDA)

This site was earmarked by Muhammed Quli Qub Shah in the late sixteenth century as a place of residence for his Peshwa, Mir Momin. In the late eighteenth century, Nizam II acquired it for his son Sikander Jah's residence from Mir Alam, a descendant of

Mir Momin. The site was extensively renovated for the purpose for which it was acquired. The main gate of this palace was built later by Sikander Jah. When he became the Nizam, however, he moved into Khilwat Mubarak (the Chowmahalla), and this palace remained unoccupied for many years. It lost its importance. It saw better days again when Nawab Nizam Ali Khan became the fourth Nizam: he and his successors added several structures to the palace; the fifth Nizam was born here, and the sixth Nizam made it his permanent residence. In 1971, Mir Barkat Ali Khan, the son of Nizam VII donated the Purani Haveli Complex to the Mukarram Jah Trust.

The complex is enclosed by a high wall, more than a mile[102] in circumference; the palace inside cannot be seen from the road. There are eleven buildings in this complex. At the centre, there are two parallel rectangular blocks; presently, there is a museum in one of them. The other palaces are put to different use: the library and the residence of the Trust's secretary, the Anwar-ul-uloom Women's College, the Setwin Office and a place for storing the old furniture of the Asaf Jahi Rulers, etc. One can assess the size of the complex when one looks at the 1914 survey sheets of Hyderabad (prepared by Col. Mackenze): it is almost two-thirds of the size of the Chowmahalla Palace.

The HEH Nizam's Purani Haveli Museum is the most famous structure in the complex. The visitors to the museum can see for themselves how much wealth the Asaf Jahi rulers had and also appreciate the contribution they made to the development of the city. There are many artifacts of cultural significance and associational value displayed in the museum. Among the most fascinating museum artifacts are the silver models of the structures planned by the City Improvement Board and the coronation chair of Nizam VII, Mir Osman Ali Khan.

Princess Esin Women's Educational Centre (Ref. No. 64, Grade III, HMDA)

This is a part of the Purani Haveli Palace complex listed separately (as another heritage component) by HMDA. The institute was set up in Palace No. 5 in 1973. The palace is designed with internal courtyards both big and small. The plan of the palace is symmetrical with a fountain in the large courtyard. The upper (fixed) part of the panelled door with fanlight has beautiful tracery in it. The semi circular arches and the big elliptical arches define the movement and circulation in the palace. There is a keystone in centre of the arches and the mouldings are done in lime. The façade of the palace gets a curved shape at some places, evidently inspired by the Palladian villas of Europe. The palace has been put to a good re-use and is being landscaped well. Happily, it is being maintained reasonably well.

A Majeed Khan's Residence (Ref. No. 134, Grade III, HMDA)

Also known as Bait-ush-Shifa, this heritage structure is located on the left-hand side of the road to Dabirpura, just before the State Bank of India. It was once the residence of Imtiazuddin, a royal *tabeeb* (doctor); Mohmod-ur-Rehman, a renowned *hakeem* of his times, also lived in this house (on rent) for some length of time.

Some of the interesting features of the house are its tri-foliated arches around the doors and the flowing wooden tracery on the glass-fitted ventilator atop the door, among others. The *chajja* in front of the first floor has a sloping roof with a triangular dormer at its centre; the paired wooden brackets supporting this chajja, is a feature not commonly seen in the city's contemporary structures. The perpendicular ends of the exterior walls are decorated with pilasters similar to the Corinthian capital. The house has a courtyard in the front, which at present is partly covered with the shops facing Dabirpura-Purani Haveli Road.

Opposite the house stands a historic mosque with a skilfully extended portico. The Dabirpura-Purani Haveli road further leads to the Dabirpura Gate.

Old gate of Dabirpura (Ref. No. S-3, Protected by State Archaeology Department Ref. No. S-3)

The Walled City of Hyderabad is said to have had seventeen gates[103] at one time; only two survive today: the Dabirpura Gate and the Puranapul Gate. The Dabirpura Gate was built between 1724 and 1740 as a part of the city walls. The gate has a pointed arch and is flanked by two bastions. The wooden door of the gateway still survives with both its panels.

Dabirpura, one of the oldest residential localities of the city, was patronised by Dabir-ul-Mulk; *Dabir* means a scholar.

Devdi Shamsheer Jung is located on the road that links the Charminar–Afzalgunj Road to the Yakutpura MMTS Railway Station.

Devdi Nawab Shamsheer Jung (Ref. No. 132, Grade III, HMDA)

Nawab Shamsheer Jung's *devdi* is situated in Yakutpura. Shamsheer Jung Bahadur I, the father of the nawab, was the contemporary of Salar Jung I. The nawab worked as Chief Magistrate and Additional Sessions Judge.

An interesting mix of different architectural styles can be observed in the blocks of this devdi. The façade from the side of the road immediately catches the visitor's eye. The dark-shaded corners of the building are in contrast with the rest of the wall that is plain. The lower storey of the structure facing the road is treated with rusticated stone finish. The central block of the devdi has the entrance porch. The front façade of this part has a tri-foliated arch, surrounded by two other same but smaller arches. The three arches are together enframed by one semi-circular arch which is flanked by two towers. Each tower is punctured by two openings: the lower opening is in the shape of a pointed arch and the upper opening is circular. Both the towers are topped by the small domes standing on an octagonal base. The central portal ends with a band of Metope and Frieze (above the arches) which runs on the towers as well, at the same level. On this band, there is the cornice with a broken scroll pediment – an element from the European architecture. In the centre of the pediment one can see a feature, in lime, perhaps the insignia of the Nawab's family.

Sheikh Faiz ki Kaman (Ref. No. N-13, Grade I, HMDA)

This entrance gateway stands on the northern side of the Yakutpura and has the shape of a multi-cusped arch, made with brick and lime mortar. The height of the structure is about 25 feet and its width is 20 feet. It is said to be one hundred and fifty years old. As per the 1914 survey sheets of Hyderabad, there was a structure, *Devdi Faiz Khan*, near the Kaman; it does not exist anymore. There is a mosque, though, on the eastern side of this gateway.

NORTH-WESTERN QUARTER

The north-western quadrant was originally meant to be the place for *Jagirdars* to settle in; later, a part of it, like the Mitti ka Sher, was acquired by rich Marwari traders (Ratna Naidu 1990)

Mitti ka Sher (Ref. No. N-11, Grade I, HMDA)

Mitti-ka-Sher refers to a small statue of a lion standing on the roadside (road to the west); it is understood to be more than one hundred and fifty years old. The locality is named after the statue. The area around the statue is being used residentially as well as commercially.

From Mitti ka Sher one needs to come back to the Gulzar Houz, and further to left, the Patharghatti Market.

Patharghatti Market

This market, on both sides of the main road in the north of Charminar, (from Gulzar Houz to the Mir Alam Mandi Crossing) was built as a part of the City Improvement Board's post-flood development Scheme. *Pathar* refers to stone, built entirely of granite; this market has shops for clothes, jewelry, perfumes, footwear, and other items of interest for tourists and local shoppers. The plan of the market displays an influence of the Rajasthani architecture. It is a two-storeyed structure, with arcaded verandahs on the ground floor to provide a shaded walkway for the visitor.

Beyond the Patharghatti Market, right at the crossing, stands the western gateway of the Diwan Devdi; it can be visited on the way back from the Badshahi Ashurkhana located in the north of the Madina Building.

Badshahi Ashurkhana (Ref. No. S-2, Protected by State Archaeology Department, INTACH Awards 2006)

This structure is renowned for its enamel-tiled mosaics (refer to Chapter 4, surface decoration) in Persian style, similar to the ones found in Lahore and Multan. It was built by Mohammed Quli during 1593-96 and, architecturally, belongs to the early Qutb Shahi period. Badshahi Ashurkhana is among the oldest *imambaras*[104] and *ashurkhanas* in the country.

The entrance gateway of this structure, too, is of considerable architectural significance. It has a huge semi-circular arch with a key stone in its centre. The springing points of the arch rest on pilasters that have simple lime moulding. The arch is enframed by a three-sided moulding. The gate has arched punctures on its top and a small minaret on a pedestal on its either side; its huge wooden doors have survived the centuries gone by. The gateway was built during the reign of Asaf Jah II.

The parapet wall of the *ashurkhana's* main structure is quite impressive; its small, multi-cusped arched openings lend it a look of solid and voids. Numerous floral motifs and the row of ornamental leaves above the arched openings crown the building. While these motifs and the miniature minarets on their pedestals seem to lace the *ashurkhana* structure, the taller minarets at its ends add verticality to it. The timber colonnades (in the period of Mir Nizam Ali Khan, Asaf Jah II) and the wired grill in the façade are subsequent additions to the *ashurkhana*.

After visiting the Ashurkhana, one returns to the Charminar Road; on its left (to the east) stands the main gateway of the Diwan Devdi.

Gate Portion, Dewan *Devdi* *(Ref. No. 6, Grade I, HMDA)

Dewan Devdi has a significant place in the history of Hyderabad. It was the residence of the well known Salarjung family from which came several prime ministers of the Asaf Jahi Hyderabad. Originally, the palace is understood to have been the possession of Mubariz Khan who was appointed the *Subedar* of Deccan in 1724 by the then Mughal emperor. Later, in the early phase of the Asaf Jahi rule, it was occupied by two prime ministers of the Asaf Jahi court:

Dewan Devdi, western gateway

first by Mir Alam, and then by his son-in-law, Nawab Muneer-ul-Mulk. However, the *devdi* acquired its exceptional significance only when Sir Salar-Jung became the *diwan* (prime minister) of Hyderabad. Many extensions were made to this devdi during his time. The palace does not exist anymore; however, the architecture of the two gateways that still remain amply reflects the dynamic personality of its patron, Sir Salarjung. The gateways have been listed as heritage components.

The double-storeyed northern gateway displays the influence of Mughal and Rajasthani architecture. It has a large semi-circular entrance arch in the centre incased in two multi-foliated arches; all the three arches are concentric. The entrance arch is flanked by three smaller multi-cusped arches on its either side, beginning at the first-floor level. The window on each side of the entrance is canopied probably, for the convenience of the drum-beaters who sat there.

The western gateway, on the main road displays the influence of European architecture. It has a semi-circular arched entrance flanked by two bastions with octagonal façade rising up to the second storey. It is said that different gateways were meant to please the sensitivities of both, the Indians and the Europeans. Owing to unplanned commercial development and indiscriminate placement of the sign-boards on the structure, some of the elements of these gateways are now lost.

The western gate facing the Charminar–Falaknuma Road is in a bad way. The northern gate facing the Chatta Bazaar is, relatively, in a better state.

Kaman Chatta Bazaar (Ref. No. 7, Grade I, HMDA)

Kaman Chatta Bazaar is locally known as Chatte-ki-Kaman. It is said to have been built during Abul Hassan Tana Shah's rule (1674–1687). This entrance arch is famous for its lofty structure, width and magnificence. In the east, the *kaman* leads to the Purani Haveli Complex (see the north-western quarter). In the eastern and northern direction, the *kaman* leads to Nayapul. Over the roof of the Chatte-ki-Kaman, there was a long, concrete construction- stretching from south to north upto Diwan Devdi in the south. It went till Lakkad Kot[105] in the north. Above the apex of the arch, there are three small wooden windows facing Purani Haveli in the east and Diwan Devdi in the south side.

Entrance gate of Mecca Masjid

THE SOUTH-WESTERN QUARTER

This quadrant of the Walled City was originally reserved for the palaces of the king and the Paigah nobles. The western part of this quadrant—the Hussaini Alam (Old Kabuter Khana)—is said to have been occupied by Marwaris and Bohras[106]. The trip to the south-western quarter can begin from the Mecca Masjid—a grand historic structure of the Walled City.

Notice the original elevation of Mecca Masjid

Mecca Masjid (Ref. No. S-1, Protected by State Archaeology Department)

Built by Sultan Muhammad Qutb Shah in 1617, and completed by Aurangazeb in1693[107], the Mecca Masjid is the principal mosque of Hyderabad; it is also the second largest mosque in India. The entrance gateway of the mosque faces the main road. On entering the gate, one finds a number of steps leading to the majestic mosque–225 feet long, 180 feet wide and 75 feet high. There is a rectangular tank right opposite the mosque. The mosque is built with the local granite stone and has fine grain finish. It has three bays inside. There are five pointed arches in the front façade of the mosque.

When the mosque was built, its plan was simple and symmetrical. After the burial of the Asaf Jahi ruler Nizam Ali Khan, in 1803, a part of the courtyard at the south end became a graveyard. This place became a traditional graveyard until 1911, when Mir Mahbub Ali Khan, the sixth Nizam, was buried here. The roofing on the graves came up in 1914; with this, the front elevation and plan of the mosque underwent a change.

The large gateway of the mosque also deserves a mention here. It is contemporary to the mosque and has a wooden door, encased in a pointed-arch; this arch in turn is enframed by a bigger pointed-arch with a quasi-dome. The big pointed-arch is adorned with a band of niches on three sides. These niches are shaped as the multi-cusped arch and one more geometrical form (typical to the Mughal architecture). A small postern in the door is provided for controlled movement. The structure is topped with two minarets and has platforms for the guards to sit on.

After visiting the Mecca Masjid, one can return to the Charminar and take a left turn (to the west). From here up to the Mehboob Chowk, the street is known as Laad Bazaar. A turn to the left, at the end of this street, leads to Hussaini Alam and Shahgunj.

Laad Bazaar

Laad Bazaar connects Charminar with Golconda, via Puranapul (the famous historic route). The street is said to have existed since the Qutb Shahi period; the market, however, dates back to the Asaf Jahi period. This market has been the commercial spine of the city ever since its inception. One of the most famous historic bazaars of India, Laad Bazaar is renowned for manufacturing and selling bangles. In addition to the famous bangles, the bazaar deals in *itr*, *mehndi*, *surma*, laces, *zari* (the brocade), bridal wares and other items required for wedding.

Most structures in this street are two-storeyed, called *magdis*. The ground floors of the *magdis* were designed for shops and the first floors for workshops. A small-scale door can be seen on the street-facing façade of each *magdi*, leading to the first floor. Many of these *magdis* exist even today.

The street is about 350 metres long and 9 metres wide. The restoration of the Laad Bazaar is currently in progress under a scheme prepared by the GHMC.

The narrow alleys here present interesting views of the majestic minarets of the Mecca Masjid. One of these alleys the Laad Bazaar has two simple yet interesting arched gateways. This alley serves as a secondary entrance to the Mecca Masjid.

Gate Portion – Shahi Jilu Khana[108] (Ref. No. 9, Grade I, HMDA)

On the Laad Bazaar Road, between the rows of shops, a famous heritage component often goes unnoticed: the entrance gate to the magnificent Chowmahalla. It was built during the reign of the first Nizam and is greatly influenced by the Mughal architecture. One cannot miss a large multi-cusped

arch in the gateway; it is built with rubble stone masonry and smooth lime plaster. There are two typical Mughal-style *Jharokha* windows, one on either side, which lend a royal look to the gate. Small domed kiosks in the simple parapet wall crown the structure. One can notice traces of beautiful lime work in the three-sided border of the big central arch.

Presently, the gate portion is in a sorry state; the small shops in and around the gateway (came up later) do not help the situation in any way.

There is a crossing past the Laad Bazaar Street; on the left at this crossing lies the Moti Gali (a street) that leads to the Chowmahalla Palace complex (now a museum). The first structure of this complex is known as Aiwan-e-Ali.

Aiwan-e-Ali (Ref. No. 72, Grade IIB, HMDA)
Aiwan-e-Ali was once an integral part of the Chowmahalla Palace complex, used as the *Diwan-Khana-e-Aliya* or the office of the *Sarf-e-Khas* (Privy Purse) till 1948. It was the seat of royal culture then, and people had to observe various formalities when entering its premises. But now, there is a wall separating it from the rest of the palace complex. This heritage structure is being used as a function hall presently, and the main palace is the Chowmahalla Palace

Museum. Aiwan-e-Ali was constructed with the other structures of the Chowmahalla, probably in the period of the second Nizam. The structure has a façade of five multi-cusped arches in front and is accessed by a flight of steps added recently. It has two big halls now used for functions. On the wall of the hall, there are pointed arched-niches perpendicular to the multi-cusped arch panel.

On the road opposite the Aiwan-e-Ali stands the Pension Office, once, the Shahi Khazana building. It can be easily identified because of the unique pineapple-shaped elements on the pylons of its entrance gate. Next to the Aiwan-e-Ali is the Chowmahalla Palace Museum.

a) Chow Mahalla – main palace (Ref. No. 35a & b, Grade IIB, HMDA)
b) Other Palaces – Chow Mahalla
c) Shahi Khilwat Khana (Ref. No. 53, Grade IIB, HMDA)

Chow Mahalla (*chow* means four and *mahalla* - the palaces) was built in 1750 by Salabat Jung II, the successor of the Nizam-ul-Mulk; this is the first of the several Asaf Jahi structures that he went on to build. As the name suggests, Chowmahalla forms a complex of four main palaces, all clustered around a courtyard. Each one of the four palaces was meant for a different function: the Shahi Jilu Khana (Ref. No. 9) was the main entrance to the palace complex, opening into the Laad Bazaar. The palace on the north side is the Darbar Hall, the court in Mughal tradition held here. The south palace Afzal Mahal was meant to receive dignitaries, and the structure in the west—believed to be a copy of the Shah's palace in Tehran—was the Nizam's palace. The eastern palace housed the office of the Nizam. Though the complex was built over a period of time, the structures display a remarkable unity of design. The palace complex was once spread over nearly one-fifth of the entire walled city area, bounded on all four sides by the Laad Bazaar Road, the Aspan Chowk[109] Road, the Panjmahalla Road and the Shah Gunj; the area of the complex has now dwindled to around 12.7 acres.

Chowmahalla has two main courtyards: in the first courtyard, accessed from the main entrance, stands the Khilwat Mubarak palace; right in front of this remarkable structure, there is a cistern in line with the entrance gate. There is a structure on each side of the Khilwat Mubarak palace: Sise Adalat on the western side and Bara Imam on the eastern side. The other entrance gate to the palace has a clock tower; this is presently closed. At the end of the courtyard, there are two smaller, symmetrically placed gateways on either side of the Khilwat Mubarak; these lead to the second courtyard which has several palaces: Afzal Mahal in the south, Aftab Mahal in the east, Mehtab Mahal opposite the Aftab Mahal, Tahniyat Mahal opposite the Afzal Mahal, and the Chaman Bangla in the south-east corner. There are a few more structures on either side of the Aftab Mahal and Mehtab Mahal used as stores.

Princess Esra, the former wife of Prince Mukarram Jah, undertook the restoration of the palace-complex. Several rooms in the Mehtab Mahal have now been redone with furniture and art, brought in from the other palaces of the Nizam, with a view to capture the cultural heritage of Hyderabad. The rarest of the rare maps and pictures of Hyderabad are displayed here. The royal *zenana* in the Afzal Mahal, too, has been restored to its former glory.

Built over a period of time, the structures of the palace-complex display various architecture styles: the Qutb Shahi, the Asaf Jahi, the British, the Mughal and the Rajasthani. A visit to the Chowmahalla is a special treat to anyone who is interested in the built and cultural heritage of Hyderabad.

The other structure, the Majhli Begum-ki-Haveli, is discussed in the next quadrant. To visit more structures, one has to return to the T-junction at the end of the Laad Bazaar Street; from here, the street to the left leads to Mehboob Chowk.

Old Homeopathy Hospital (Ref. No. 78, Grade IIB, HMDA)

The structure is an old palace of the Nizam called the Moti Mahal. It is located at the western end of the Laad Bazaar Street, opposite the Mehboob Chowk Clock Tower. In the early 1950s it was sold, it is believed, to a royal watch-maker. For a few years, until 1969, the structure was used by the Indian Medicine Department. From 1969 until a few years ago, there was a Homeopathy Hospital in the first floor of this building. There are a few shops in the ground floor of the structure. The elevation of this heritage structure has a beautiful elliptical arch which in turn is surrounded by semi-circular arches. The Moti Mahal, and the clock tower that stands opposite it, complement each other; displaying similar European architectural features.

Clock Tower – Mehboob Chowk (Ref no. 92, Grade III, HMDA)

The Clock Tower at Mahboob Chowk is one of the most famous landmarks of the city. This five-storeyed structure has a square plan and is located in the park opposite the Chowk Mosque. The Clock Tower was built in 1892 by the Paigah noble, Sir Asman Jah. It took two years to build; the clocks were installed in it after its completion. To the south of the tower, there is a market built by Sir Salarjung I (1853-1883).

The first storey of the clock tower has rusticated stone finish and there is a semi-circular arch on each of its four sides. The next storey has a door with pilasters on both sides with a tri-foiled arch rising from the end of each pilaster. The level after this has a beautiful cast iron railing. The parapet with cast iron railing at the next level is supported by beautiful brackets. A small flower motif fills in each intra-bracket space. All levels of the clock tower have been tastefully ornamented. The ornament at the third level is in two sections: there is a big elliptical arch at the lower section and a semi-circular arch at the upper section. The arch at each section have a glass panelled door and a louvered window. The next level of the tower has the clocks and a door placed in a frame that is topped with a segmental arch. The topmost level of the tower has semi-circular arches to support a dome with a spire. Although built in different architecture styles, the clock tower and the mosque stand in harmony on the same site.

Mehboob Chowk Mosque (Ref. No. 87, Grade III, HMDA)

This mosque was built by Khwaja Abdulla Khan in 1817. To the people of the old city, it is the Chowk Mosque. This structure stands on a high terrace in the

View of the clock tower from the courtyard of the Chowk Mosque

العافى أنثككك عن ثككاب زاذكطلك
نهمة ابدا ولى نه بنم للل باطتابدى س

west of the Charminar. The mosque still runs on a self-sustainable traditional system that was established way back in the past. Under this system the shops on the lower level of the mosque pay rent to the mosque committee; the money thus obtained is spent for the regular expenses of the mosque. Mehboob Chowk locality owes its historic character not only to the mosque but also to these shops: the metal wares, the antique books, and the various traditional eatables, namely: *naan*, biscuits, *kebabs*, etc., are an integral part of the intangible heritage of Hyderabad.

The mosque has three multi-cusped arches in its main façade with a minaret at both its ends. There is a portico in front of the mosque and a beautiful water tank in the centre of the courtyard. To enter this courtyard there is a small gateway with a pointed arch. The attraction of this gateway is greatly enhanced by the four minarets that stand on its top. On either side of the entrance gateway stands a small structure resembling the <u>bangladar roof pavilion</u> in the Mughal architectural tradition of Hyderabad. A left turn at the Chowk leads to the street known as Amir-e-Kabir[110] Gali – the location of the Paigah family devdis. The first structure here is the Devdi Asman Jah.

Devdi Asman Jah (Ref. No. 81, Grade III, HMDA)

At one time the High Court of Hyderabad was located in this devdi; that was when Sir Asman Jah was the Law Minister of the State. Sadly, only the part facing the road of this devdi remains today. This *devdi* – the residence of Sir Asman Jah Paigah, was built in the late nineteenth century with *mahals*, *jilu khana* and the stables, right behind the Nizam's palace-complex. Most of the external elements of the structure – or what is left of it – that display European influence are the rusticated lower storey, the openings capped with pediments and the circular arched windows. The structure is made with bricks, lime and iron joists.

There is an *Aabdarkhana*[111] standing right in front of this *devdi*.

Baradari of Nawab Khursheed Jah Bahadur (Ref. No. 54, Grade IIB, HMDA)

This *baradari* was built around 1880–90, and designed by Nawab Fakhruddin Khan, Sir Khursheed Jah Bahadur's grandfather. In better times, this was one of the most prominent palaces of the Asaf Jahi Hyderabad; today, it has the Girls Junior College located in it.

The palace stands on a high plinth; it has a big flight of steps for its entrance, on the pattern of a European mansion. The façade of the structure has eight ionic columns supporting the *pediment*. The top floor of the structure has a barrel roof vault which gives an uncommon look to the structure. The beautifully decorated lime mouldings, the grand timber staircases, the huge halls with jack arch roofing, and the timber false ceiling are the main features of the *baradari*. The heritage building is in a bad state of preservation. Its small beautiful entrance gateway with semi-circular arch in centre resembles the two gates inside the Chowmahalla; it is also in a bad state and needs immediate attention.

Devdi Iqbal-ud-Daula, Shah Gunj (Ref. No. 56, Grade IIB, HMDA)

This *devdi* was built in the late nineteenth century; it is located in the Amir-e-Kabir Street of the historical locality of Shahgunj. *Iqbal-ud-daula* refers to the title conferred on Sir Vicar-ul-Umra; he was the Prime Minister of the Hyderabad State from 1894 to 1901. This heritage structure has weathered well and exists with most of its parts intact. Here is a sketch of one of the columns.

Devdi Iqbal-ud-Daula

The devdi is designed with bold Palladian façade. At present the structure has a mix of re-uses: a part of the devdi is a *shaadi khana* (a Function Palace); the other is a school, and the rest of the building is being used as small residential quarters.

The existing structural condition of the building in several places is poor. The entrance to the *devdi* is from the main road, through the *jilu khana*; it also stands in a bad structural condition. On entering the *jilu khana*, one finds a big open courtyard that provides access to different structures. To its right is the entrance to the Ethics School. Several steps up a stairway here, there is a classroom; the walls and the ceiling of this space display attractive floral patterns in their lime plaster – indicative of the significance this room had in this palace in the good old days; but now, their condition is fast deteriorating. Crossing the entrance courtyard, going through a narrow passage one finds a grand Hall. It is said that it functioned as *Diwan-e-Aam* (Hall of Audience). The hall displays large multi-cusped arches and intricate lime plaster work. This site needs to be cleaned and restored.

THE SOUTH-EASTERN QUADRANT and down south side

In the late Asaf Jahi period, a part of the south-eastern quadrant of the walled city had the residence of Maharaja Kishen Pershad Bahadur[112]. This trip can begin with the Unani Hospital, opposite the Mecca Masjid.

Government Unani Hospital, Charminar (Ref. No. 75, Grade IIB, HMDA)

This hospital was built in 1929, under the scheme for the post-flood developments in Hyderabad. It is one of the most important Unani and Ayurvedic hospitals of India today. The structure was designed by the architect Vincent Esch. It has big inner courtyards and is yet another specimen of the Indo-Saracenic architecture of Hyderabad. Although built much later, it fits in well with its much older neighbours, the Charminar and the Mecca Masjid.

A few hundred metres to the south of the Unani Hospital on the same road (i.e. the Charminar Falaknuma Road) is located the next heritage component, the Manjhli Begum ki Haveli.

Manjhli Begum ki Haveli (Ref. No. 18, Grade I, HMDA)

Manjhli Begum ki Haveli is accessed by a street to the right of the Pista House – a confectionary shop and restaurant. When the second Nizam shifted his capital from Aurangabad to Hyderabad (1763-1803), he constructed many buildings and palaces in the city; among them is this structure built for his daughter, Fakhr-un-Nisa or the Manjhli Begum, who lived in it all her life. Fakhr-un-Nisa was married to Zafar Yar-ud-Daula. She was a pious lady and had a great respect amongst the city nobles. Mubaraz-ud-Daula, the son of the fourth Nizam Nawab Sikander Jah, and a prominent participant of the first war of independence in 1857, was born in this *haveli*. Hence, other than architectural and historical value, the palace has political value as well. Presently, the *haveli*, or what is left of it, is being used as a marriage hall. The structure is an important heritage component of the city; the woodwork of the arched verandah at the entrance, with its ornamental niches made in lime, is considered to have a great architectural significance.

Devdi Maharaja Kishan Pershad Bahadur (Ref. No. 133, Grade III, HMDA)

The structure stands in Shah Ali Banda, another historic locality of the walled city. It is located past the Hanuman Temple,[113] on the left side of the street after the Khoya Gali. Khoya Gali was originally known as the Maharaja Peshkar Devdi Street, as it led to the property of Maharaja Kishan Pershad, the Nizam's prime minister and peshkar. The palace was constructed in 1802 by Maharaja Chandulal the great-grandfather of Maharaja Kishan Prasad; later, Kishan Prasad made several additions to it. The complex contained a *jilu khana*, *aina khana*, *bala khana*, *khas bagh*, *zenana mahal*, *serais* and *baradaris*. Besides, there were stables for Maharaja's horses, a *Feel Khana* for his elephants and the *Moti Khana* for his cars. In late 1980s, a part of the palace – the 'Shad Mansion[114]– was acquired by the Suraj Bhan Bhagwati Bai Maternity Home.

Walking past the Kishen Pershad Devdi, one reaches the Charminar-Falaknuma Road. A couple of hundred metres away on this road, to the south, stands the gateway to the Devdi Shamraj Bahadur. From here, the visitor can head to some of the tomb-complexes in the south-eastern part of the walled city: Daira Mir Momin, Makbara Kalyani, the Moghulpura Tombs, and Khairat Khan's Tomb located in the east and the north-east direction, about two hundred metres from this *devdi*.

Daira Mir Momin

Daira Mir Momin is a large graveyard named after Mir Momin, a prime minister and an architect in the Qutb Shahi period, who bought this land and converted it into a graveyard. Daira Mir Momin has the distinction of being the resting place for several important people of their time. The dargah of the renowned saint, Shah Chirag of the Qutb Shahi period is located in this graveyard. Shah Chirag's ceaseless efforts for the enrichment of the city's culture are priceless. When he passed away in 1543, his dargah was built at the southern end of the Daira Mir Momin. This graveyard has been the burial ground of the Salarjung family. The music maestro Bade Ghulam Ali Khan, who died recently, is also buried here.

Daira Mir Momin

Makbara Kalyani

This is the tomb of the saint Mirza Kalyani; it was built during the transitional period between the Mughal and the Asaf Jahi rule. It is located in the east of the Mughalpura Tombs, and can be seen from the Itebar Chowk Road. Built with Qutb Shahi construction techniques, this heritage component is in a poor state of repair. The tomb will be worth restoring as it will be a good demonstration of the historic building art and architecture.

Moghulpura Tombs (Ref. No. 39, Grade IIB, HMDA)

These tombs are located in the dense area of Mughalpura; they are built with square plans. The graves in the tombs are placed on elevated plinth. The first tomb near the entrance belongs to Qutb-ud-din, alias Nimatullah and the second tomb belongs to his son, Mirza Sharif. Both of them were members of the Qutb Shahi family. Mir Nimatullah was the maternal uncle of Prince Abdullah, the son of Muhammed Qutb Shah VI (1612-1626). Nimatullah was also the Prince's tutor. It is believed that the king was warned by his priests against seeing his son Abdulla's face till he had attained the age of twelve. One of the tombs has a domed roof and the other one is flat. Both the tombs display Qutb Shahi architectural features: the pointed arches, the stucco work and the onion dome.

Khairat Khan's Tomb (Ref. No. S-16, Protected by State Archaeology Department)

This tomb is located in the Sultan Shahi area, in the street opposite the Mughalpura Police Station. This area comes under the south of Gaulipura. Khairat Khan was King Abdullah's ambassador to Persia. He died in 1655. There are actually two tombs on this site: the larger one contains the graves of Khairat Khan and his son, Baba Abdullah; the adjoining tomb is said to be of his wife. The tombs are built with stone and lime mortar. The post of the door and the *jaali* panels, done with stone, are the main characteristics of the structure. The tombs stand on stone plinth. The entrance to the main tomb is through a small flight of steps. The façade at the entrance side has a rectangular door within a pointed arch. There is a *jaali* panel in the space between the door and the arch apex. The cantilevered part of the roof of the structure is supported by stone brackets. Below the brackets, there is a row of rectangular niches–seven in the smaller face and eleven in the larger face. On the top of the roof there is a parapet punctured by rectangular elements and crowned by floral motifs – quite common in both, the Qutb Shahi architecture and the Mughal architecture. As in any other Qutb Shahi structure, there are minarets in all the four corners, standing at the parapet level. The elevation at the entrance side has a central arch flanked by arched niches, one on either side. The main tomb is covered with a flat roof. The ceiling inside the tomb seems to be made in three parts; each part has a skylight in it.

The smaller tomb is covered with a dome that has a square skylight at the top. The dome stands on an octagonal plan, rising from the top level of all the four pointed arches with squinches.

After visiting the tombs, one can return to the Charminar–Falaknuma Road and head south for more heritage components.

Gate Portion – Shamraj Bahadur (Ref. No. 93, Grade III, HMDA)

Raja Rai Rayan Bahadur[115] was in-charge of the office of revenue in the Hyderabad State. In the front part of his palace, he built a tall gateway, in 1904 (inscribed on the gateway) with a clock on it facing the Charminar–Falaknuma Road.

The entrance gateway has a pointed arch within a multi-cusped arch. The gateway's entrance level is surrounded by four small domed canopies, one on each corner. From the centre of the gateway's roof, a tower-like structure rises to three storeys; the clocks are installed on the second storey. Only two clocks are visible at present, the one in front, and the one on the rear side; the other two sides of the tower-like structure are hidden from sight by the newly built structures right next to the structure. The parapet of the main gateway structure connects the two domed canopies, and this forms a beautiful crown on the front and the rear side of the gateway. The top most level of the tower has eight semi-circular arches supporting the dome, with a lantern (in the shape of a domed canopy with four arches).

Because of the unrestricted growth on this road, this spectacular gateway with beautiful lime stucco work goes unnoticed. The structural condition of the heritage component is not very good at present.

Five hundred metres to the south from the gateway stands the Aliabad Sarai on both sides of the main road.

Aliabad Sarai (Ref. No. 10, Grade I, HMDA)

This *sarai* is located near the Aliabad locality to the south of Charminar, on the way to Falaknuma. It was constructed in 1740, during the reign of Asaf Jah-I. The gate constructed with the *sarai*, is known as the Aliabad gate. The *sarai* was attached to the city wall; this part of the wall still exists. Presently, there are eighty shops in the *sarai* – forty on either side of the road. On the first floor, to the west, there is a mosque built in the same period as the *sarai*; the extensions to it were made later. Opposite the mosque, on the eastern side of the road, can be seen what is left of the *sarai's* gateway. Another gate in the west provides access to a graveyard and the residential locality inside.

The next component, the Durgah Hazrat Syed Shah Rajuddin, is located in the south-west of the Charminar; for the visitor's convenience it has been included in this trip. It could be accessed by taking a street next to Aliabad police station, leading to the Charminar – Falaknuma Road.

Dargah Hazrat Syed Shah Rajuddin, Gazibanda (Ref. No. S-32, Protected by State Archaeology Department)

This *dargah* is situated in the south of the Fateh Darwaza of the old city, along the road to Misrigunj and Jahanuma. Next to the entrance of the *dargah* stands the Mehboob Function Hall.

Syed Shah Rajuddin, or Shah Raju-II, was the nephew of Hussain Shah Wali; when he passed away, the Qutb Shahi ruler, Abul Hassan Tana Shah, built this magnificent tomb on his grave in 1684. Tana Shah was a great devotee of the saint, and was also married to his daughter.

The tomb stands on a square plan. The *dargah* structure has a 20 feet high verandah on all four sides, standing on octagonal columns. The dome, with a tall drum (the cylindrical part of the dome), rises from the first floor roof. There are openings in the necking to provide light and ventilation to the domed chamber. The necking ends with beautiful floral and torus shape lime moulding made several rows. Floral moulding appears to be lacing the drum of the dome.

It is the second biggest tomb in Asia after the Gol Gumbaz of Bijapur. The devotees throng here from all over the city to celebrate the annual *urs* of the saint. The tomb deserves better attention and a regular maintenance programme.

From here, one must return to the main road; the access road to the next component is located near the Falaknuma Police Station, one and a half kilometres to the south of Aliabad police station.

Falaknuma Palace

Falaknuma Palace Main Palace (Ref. No. 55a & b, Grade IIB, HMDA)
Other Palaces

'Falaknuma' means the 'mirror of the sky'; it is indeed the most famous and grand palace. To reach the Falaknuma Palace, one takes the Charminar-Falaknuma Road and travels towards the south of the city[116]. On the right, there is a huge, 2000 ft. high hillock with several palatial structures dotting the hill cannot fail to catch the visitor's attention. (Sadly, the increasing pace of development has begun to mar this heavenly view). The road to the right beyond the Falaknuma police station leads to the top of the hillock known as Koh-e-Tur; here, the visitor is welcomed by a lavishly ornamented gateway with a clock at the top. On entering this gate, one finds a group of beautifully crafted structures. Falaknuma Palace was built by Nawab Vikar-ul-Umra (also referred as Iqbal-ud-Daula), the Paigah, in 1892; it was designed by an Italian architect and it is planned in the shape of a scorpion. The palace was later purchased by Nizam VI.

The front elevation of the main palace is similar to any European mansion and the materials used in the interior surfaces of the palace were imported mostly from the European countries. Drapes and upholstery were imported from France, and the marble used here, is Italian. The paintings done on the ceiling are one of its kinds in the city. Its collection of jade objects is considered unique in the world. The library of the Falaknuma is also unique; it is rich in interiors and contains numerous rare books collected by the Nizam himself. The palace is being converted into a hotel by the Taj Group of Hotels.

Many of the scholars believe that the Falaknuma Palace resembles the palace of Versailles. It is considered unique in style and design among its contemporary palaces in India. The sixth Nizam died in this palace; considering this a bad omen, the seventh Nizam chose not to use it as his residential palace; instead, it was made a guest house for important state visitors and the royalty.

The palace has a beautifully designed and well maintained garden overlooking the city.

The next three structures in the surroundings of Charminar can be accessed from the National Highway 7 which begins at Nayapul in the south. Since the Mir Alam Tank and the Zoo Park are accessed from the National Highway, they could be included in the Karvan Trip. The *dargah* is located in the south-western direction, at a distance of two and a half kilometres from the Kishan Bagh Crossroads.

Mir Alam Tank and Zoo Park

The tank was named after Mir Alam (Syed Abdul Khasim), the Prime Minister of Hyderabad during the reign of Sikander Jah, the third Nizam. Mir Alam Tank used to cater to the city's need for drinking water. The tank has a long serpentine bund with   21 arches. This bund is an illustration of the engineering skills of the Asaf Jahi period. Andhra Pradesh Tourism provides a facility for boating in the tank; for this, one must enter from the zoo.

Spread over 300 acres of land, the Zoo Park is one of the largest in Asia. It has a collection of a large number of wild animals, birds and reptiles. The entrance to the park is from the western side of the National Highway No 7.

Kishan Bagh Temple (Ref. No. 90, Grade III HMDA)

Kishan Bagh Temple is one of the biggest and the oldest temples of Hyderabad; it is located at Bahadurpura. A U-turn on national Highway from the Zoo Park leads to the Bahadurpura Crossing (location for another historic temple of Lord Hanuman, contemporary to Kishanbagh Temple) located at a distance of seven hundred metres from the Zoo Park. A road to the west from here, leads to the temple, and then, to the dargah.

Kishan Bagh Temple was built by Raja Raghuram more than a century and a half ago. He worked as a Vakil (ambassador) of different *Samasthanas* under the Nizam. The huge entrance gateway of the temple has little ornamentation. There is a high wall surrounding the temple; within this wall, besides the temple, one finds a garden and a few living quarters for the temple's employees. There is a play-school, too, (started a few years ago) on the premises of the temple. The Shikhara of the main structure is dotted with small statues of men, animals and birds.

Before the enactment of the Urban Land Ceiling Regulation Act, the temple used for its maintenance the revenues it received from its several *jagirs* (lands). The calm and peaceful environment of the huge temple complex makes the visit here worth its while.

Dargah Syed Shah Mir Mahmood (Ref. No. 40, Grade IIB, HMDA)
About a kilometer and a half down the road[117] to the left from the Kishan Bagh
Crossing, a narrow meandering road to the left leads up the hillock and ends at
the Syed Shah Mir Mahmood Dargah; from here a number of steps lead to the
main complex. The steps end at a rectangular gateway that opens on the dargah
complex.

Syed Shah Mir Mahmood came to Hyderabad
from Najaf in Iraq during the reign of Sultan
Abdullah Qutb Shahi (1626-72); he chose to stay
on the hillock situated near Mir Alam Tank, five
miles to the west from the city of Hyderabad.
When the holy saint died in 1692, he was buried
on this hillock; his devotees celebrate *Urs* here
regularly and maintain the dargah premises.

The architecture of the main shrine conforms to the Qutb Shahi style. The
simple looking main structure of the *dargah* has a group of arches to take the
load of the huge dome which has a big drum for the dome's base; the netting of
the arches can be seen in the drum of the dome. Besides the main sanctum
sanctorum there are a few more structures in the complex with impressive
architectural features. From the rear side of the *dargah,* one gets to see a
breathtaking view of the Mir Alam Tank.

AFZALGUNJ- BEGUM BAZAR and the road parallel to the Musi River (on both the sides)

Afzalgunj located on the north bank of river, was named after the fifth Nizam
Nawab Afzal-ud-Daula. The Begum Bazaar is also located in the north of the
river and in the west of Afzalgunj; it was named after the Queen Mother
Qudsia Begum. The Begum Bazaar is the biggest general merchandise market
of Hyderabad. The market was rehabilitated after the floods of 1908.

THE NORTH BANK OF MUSI: This trip will take the visitor to the
structures of Late Asaf Jahi Period.

Devdi Bansilal (Ref. No. 115, Grade III, HMDA, INTACH Awards 1998)
The building is owned by the Pitti family[118] of Hyderabad; it stands in the busy
locality of the Begum Bazaar. It was constructed in 1930—in Raja Bansilal

Pitti's period—under the supervision of Nawab Mehdi Nawaz Jung. The structure belongs to the category of vernacular buildings of the city. It is designed with European features in the main elevation. The entrance is through a segmental arch standing on a pair of round pilasters. The sloping roof of the first floor *chajja* has <u>tri-foliated gables</u>[119], to break the monotony of the horizontal lines of the roof. The street side elevation displays a combination of different architectural elements. The main façade is done with timber, coloured glass and cast iron railing. The covering of the balcony, from the parapet railing up to the slab level, is probably a later addition. The devdi has internal courtyard, with carefully maintained interiors.

Osmania General Hospital (Ref. No. 61, Grade IIB, HMDA)

The hospital was constructed during the reign of Mir Osman Ali Khan, the seventh Nizam; it is situated in the busy locality of Afzalgunj, overlooking the river Musi; the Afzalgunj Bridge on the river links the Walled City to rest of the Hyderabad. This is one of the most important constructions by the City Improvement Board. Looking at the skyline of the heritage structure across the Musi River (on the southern bank) one gets the impression of it being another palace of Hyderabad, with its soaring domes and minarets surrounding the main dome. The domes, designed by Vincent Esch, are different here from the Qutb Shahi domes more massive and round in shape.

At the time it was built, this hospital was considered one of the best equipped hospitals in India. The main entrance to the hospital is from the river side and another from the Afzalgunj side. The entrance from the river side has a park in front called Osmania Park (refer to Chapter 4). This park has a Tamarind Tree which saves the life of many people during the flood of September 1908.

Afzal Gunj Mosque (Ref. No. 37, Grade IIB, HMDA)

This mosque was constructed in the period of Nawab Afzal-ud-Daula, in 1857. It displays an impressive combination of elements from both the Qutb Shahi, and the Mughal architecture. The main elevation of the mosque has all the features of the Qutb Shahi[120] architecture. The cloister around it has the multi-cusped arches that stand on

Afzalgunj Mosque original elevation

the angular fluted columns (not with the round flutings) facing the courtyard. The entrance to the mosque is from a 20 feet high wooden door fixed in a pointed arch-shaped opening. After climbing a couple of steps, one enters a big courtyard. Facing the courtyard is the verandah made with cement concrete and belongs to a later period (refer to the sketch on the cover page of this Circle displaying the original façade of the mosque). After crossing the verandah, one sees a panel of three arches that support the domes. There are six domes (three in each row) that form the roof of the mosque. The thickness of the arch is rendered with simple lines in lime plaster (multi-tiered arch). The arched openings in the front have been closed with a wired grill at present.

The architectural features of this mosque appear to be similar to the Mehboob Chowk Mosque (1817).

State Central Library (Ref. No. 68, Grade IIB, HMDA)

This library was formerly known as Asafia Library, after the name of the Asaf Jahi dynasty; it was founded in 1891 by one of the famous personalities of Hyderabad, Moulvi Syed Hussain Bilgrami. Initially, it was located in an old bungalow in Abids, at the site of the present GPO. The library was once known for its Urdu, Arabic, Persian and English books, besides numerous manuscripts; these have since been transferred to the State Archives Library in Tarnaka.

The architecture of this building displays a judicious mix of the architecture in different parts of the Nizam's dominions[121]: the main entrance appears to be similar to the one in Buddha *Viharas* of Ajanta, and the semi-circular vault-like structure in the front elevation is a reminiscent of the sun window of the *Vihara*, originally made in wood and stone. The plinth of the structure is kept high. There is a circular *jaali* designed over the entrance door and the external surface of the walls of the structure display beautiful plaster work done in lime.

The State Central Library building was constructed by the seventh Nizam, Mir Osman Ali Khan in 1936; it is situated near the bank of the river Musi, close to the Afzalgunj Mosque.

THE SOUTH BANK of Musi River: Most of the structures in this trip date back to the late Asaf Jahi period.

Salarjung Museum

The Salarjung Museum was originally housed in Diwan Devdi (the house of the *diwan*) near Charminar; in 1968 it was shifted to this complex. The museum was started by Salarjung I, the *diwan* (prime minister) of Hyderabad (1853–1883). He started collecting unique articles which he acquired during his visits to Europe. His eldest son, Salarjung II and after him his son, Salarjung III, continued the good work of adding artifacts to the museum. Mir Yusuf Ali, Salarjung III, is said to have made a major contribution to the museum collection.

The Salarjung Museum, with its 43,000 objects, is one of the largest private collections in the world. The library of the Museum complex has a remarkable collection of about 50,000 books in several languages – English, Urdu, Persian and Arabic.

Victoria Maternity Hospital (Ref. No. 73, Grade IIB, HMDA)

The Hospital was founded in 1902, in the memory of Queen Victoria of England. According to a different source, the foundation stone of this hospital was laid on the bank of the river Musi by the Price of Wales, in 1906. The big flood in the Musi River in 1908 washed away many parts of the Hospital; all the patients in the hospital are said to have lost their lives. The hospital was rebuilt after 1911, during the rule of the seventh Nizam.

The entrance to the hospital is from the north and its main façade is in the south. In front of the main block there is a well-laid garden, with a small rectangular pool at the centre. At the centre of the pool, there is a carved stone column. As per the local scholars, the stone column dates back to the Qutb Shahi period and was discovered at the site during the construction of the hospital.

With its turrets, minarets and canopies the hospital building has the appearance of a palace complex. It displays an attractive combination of semi-circular and Osman Shahi arches – the roofing is jack-arched, and the plinth is made of stone. The site is full of green trees, which screen the view of the main structure from the road.

City College (Ref. No. 62, Grade IIB, HMDA)

This structure was constructed in 1921 as a part of the City Improvement
Board's project. The structure is a remarkable specimen of the Indo-Saracenic
architecture of Hyderabad. The building can be accessed from the City College
Road on the banks of the river Musi. The plinth of this heritage structure is
made in stone. The walls are punctured with arched doors and windows. Some
windows are fixed in the arched openings, leaving the multi-cusped shape for
the ventilator. The entrance is adorned by an Osman Shahi arch after a flight of
steps. The skyline of the building is dotted with high domes, some smaller
domed-kiosks, the crenellated (pointed arch type) parapet wall, and the *chajja*
that is supported by brackets.

A.P. High Court (Ref. No. 74, Grade IIB, HMDA, INTACH Awards 1996)

After crossing the river from the north of the city one sees grey-coloured
domes contributing to the Old City's skyline towards the Charminar locality.
The High Court building is one of the most magnificent works of the Indo-
Saracenic architecture in India; it was designed by none other than Vincent
Esch. The structure stands at the south end of the river Musi; it was built
during the rule of Mir Mehboob Ali Khan, the seventh Nizam, as a part of the
post-flood development project of the City Improvement Board. A
monumental flight of steps provide access to the structure.

A big central dome adorns the entrance portal with an Osmanian arch that contributes symmetry and balance to the superstructure. The ceilings in many rooms are kept high, and a play of different levels can be observed in different blocks. The plan of the High Court comprises inner courtyards with a well maintained exterior garden that provides cool breeze all around. Before visiting the structure, a special permission must be obtained from the concerned authority. The other structure, next to the heritage building, is an extension to the original one.

Dar-ush-Shifa and Mosque (Ref. No. 33, Grade IIA, HMDA):

Dar-ush-Shifa was built by Mohammed Quli Qutb Shah in 1595, to provide free medicine to as many as 400 patients at a time. It was a Unani Medicine hospital and a residential college; physicians from different countries came here to attend to the sick. The structure also had a caravanserai for the patients on the waiting list. Presently, a school and a few shops are located in the Dar-ush-Shifa structure. The shops can be seen from the main road (north-south). In the courtyard of the Dar-ush-Shifa, there is an *Ashurkhana* (the mourning hall) which has in it the *Sar Tafu Alam*[122], associated with the fourth Shia Imam, Hazrat Zainul Abidin. Dar-ush-Shifa is unique structure in the whole range of Secular architecture of Deccan.

Opposite the entrance gateway of the Dar-ush-Shifa there is a beautiful mosque. Originally, the mosque is a Qutb Shahi structure; the big domed-hall, with hexagonal RCC columns, is a later addition to it, to accommodate more people inside the mosque. The original Qutb Shahi construction system and ornamentation could easily be differentiated from the modern one. The beautiful Qutb Shahi calligraphy on the medallions (the enamel tiles around pointed arches in the main, and original, façade), to add brightness to the façade, cannot go unnoticed.

Old M.C.H. Office (Ref. No. 135, Grade III, HMDA)

This heritage complex is located in the south of the Dar-ush-Shifa crossing, near Aza-Khana-e-Zehra. Curently, different government agencies are functioning from this complex including the office of QQSUDA (Quli Qutb Shah Urban Development Authority). The MCH office was shifted to this complex in 1906. This complex was also used as Madrassa-e-Aizza, and the Mint in the past.

There is a big courtyard in this complex, in and around which there are several blocks; some of these blocks are later additions to the original complex. The entire complex stands in a poor state of repair. The site has an architectural value as it displays various construction systems and attractive architectural features made in wood. It needs to be restored urgently.

Aza Khana-e-Zehra (Ref. No. 88, Grade III, HMDA)

This is also known as 'Madre-e-Deccan' Ashurkhana. The Aza Khana-e-Zehra, a large white building with domes and *jaalis*, is located at a distance of 135 metres to the east of the Salarjung Museum. It can be seen from the north bank of the river Musi. This structure was built in 1930, by Mir Osman Ali Khan, the seventh Nizam of Hyderabad, in memory of his mother Zehra. It is one of the largest *ashurkhanas* in the country.

The remarkable interiors of this structure are worth visiting. The walls and the ceiling of the hall are covered with extraordinary enamel work.

The Charminar Precinct (as declared by the HMDA)

The Heritage Precinct declared by the HMDA starts from the Salarjung Museum Road and Purani Haveli Road in the east corner goes till Daira Mir Momin.   Moving towards west side, along with Mughalpura Akkanna Madanna Temple, Hari Baoli, Shah Ali Banda, Kazapura touching Doodh Baoli Darwaza and Hussaini Alam, touching City College and City College Road comes back to the same junction of the Aza Khana-e-Zehra (refer to the boundary of Heritage Precinct No. 14). Though the precinct covers most of the listed and protected heritage structures, yet is different from the walled city map; and there are many more monuments with or without list waiting for the protection from the city's pressure[123].

The boundaries of the precinct exist on the paper for the precinct, as a part of regulation; but for the visitor, it is the essence of the old city which can be felt in different pockets of the heritage precinct.

Only effort required for the future of the city is to keep the heritage alive; to create a sense of belonging in the citizens so that they themselves contribute to lessen the burden of economic pressure in and around the historic core of the city.

The Circle VI- Dilsukhnagar and surroundings will be discussed in the next section.

CIRCLE VI

DILSUKHNAGAR and SURROUNDINGS

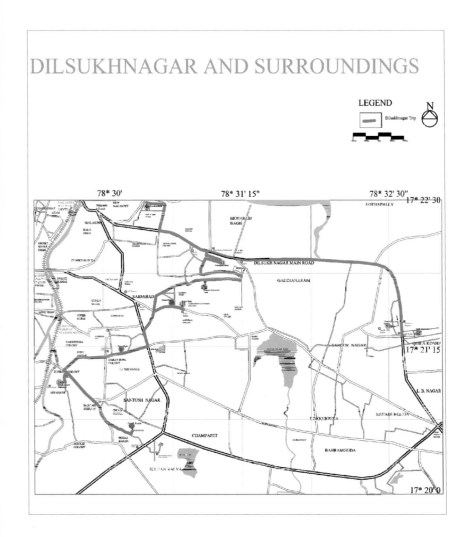

This locality is in the south-eastern part of the city and on the southern bank of the river Musi. Dilsukhnagar can be accessed after crossing Moosaram Bridge. In the surroundings of Dilsukhnagar there are some historic localities, associated with different people. For instance, Asmangarh is associated with Paigah Noble Sir Asman Jah; Malakpet[124] is with the sixth Nizam and Saidabad is associated with another noble in the Qutb Shahi Court. The National Highway No. 9 between Mumbai and Vijayawada is the south of Dilsukhnagar, there is going to in the east. All the structures discussed in this section can be covered in one trip.

The first structure in this trip is the huge Asaf Jahi palace.

Victoria Memorial Home (Ref. No. 57, Grade IIB, HMDA, INTACH Awards 2003)

The Victoria Memorial Home and Industrial School—earlier known as Victoria Memorial Orphanage—is located in a huge Asaf Jahi palace at Saroornagar[125] in the west of the Dilsukhnagar Main Road. The heritage structure was originally meant to be the palace of Mir Mehboob Ali Khan, the sixth Nizam. However, while it was still under construction, the Nizam fell ill. Considering this a bad omen, the king decided against using the structure as his future palace so its construction was halted. Almost at the same time, in 1901, Queen Victoria of England died. Sir David Bar, the then British Resident of India, wished to set up an institution that would perpetuate the memory of the diseased queen. This structure suited his purpose. So, with the Nizam's permission, the construction of the palace was completed, and in 1903, Victoria Memorial Home was instituted here.

The structure is the biggest of its kind in the State of Andhra Pradesh. There are six big rooms, a large hall and a number of smaller rooms being used for a residential school. A big flight of steps leads to the main entrance hall built on a monumental scale. Across the verandah on the same axis there is a huge courtyard, possibly meant for large gatherings in the palace. The roofing in most of the spaces is jack-arched. The massing of different blocks appears an interesting composition when viewed from the front. There is also a mosque in this palace complex, close to the main block on the western side, probably built in the same period.

Qila Kohna and Mosque[126] (Ref. No. 41, Grade IIB, HMDA)

Saroornagar was once the suburban area of the city of Hyderabad. It was renowned for its healthy climate, but its water was not fit for use. This could explain why a large palace lies here, incomplete. Ibrahim Qutb Shah is said to have started building a fortress here in 1560. On one of his visits to the site of the construction, he fell ill. His courtiers considered this a bad omen and the construction was stopped. The incomplete structure has been lying in ruins for the past many years.

The site is important for its historical value, but more so, for its educational and architectural value. It deserves to be cleaned and restored. It has the educational and the architectural value, other than the historic value. The students of architecture, history and archaeology can learn about the building material and construction techniques of that period from the structural components lying abandoned in the open space. This site exits in the east of Dilsukhnagar Main Road, opposite Victoria Memorial Home.

Close to Dilsukhnagar Main Road, Saroornagar Lake is another site for recreation. Cleaned and maintained by HMDA, this is one of the biggest lakes of the city.

Hayat Bakshi Begum Sarai and Mosque[127] (Protected by State Archaeology)

The huge complex of the Hayat Bakshi Begum Mosque is located on NH 9, the road to Vijayavada. It has a caravanserai, a mosque and a large well. The road right opposite the entrance arch of the RTC Colony leads to the mosque. There is an Indian Oil petrol pump and a showroom of the Honda Motors on the National Highway No. 9, the *minars* of the mosque are visible behind them.

Hayat Bakhshi Begum[128] was Sultan Abdullah Qutb Shah's mother and daughter of Mohammed Quli Qutb Shah. The mosque was built during the reign of the Sultan some time between 1626–72. The large mosque has a caravanserai around a 150mx130m courtyard. There is also a large well-known as the Hathi Baoli–on the north-east of the mosque. One of the walls of this well displays the remains of some lime murals. The caravanserai has four

entrance gateways topped with a combination of domed and flat ceiling built
with stone and lime mortar. The front elevation of the mosque has five Qutb
Shahi arches and *minars* at its ends. The *minar* has a miniature balcony, above
which the round shape shaft of the minar takes the shape of an *amalaka*[129], an
interesting feature, unique to this mosque.

The rear side of the mosque is similar to that of the Khairati Begum's mosque
and the Kulsumpura Mosque. All the smaller elements, used in the Qutb Shahi
ornamentation, are present here; the parapet of crossed arches, the stone
brackets in the Gujarati style, the rectangular stone water spouts are all a treat

Main Gateway - Mahboob Mansion

for the visitor interested in history, art, architecture and photography. The site
stands in the serene surroundings of Hayatnagar. The open plot of land next to
the Hathi Baoli is reserved for a park; the boundary wall of this plot has
recently been built by the Municipal Corporation.

Mehboob Mansion (Ref. No. 50, Grade IIB, HMDA)
Mehboob Mansion used to be one of the palaces of the sixth Nizam, Mir
Mehboob Ali Khan. The Nizam lived in this palace for a short span, as he lived
in Purani Haveli for most of the time. Nizam built a race course, considered to
be one of the best in the country, along with a palatial residence amidst a
garden. This residence is Mehboob Mansion. The mansion can be accessed
from State Highway No. 9, by taking a street through the Grain and Seed
Market, Malakpet.

The visitor is greeted by the ceremonial entrance to the mansion, which is quite similar to the one made for the European mansions. A big semi-circular arch is flanked by two small arched alcoves, on the lower level of the gateway. This arch is topped with a pediment. The pediment has some plaster decoration in it and is further enhanced by the crenellated wall and two small barbicans. The central arch of the gateway has single storeyed structures designed symmetrically on both the sides. These small structures were probably meant to house the guards. There is one more entrance gateway smaller than the main one, located on the road to the west of the main entrance, probably served as a secondary entrance to the mansion.

The physical condition of both the gateways is fair. Inside this gateway, the beautiful palace was located on a high platform with many staff quarters, a beautiful cistern and a huge area around it. Slowly, many new residential colonies like Saleem Nagar Colony, Andhra Colony, New Malakpet, Professors Colony and Dilsukhnagar Colony came up in the vicinity of Mahboob Mansion. In the mid-1980s the mansion and the land around it had been acquired by the State Government and all the trees around it were cut down[130].

The building is a fair example of Indo-European architecture and was built in late nineteenth century. The plinth of the gateway and the main palace is made of stone. The ground floor has semi-circular arches displaying a dominance of European architecture. The first floor displays more of Mughal influence with the multi-cusped arches. Palace had beautiful interior and exterior surfaces. Ornamental painting was done on the walls of the rooms. Traces of this paint can be seen in some of the walls in the upper storey, close to the beam level. The structure is covered with Madras terrace and jack-arched roofing techniques.

There are a number of semi-permanent structures/huts come up right next to the mansion, because of which the main access to the palace is blocked, and it is difficult to see the structure from inside.

Asmangarh Palace (Ref. No. 51, Grade IIB, HMDA, INTACH Awards 2004)

The palace is located opposite the Salim Nagar Colony on the way to Saroornagar. The site is close to the Hyderabad TV Tower and can be reached

by a road branching off the State Highway No. 9. This road turns around the tower and ends at the palace.

The palace designed and constructed by Sir Asman Jah, a Paigah noble and the Prime Minister of Hyderabad State, stands on the top of a hill with beautiful granite turrets and pointed arched windows. Asmangarh Palace is built in the pattern of a European Castle. The roofing is done with jack-arch and Madras terrace technique. The buttresses are constructed to enhance the stability of the structure. A view of the palace with crenellated parapet wall and gothic pointed arches can be seen from the nearby hillock, the site of Raymond's Tomb, another heritage site of the neighbouring area.

Presently, there is St. Joseph's School functioning in the grounds of the palace. The three-storeyed block of the school is a later addition to the site. The heritage structure is being used as a part of the school and regular classes are being conducted in it. Permission from the school authority is required prior to the visit.

Mons Raymond's Obelisk (Ref. No. S-18, Protected by State Archaeology)

This heritage site is located in the New Malakpet. A seven-metre high granite obelisk marks the grave of a French adventurer, Michel Joachim Marie Raymond, who served in the Nizam's army. Raymond came to Pondicherry as a trader at the age of twenty and later joined the army of Tipu Sultan. After the defeat and death of Tipu Sultan in 1785, he enlisted in the Nizam's army (the second Asaf Jah, Nizam Ali Khan,) in Hyderabad.

Raymond was responsible for building the Gunfoundry (refer to the Abids section) used for training a large number of troops. He was quite popular among his troops; even today the descendents of his troops gather at his grave for *Urs* on his death anniversary. He was affectionately known as Musa Ram by the Hindus and Musa Rahim by the Muslims. The area surrounding the grave is known as Musa Ram Bagh. A pillared structure with a pediment on top, standing next to the granite obelisk is used to store the material required for the *Urs*. The faded grave stone nearby belongs to Anne Elizabeth Jenkins. Not much is known about Anne or her relations with Monsieur Raymond.

Ameen Manzil (Ref. No. 24, Grade I, HMDA)

Ameen Manzil is located in Saidabad[131]. It was constructed in the late nineteenth century and was once the residence of *Nawab* Amin Jung, the private secretary of the sixth Nizam. The part of this house that had the library of the nawab has been listed by HMDA. Besides political and associational value, Ameen Manzil has architectural value as well. Its unique architectural feature is its window sun-shades; they are designed in the shape of a pediment at the lower level, supported by scroll-shaped brackets. The brackets stand on the capital of a pilaster with semi-circular shaft. This pediment has been adopted from the European architecture and has taken a local shape in Hyderabad. It has a bas-relief[132] designed with the crescent moon and a star with floral pattern around it. The side elevation of the structure has a semi-circular arch with a prominent key-stone at the centre. This part of the structure is surrounded by a pilaster on either side with crown moulding at the top and is covered with a bangladar roof, *chau-chala*[133] type. The metope of the crown here is decorated in the local style – with a flower-shaped element. This element has been repeated on the curved panels formed on all four sides of *bangladar* roof. The openings have now been barred with iron grill for security. There is a wall between the residence and the library now; the entrance to the two parts of the structure is separate and next to each other.

Baquer Bagh (Ref. No. 131, Grade III, HMDA)

The family of Abdul Baquer Khan is staying in the Baquer Bagh. It is situated on the main road in Saidabad (west to east) towards west and close to Ameen Manzil. The residence stood amidst a beautiful garden once as a separate entity; it seems to be subdivided now. The main feature of the structure is its beautiful elliptical arch which has enframed in it three gothic pointed arches – the big one in the centre, and the small one on its either side. On the first floor stand two columns and two pilasters—symmetrically placed—which make way for a semi-open space on this floor. There are pivoted windows[134] on the first floor verandah that seems to have been added at a later point of time. The parapet of the top floor is another admirable feature; the vase-like objects standing on the pedestals seem to crown the structure. In the interiors, the openings are designed with, a gothic pointed arch with moulding enframing the door and the windows individually. The springing points of the arch rest on the capital of ornamental pilaster. The floral pattern of the wooden tracery enhances the beauty of the semi-circular fanlight here. The roofing is done with a combination of primary and secondary wooden beams.

Old Idgah, Madannapet (Ref. No. S-41, Protected by State Archaeology)
The *Idgah* is located in Edi Bazaar and was built by Sultan Mohammed Qutb Shah (1612–1626). When another *Idgah* was built near the Mir Alam Tank[135], this former one understandably came to be known as the Purani Idgah. It is a massive and imposing structure and is protected by the State Archaeology Department. The word *Idgah* refers to an open place meant for the community to gather and offer prayers on the festival of Id.

If one comes from the Saidabad police station and proceeds towards south, one finds a road which leads to Santosh Nagar. To the right there is a road that leads to the Rein Bazaar; if one turns right, one cannot miss the huge structure of the Idgah. It is located in a narrow lane to the right on this road. A single bay structure, with three arches and two large *minars*, surprises the visitor by the very scale on which it is built. It presents an attractive composition of horizontal and vertical components. The *minars* have the rings on the base and the main shaft. Each *minar* has a gallery of multi-cusped arches which starts at a level higher than the parapet wall of the main mosque. The structure of the mosque is made, primarily, of stone and lime. A staircase in the *minar* leads to the roof-top.

The ceiling of the structure is domed, and each dome stands on polygon formed by the crossing of the four arches. The apex of the arches and squinches are decorated with a floral motif made with lime stucco. The remains of a lime pendant at the centre of the dome can be easily noticed. The Qutb Shahi arches in the front façade have medallions on the external surface. A row of stone brackets support the cantilevered roof. On the top of the *chajja*, stands the parapet wall, with a series of arched openings and minarets.

One must not forget to look at its side elevation, which is quite uncommon. Breadth of the mosque measures less than half of the length. The side elevation has unusual rows of six concave hemispherical niches and the seventh one is divided into two halves and placed back symmetrically on left and right of this row. There are three such rows. This structure is different from a regular *Idgah*, which usually has just one wall, with a prayer niche in its centre. This wall stands in a courtyard (open to the sky), facing west. The structure seems to be quite similar to a covered mosque.

Dargah Hazrath Shahjuddin (Ref. No. 38, Grade IIB, HMDA)

This well known *dargah* of Hazrat Mir Shajuuddin Saheb is located in Edi Bazaar. The saint was born in 1744 AD at Burhanpur and came to Hyderabad in 1779, when the third Nizam Nawab Sikander Jah was the ruler.

The Nizam was one of the great devotees of Hazrat Shajuuddin. The saint died in 1848, at the age of seventy-four.

The tomb stands in a complex with two-storeyed *Naqqarkhana*, a mosque and a graveyard. The verandah of the main tomb has five multi-cusped arches on all the four sides. The structure is made of lime and rubble stone masonry. The three-storeyed structure is topped with a dome. The ground floor has five multi-cusped arches in the elevation. The first floor structure has nine arches façade, same on all four sides. The parapet of this storey has small minarets on it, enframing the dome. At the third level, there is a huge dome covering the structure. The surface of the dome's necking is patterned with two rows of flower petals on it.

On the roadside, a verandah in RCC has been added to the tomb of Hazrat Shajuddin. The grills of the verandah, painted in green, are a recent addition. The courtyard opposite the dargah has graves with beautiful tombstones; it also has a small, single-storeyed structure, with three arches in its façade on all the sides.

Shams-ul-umra Tombs (Paigah Tombs), Phisal Banda (Ref. No. S-40, Protected by State Archaeology)

Fondly referred to as the Taj Mahal of south India, this complex seems to have lost much of its original glory; still, there is a lot to save, restore and admire here even today. The site is known as the Paigah Tombs, as this is the burial ground of the members of the famous Paigah family of the   Asaf Jahi period.

Shams-ul-umra Tombs is located in Phisal Banda, near Santosh Nagar[136]. The entry to the complex is through the *Naubatkhana* – a traditional doorway. Inside the tomb complex there is a beautiful mosque with a tank and a store house. In the courtyard of the mosque there are a number of tombs – the tombs of the top-ranking nobility of Hyderabad. The structure of this mosque displays a mix of the Qutb Shahi and the Asaf Jahi architectural features – the main façade has three pointed arches and two minars.

The presence of a mosque in the tomb complex is a deviation from tradition; not only does the site provide a place for people to pray but also for their prayers to resonate over the graves of the 27 members of the *Paigah* family buried in them.

The main feature of these tombs is their *jaalis* that, although made in lime, appear like the ones made of marble in the Mughal architecture. The multi-cusped arches and their springing points stand on the lotus capital with fluted shafts; this creates a long isle in front of the main tomb complex. Perpendicular to this nave, there are wooden doors enframed – typical of a *bangladar* pavilion style canopy; this is a unique architectural feature of this complex. The two panelled doors, done in wood, are richly ornamented with wooden *jaali*; they act like a screen, for the graves of the great *Paigah* family.

The experienced guides from the Department of Archaeology and Museums narrate to the visitor, the family-tree and beauty of even the tiniest element in the complex in a unique manner. Though the site of the complex is small, one needs to spend some quality time here to see the intricate, elaborate work of the craftsmen.

Paigah refers to pomp and rank in the Persian language. The second Asaf Jahi king conferred the honorific title of *Paigah* on the estates held by Abdul Fateh Khan Taig Jung Bahadur in appreciation of the services rendered to him.

From here, we will move to the last part, Circle VII– The north-east of the city.

CIRCLE VII

EAST OF THE CITY

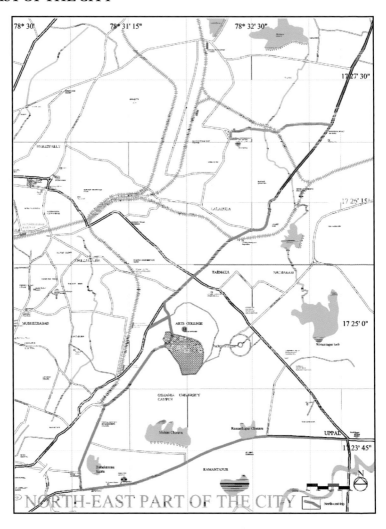

This Circle includes the remaining historic localities and sites in the east of Hyderabad, which includes Uppal, a part of the historic trade route, Amberpet, a well-known locality close to Dilsukhnagar (but on the north side of the river) dating back to the early Asaf Jahi period (could be even earlier than that), Adikmet village, the site of the Osmania University and Maula Ali among others.

Uppal Mosque (Protected by State Archaeology)

This Qutb Shahi mosque is situated in Uppal, in the eastern part of the city of Hyderabad along the Warrangal Road. It can easily be located when driving on the National Highway No. 202 towards the east, about 300 metres from the busy Uppal Crossing on the left. It was built during the reign of Abdullah Qutb Shah (1626-1672) when he camped at Uppal on his way back to Hyderabad from Machlipatnam.

The mosque has a façade of three Qutb Shahi arches in the front and is approached by a flight of steps. The arches are adorned by plain round medallions which are supported by curved brackets. These are termed as Grecian Horns by some scholars and are seen as a three-dimensional ornamental feature in the different Qutb Shahi mosques and Paigah Tombs built later. It appears that the construction of the mosque was finished in a hurry as the mosque displays very little ornamentation. This notwithstanding,

the structure has a clean and minimalist appearance. The mosque has a single bay with a prayer niche at the centre. The arches support a domed ceiling with squinches. These domes stand on a polygonal base formed by crossing of arches. A part of the polygonal minarets in the front becomes square in shape (cuboid in form) at the parapet level. There is an arched gallery at parapet level of the mosque. The entire structure is made from granite stone.

The shed at entrance, made of trusses and steel, is a recent addition.

From the Uppal Mosque, one can take a U-turn back to the National Highway and arrive at the Amberpet Locality after covering a distance of about five kilometres.

Amberpet Burj[137] (Ref. No. 3, Grade I, HMDA)

Amberpet Burj stands on the eastern side of the National Highway No. 202, next to a school in a narrow lane of Amberpet locality. It is named after Hazrat Amber Mian, a saint, whose sanctum sanctorum is located near the *burj*. Amberpet Burj is a two storeyed structure made of stone. It served the purpose of an outpost during the early Asaf Jahi period. This is another uncommon typology in the list of the heritage components. The *burj* displays rubble masonry and its beautiful oriel windows spell the influence of Mughal architecture in the city.

Dargah Hazrat Amber Mian is on the other side of the road, 100 metres to the east. The dargah is a simple structure with a square plan. It stands on a platform with three Qutb Shahi arches in all the four facades. The entrance to the dargah is through the central doorway. Opposite the dargah stands a gateway opening on a residential locality.

Back on National Highway No. 202, one has to go further down to the east and at the crossing take the Sivam Road that meets the University Road.

Osmania Arts College (Ref. No.14, Grade I, HMDA, INTACH Awards 2006)

Standing on Jamia Osmania Road, the building for the Arts College was designed by Moneieur Jasper and its foundation was laid on 5 July 1934 by the seventh Nizam of Hyderabad, Mir Osman Ali Khan. The construction of this building was supervised by Nawab Zain Yar-Jung. A team of designers is said to have gone not only to the different parts of the State of Hyderabad but across the world to study various architectural styles before finalising the design of this building. This is quite evident by the architecture of the superstructure that displays a harmonious blend of several styles: the arches used in façade are trefoil Moorish arches; the pointed arches used in the interiors of the structure are Osman Shahi, and the form of the column is similar to that of the ones in Ajanta and Ellora. The building material used and the techniques employed in the construction are a mix of the modern and the old—the huge RCC dome, measuring 12 metres in diameter, in the centre of the main hall substantiates this statement. The octagonal base dome is punctured by a number of openings to provide screened light to the hall.

Arts College, Osmania University

The Arts College building is 110 metres wide and 119 metres long. The entrance hall is square in plan, and designed with terraced floor. The growth of the university is phenomenalthe Arts College building is just a part of the huge campus of the University. The college was at first located near King Koti (1919); it was moved to its present location in 1934. Ownership of the building lies with the university. The heritage structure the Arts College is maintained on a regular basis; it received INTACH Heritage Award in 2006.

The Landscape Garden is opposite the university library, close to the Law College of the Osmania University. The garden is spread over a vast area and is used by students for studying during college hours. It has some shaped stone blocks which were left over after the construction of the university convenient for the students who use them as seats. The garden has a small Lord Shiva temple. There is a small organic-shaped pond here as well.

Malaqa Chanda Bai's Well

It is one of the oldest universities of Andhra Pradesh and the first one to use Urdu as the medium of instruction. On the other side of the Jamia Osmania Road is the English and Foreign Language University (EFLU), previously known as the CIEFL (Central Institute of English and Foreign Language). The EFLU complex proudly owns a heritage stepped-well, known as the Mahalaqa Chanda Bai's[138] well.

Maula-Ali–The inseparable built and natural heritage site (INTACH Awards 2008)

Maula-Ali is four kilometres from the Tarnaka Crossing on the Tarnaka–Maula-Ali Road. The locality is known for its cultural and religious past as well as its industrial development. Maula-Ali lies in the north-eastern part of the city. It is a huge granite rock 2017 feet above the sea level. On the top of the rock, there is a shrine dedicated to Ali; this is how the hill got its name, Maula-Ali. Kadam Rasul is another huge granite hill that stands out in the vicinity; a legend[139] has it that it bears the impression of Prophet Mohammed's foot. People come here on a short pilgrimage trip since Qutb Shahi Period.

It is a treat for rock lovers to climb up and feast on a clear view of the eastern part of the city[140]. Driving up and down as one reaches close to the hillock. On the side of the road small structures dating back to different periods can be seen in parts as the newly constructed structures have covered the heritage facades. This road ends with a big entrance gateway known as Maula Ali Kaman–a much wider road starts from here which is a highway leading to Tarnaka.

Different approaches to the Dargahs on the rocks are highlighted by the gateways built at the foothills. The steps to the Maula Ali Dargah are cut in the rocks. Midway to this dargah, there is a small natural water body. One can relax here for a few minutes before continuing the climb. On top of the rock there is a huge open space where a big gateway welcomes the visitors. The main dargah conforms to the Qutb Shahi architecture. On the way to Maula Ali Kaman from Radhika Theatre, to the right, one finds Chanda ka Bagh; Mahalaqa Bai Chanda's Baradari (late 18th century) is located here. This complex includes a *baradari*, a mosque, a *baoli* and a domed pavilion with two graves (*See picture above*). The access to this complex is from the street.

After Chanda ka Bagh, one comes to a small crossing; on the right[141] stands Moseri Sahib ki Kaman. Predominantly in European style, this was the entrance to a residential unit that does not exist anymore. Another 100 metres and one finds a gateway opening into Afsar Khan ki Baradari, a graveyard (*See picture to the left*). The architectural features here are quite similar to those found in the Paigah Tombs and the Saida ni Ma's Tomb.

From here one sees another beautiful mosque with Qutb Shahi features that stands behind the *baradari*.

Due to the indiscriminate cutting/blasting of stones in the surroundings, the rock is fast losing its beauty and balance.

Fortification and Baradari, Malkajgiri (Ref. No. S-36, Protected by State Archaeology)

This fortified land belonged to the second Nizam, Mir Nizam Ali Khan .It was named as Bagh-e-Mahooba Begum (garden of the darling wife). It has a building *(mahal)* named as *Baradari*. This was a gift to his Begum Mahal Gabai[142]. Nizam II stayed with Begum Sahiba on Fridays, when he visited the nearby mosque Maula Ali for his afternoon prayers. The complex has two gates, one in the western side and another in the north, large enough to facilitate the movement of an elephant or a horse ridden chariot. The area also features a fountain, a large well with bathing facilities for the *zenana* and side lawns opposite the *baradari*. The multi-foliated arches and the fluted coupled columns built in the Qutb Shahi and Mughal style are features that can still be observed in the remains of the *baradari*. In front of the *baradari*, there is a water channel. The well near the *baradari* was in use until recently (8-10 years back).

In 1954, this property was sold by HEH Mubarak Hazrat Ali to Mr D.V. Rao whose son lived there and cultivated the land. Eleven years later, the property was again sold to M/s. Shaw Walace and Co. Ltd. for their liquor manufacturing company. The property was identified by State Archaeology in 1974 under the Archaeological Act 1960.

Keesargutta Temple

The Road from Tarnaka to Maula-Ali leads to the ECIL Crossing; from here, a road to the south goes via Kushaiguda to the Keesara – a village located in the eastern end of the Hyderabad metropolitan area about 18 kilometres from the ECIL Crossing. There is a temple complex here in the Keesara[143] village known as the Ramlingeshwara Temple. A legend has it that Lord Rama installed the Sivalingam in the temple here as recompense for the sin of killing a Brahmin, Ravana. Shree Rama is said to have asked Hanuman to fetch a Sivalingam from Varanasi. But Hanuman could not return with Shivalingum before the auspicious hour for the installation; and so, Lord Shiva is said to have appeared himself and presented Shree Rama with a lingam for its installation at the auspicious time. Thus, the chief lingam in the temple *garbhagriha* is known as

the *swayambhu lingam*. When Hanuman did return later with 101 lingams he is said to have placed them all in the valley with his tail. Even today, one can witness a number of lingas in the valley.

Main features of the temple complex are the huge *gopurams*, a huge idol of lord Hanuman, the *kamans* (about 200 years old), rocks and the water bodies.

The temple is quite famous among locals; all Hindu festivals are celebrated here. The temple site dates back to third to fourth century. The remnants of several Hindu and Jain temples are found on the foothills close to which the State Archaeology has set up a museum which is closed at present.

Here, we end the discussion of different circles of the city, and move on to understand the architectural knowledge system of the historic structures.

Chapter 4

Understanding Architecture Through History

An Introduction to the Architectural Knowledge System and the Dying Wisdom[144]

This chapter deals with the building system, materials and the ornamentation techniques used in the historic structures of Hyderabad. This chapter takes a holistic approach in providing very basic information about the architectural knowledge system that developed in the different phases of the architectural history of Hyderabad.

The lakes, wells and other man-made sources for collecting water, along with more reversible and sustainable practices, have also been discussed here

A series of some of the historic events in Hyderabad have been discussed here. The sequential reference of these events is meant to facilitate a better appreciation of the development of the architectural heritage of the city. The buildings under discussion belong to the category of: the residential, commercial, religious, civic and the funerary structures. The inferences on the architectural style/s developed during each phase will be drawn after discussing that phase in the history of the city.
The phases in the city's history are:

PHASE I: the Qutb Shahi rule (1518-1687)
PHASE II: the Mughal rule: the transitional phase and establishment of the Asaf Jahi rule (1687-1724)[145]
PHASE III: the Asaf Jahi rule (1724-1948)
This phase has further been divided into three sub-phases:
a. Architecture from phase I and II with an advent of **Purely European** architecture

b. A phase influenced by the European architecture

c. The mixed style, architecture of the City Improvement Board and the vernacular architecture.

PHASE I

The Qutb Shahi Period

The Qutb Shahi Kingdom[146] has its beginning in the attempts to reinforce the Golconda mud fort that was built earlier by the Kakatiyan Kings. The Qutb Shahi Period can be considered as the golden period of construction activity and architecture of the region. The art and architecture that flourished in this period was unique and set a trend for the future generations.

Some amazing structures built in this period are recognised as landmarks of Deccan. This period came to an end[147] when annexed by the Mughals.

THE QUTB SHAHI RULERS

This period is incomplete without referring to the seven rulers in the sequence.

A link between the architectural and the political events in the period of different rulers need to be discussed here.

1. SULTAN QULI QUTB SHAH (1518-1543)
2. JAMSHEED QULI (1543-1550)
3. IBRAHIM QUTB SHAH (1550-1580)
4. MOHAMMED QULI (1580-1612)
5. SULTAN MOHAMMED QUTB SHAH[148] (1612-1626)
6. ABDULLAH QUTB SHAH (1626-72)
7. ABUL HASSAN TANASHAH (1672-1687)

History

In 1363, the Rajas of Warrangal ceded Golconda to the Bahmani kings. Again in 1512, Bahmanis in turn lost control to Sultan Quli, who was the governor of the Bahmani Province. Sultan Quli's ancestors belonged to the Turkman tribe of the Qara Quyunlu of Hamadan in Iran. He achieved autonomy in 1518, and made Golconda his capital. This is how the early constructions (quite a few in number are left today) in Qutb Shahi period are greatly influenced by Bahmani Kingdom.

The ruling period of the next king, Sutan Quli's son Jamsheed was full of turmoil. He was succeeded by Ibrahim Qutb Shah[149]. During the rule of Ibrahim, who was brother of Jamsheed, Golconda became a centre of international trade. He strengthened the fort of Golconda and added a lot of structures, gardens and tanks in and around the fort. Ibrahim had proposed a township 30 kilometres to the west of the fort, with the name of Ibrahimpatnam, exists even today.

The fourth king, Mohammed Quli became famous by founding the new city of Hyderabad, inspired by his father Ibrahim. Mohammed Quli undertook construction of many civic structures, the palaces and the gardens. The Qutb Shahi kings had cordial relations with Iran and good and able people used to come from Iran to Golconda[150].

To understand the influence on architecture of Hyderabad, another important event in history needs a reference here. *The Dutch East India Company was incorporated in 1602 and in 1606 an agreement was signed between Qutb Shah by which the former granted to the latter the establishment of Dutch Factories at Masulipatnam and Nizampatnam and this was followed by the Pullicat factory in 1610.* The first English venture, an agency on behalf of the East India Company, was made during Mohammed Quli's time at Masulipatnam in 1611. The British owe their Indian Empire's origin to the Qutb Shahi grant. (MA Nayeem 1987)

The history of later Qutb Shahi kings is about the politics and trade other than the architecture. The nephew of the Mohammed Quli, Sultan Mohammed, succeeded as the fifth king in 1612. He married Hayat Bakhshi Begum, the daughter of the fourth king. Sultan Mohammed laid out some gardens and the foundation of Mecca Masjid (later completed by Aurangzeb); he was succeeded by Abdullah in 1626. The sixth king, Abdullah had no heirs. Abul Hassan, connected with the royal family, and a disciple of Saint Shah Raju was made to marry sixth king's daughter and became the successor and the last king of the lineage as well.

As the Mughal Emperor Aurangazeb moved to south, after conquering the Bijapur kingdom he marched on to Golconda. On 22 September 1687, Mughal army entered the fort from Fateh Drawaza. Golconda fell to the Mughals; the Qutb Shahi king was captivated and sent to Daulatabad. The wealth of the kingdom was taken over by Mughals and Hyderabad was annexed to the Mughal Empire.

The chronology of QUTB SHAHI built spaces in Hyderabad goes as written below:

Early Qutb Shah
1518- Jama Masjid (Masjid-e-Safa), Golconda
1552-80- Khazana Building
1550-80- Shaikpet Sarai and Mosque (by 3rd ruler)
1550- Tomb of Jamsheed Qutb Shah
1560- Quila-e-Kohna Mosque
1561- Mustafa Khan's Mosque, Naya Quila
1570- Mulla Khayali's Mosque, Naya Quila
1578- Puranapul Bridge and Gate
1580- Tomb of Ibrahim Qutb Shah
1591- Charminar,
1592- Charkaman
1595- Dar-ush-Shifa
1596- Badeshahi Ashurkhana
1597- Jama Masjid, near Charminar
1602- Tomb of Sultan Mohammed Quli

Late Qutb Shah
1617- Mecca Masjid (started)
1612-26-Kulsum Begum Mosque, Khairati Begum's Mosque and Tomb
1617- Tomb of Hayat Bakshi Begum
1618- Mughalpura Tombs
1620- Purani Idgah, Maddanapet
1625- Hayatnagar Mosque, Uppal Mosque, Premamati Mosque and Taramati Baradari
1626- Tomb of Sultan Mohammed Qutb Shah
1634- Mughalpura Tombs
1634- Goshamahal Baradari (finished in 1686)
1655- Khairat Khan's Tomb
1662- Tombs of Taramati and Premamati
1671- Toli Masjid (by the fifth ruler)
1676- Mian Mishk Sarai and Mosque
1684- Mushk Mahal, Kaman Chatta Bazar, Shah Raju's Tomb at Misrigunj
1684- Kaman Chatta Bazar (by the last ruler)

QUTB SHAHI BUILDING TECHNOLOGY, MATERIAL AND ORNAMENTATION

The typology of buildings consisted mosques, tombs, caravanserais, *baradari*, palaces, etc.

The building plans are simple display the composition of squares. A pointed arch rises from every side of the square. At the height where the arches end the arch netted pendentives (also called squinches) are formed and provide a sixteen or eight-sided polygon becoming the base of the dome.

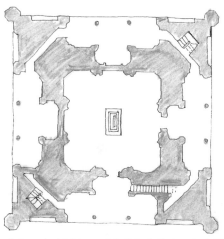

The plan of the tomb of Mohammed Quli Qutb Shah at Qutb Shahi Tombs

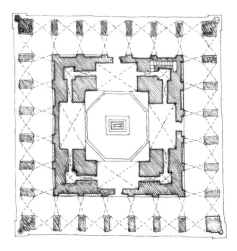

The plan of the tomb of Sultan Mohammed Qutb Shah at Qutb Shahi Tombs

The domes are made with rubble stone and lime, as observed in Purani Idgah and roof of entrance gateways in Golconda fort and gateway of Hayat Bakshi Begum Sarai. The structures of monumental scale are covered with huge domes and the one of human scale with flat roof. The combination of flat roof, vaults and domes are also found in one structure and in one complex, at the same time. Combination of flat and domed roof is observed in caravanserai structure at Shaikpet Sarai and Hayat Bakhshi Begum Sarai. Vaults are observed in Golconda Fort and Qutb Shahi Tombs. Another type of roofing is done with a group of small domes, the shallow and deep ones.

The flat roof is done with stone masonry (stone wedges are arranged in the form of a concentric square) and lime plaster (see picture in roof section). A thick layer of lime mortar is provided at the top of the roof with proper sloping for the rain water.

The walls of these structures are made of dressed/undressed stone, cemented with lime mortar. In some structures, e.g. Taramati Baradari the walls are finished with lime mortar. A group of shallow domes give a flat roof at the top. The independent deep domes end with a brass finial (of five tiers) at the top. Some structures in Golconda fort have a different type of roof also. Mulla Khayali's Mosque (1570) at Naya Quila has an uncommon type of vaulted ceiling.

The structures from Qutb Shahi period display simplicity and utility in the design of openings. The size of the ventilators is small and the door posts are made of stone. The buildings are full of ornamentation. The main form of the structure is a composition of different types of ornamental members. All the components, the structural and non-structural played their role in making the architectural vocabulary unique: the domes, cupolas, minarets, kiosks, parapets, *chajjas* are full of delicate lime work.

ORNAMENTATION

The design of medallions in the arch spandrels are main eye-catching features at the entrance. At some places use of polychrome tiles in these medallions can be seen. Row of small pots (in basalt at some places), calligraphy, multi-tiered pointed arches, the apex ornamentation, lacing of parapet in different layers, square, round and multi-surfaced minarets, (with or without miniature balcony) are the main features, which make the Qutb Shahi structures the landmarks of Deccan. Necking of the dome and the cupolas are decorated with rows of lotus petals. Gujarati brackets and *chajja*, (originally dating back to 12th century in Gujarat) are used boldly in the structures.

Solid and void effect is created through odd number of pointed arches in the parapet. Introduction of miniature *minars* in the simple parapet wall add variety to it.

Use of miniature mosque mural in interiors is a unique feature in Toli Masjid. Quasi dome in provided in the central prayer section. Ceiling is decorated with lime stucco in circular patterns *(See picture to the right)*. The ceiling of Toli Masjid is full of stucco. Treatment of apex of arch and squinches (known as arch pendentives too) is also noticed in many structures. A lot of cut stucco work is noticed in different parts of the structure. Use of coloured tiles on the wall surface is a very important feature in the interiors of Badshahi Ashurkhana. Flooring in most of the structure is kept simple but use of rich carpets was in vogue, which was noticed by different travellers.

The Dying Wisdom: is all about the traditional water supply and water harvesting system

The Qutb Shahi kingdom was rich in natural resources. Availability of a natural water resource became a condition for founding of any city. The settlements came up around the water bodies. The Qutb Shahis also followed the same rule in a more reformed manner. Durgam Cheruvu, located at a higher level provided water through pipes to the people living in the Golconda Fort. Mir Jumla tank supplied water to Yakutpura. Hussain Sagar was the main source of drinking water supply for the north part of the river Musi including British Residency. Shah Hatim Tank, Langar Houz, Maa Saheb Tank, etc., are some of the tanks constructed during the Qutb Shahi period. Use of Persian wheel was common in this period. Water was drawn from the well through these Persian wheels (Saqiya). The catchment areas of these water bodies[151] were open, free from any encroachment, allowing more surface runoff to go into the main resource. Qutb Shahis planned sites in such a way that the built part merged beautifully with nature.   Gardens were laid all over the kingdom. Bagh-e-Asar, the earliest garden of that period and presently known as the site of the Qutb Shahi tombs, was laid by the first Qutb Shahi, Sultan Quli. Durg Tank (Durgam Cheruvu) supplied water to this site. Ibrahim Bagh, the present site of Taramati Baradari and Premamati Mosque, was laid by Ibrahim Qutb Shah.

Nabat Ghat (later called Naubat Pahad, the site of Birla Planetarium), Koh-e-Tur (the site of Falaknuma Palace), Sultan Shahi Bagh are places where the Qutb Shahis planned gardens. These gardens had fruits and flowers trees. The historic maps displayed in the Chowmahalla Museum are a testimony of the abundance of groves and gardens around Charminar.

The Baoli at Qutb Shahi Tombs

PHASE II

From 1687 to 1724, the city was under Mughal control, the Qutb Shahi Palaces near Charminar are said to have been destroyed by Mughal army. For a couple of decades the building activity suffered a set back. The city was controlled by a Mughal Governor (appointed by Aurangazeb) from Aurangabad till 1724[152] and after it.

Existence of this period added some more features from Mughal architecture, to the city's pre-existing built heritage[153], built during and after Mughal rule. The first Asaf Jah who was governor of Mughals (not yet independent) built some structures in Hyderabad. One of the most important building activity is the completion of Mecca Masjid in 1694, which was started by Sultan Mohammed in the year 1617.

PHASE IIIA   EARLY ASAF JAHI

Qutb Shahi kingdom is responsible for the strengthening of Golconda and formation of Hyderabad. The Asaf Jahi lineage gave birth to modern Hyderabad and worked for the public reforms, too.

The seven Asaf Jahi kings are listed below:
1. Mir Qamar-ud-Din Khan, Nizam-ul-Mulk (1720-1748)[154]
2. Nizam Ali Khan (1762-1803)
3. Nawab Sikander Jah (1803-1829)
4. Nasir-ud-Daula (1829-1857)
5. Afzal-ud-Daula (1857-1869)
6. Mir Mahabub Ali Khan (1869-1911)
7. Mir Osman Ali Khan (1911-1948)

The first Nizam Nawab Mir Qamar-ud-Din Khan was the governor of Mughal Empire. After the disintegration of the Empire, the Nizam-ul-Mulk declared the autonomy. Nizam continued to rule from Aurangabad. The real construction activity began, when the second Asaf Jah[155] came in rule. The seat of power was shifted to Hyderabad and it became the capital city again. In 1798, after the Subsidiary Alliance, the intervention of British in the politics of Hyderabad started increasing; it promoted the construction activity in the city. These structures were first purely European and slowly opened the avenues for Indo-European forms. The important structures in the city were patronised by the Nizams, the Paigah, the Salarjungs and some more influential nobles of the courts. They chose to build a whole or a part of the new European forms, along with their old existing Qutb Shahi and Mughal type forms and spaces. The period of the late Asaf Jahi kings was the period of mixture of different cultures. The idea for the construction of a structure/space was very individual and local but the ornamental features, and many times even the complete form was adopted from European architecture.

There is a list of some prominent structures come up in different phases of architectural history of the city.

1724-40 - Construction of the city walls, Dabirpura Gate
1724- Pavilion in Bhagwandas Garden
1734- Shahi Jilu Khana
1740- Aliabad Sarai
1734-1803[156]-Malkajgiri Baradari
1750- Khilwat

Multi-cusped arches, along with multi-tiered[157] and simple pointed arches and *Jharokha*/canopied windows[158] are found in the structures of this phase, in the city. Material for constructions remain similar to the earlier phase, i.e. stone, brick, lime and wood (structural and non-structural)

The wall panels were decorated in lime, similar to Mughal architecture and the technology to cover the roof remains similar to Qutb Shahi structures. Introduction of the Mughal style roofing technique is also observed in early Asaf Jahi structures (roofing of the Jilukhana Gate, Laad Bazaar). The Mughal architecture brought the *bangladar jharokha* window/kiosk. The Mughal fluted coupled columns, with vegetal capitals and acanthus leaves base are also introduced. Parapet remained similar to the ones in Qutb Shahi structures (compared with defense structures, like fort wall), e.g. Malkajgiri Baradari. In this complex the remains of the Baradari structure, display coupled columns (typical to Shahjahan's period in Mughal architecture). The construction system is also similar to Mughal period. Architectural and planning features from Mughal architecture are observed in many *devdis* in the walled city.

PHASE IIIB MID ASAF JAHI
1763- The Nizam II shifted his capital back to Hyderabad. Role of British starts, in the city's politics
1774- Mosque near Jhamsingh Temple
1784- Purani Haveli, Majhli Begum ki Haveli, Pavilion in Bhagwandas Garden
1786- Gunfoundry
1790- Shams-ul-Umrah Tombs (started)

In the year 1798, Subsidiary Alliance becomes the main reason for the European style of construction.

1798- Grave of Mons Raymonds
1805- British Residency [159]
1834- Zenana Mahal, Purani Haveli
1839- Chaderghat Bridge
1859- St. Mary's Cathedral
1860- Secunderabad Clock Tower
1861- Nayapul (also called Afzalgunj Bridge, started in 1857)
1867- St. Georges' Church
1869- Afzal Mahal at Chowmahalla (started in 1857)

The foreign officers built a few structures independently, which were purely European in nature. The building construction was supervised by Europeans, and was actually done by the Indian masons. The most important structure of this period is the British Residency made with semi-circular arches, domed and jack-arched roofing, and vaulted roof in the basement. Use of steel as a reinforcing member became common.

The Roman façade and Palladian façades became popular amongst the city nobles. The complete vocabulary of classical architecture and ornamentation is displayed in British Residency. There is a change which can be observed in the small elements of the prime structures of the city after the role of British starts in politics and construction of British Residency.

Introduction of semi-circular/classical arches, with circular columns and pilasters became some of the main features of the building. The classical style of railings with the Palladian [160] and Victorian facades, were appreciated, though the Qutb Shahi and Mughal features were also getting constructed in the city. Square Columns, pointed arches, trussed roof, use of timber as a structural material became a part of common practice in the buildings of the city. Devdi Khursheed Jah (1880-90) is a beautiful example of the Indo-European mixed way of construction. In this building the elliptical arches in the interiors give a grand look. The wooden flooring was provided in formal spaces.

The jack-arched roofing [161] and Madras Terrace technique made their way to the city structures. The stucco work was borrowed from the British Pattern Books.

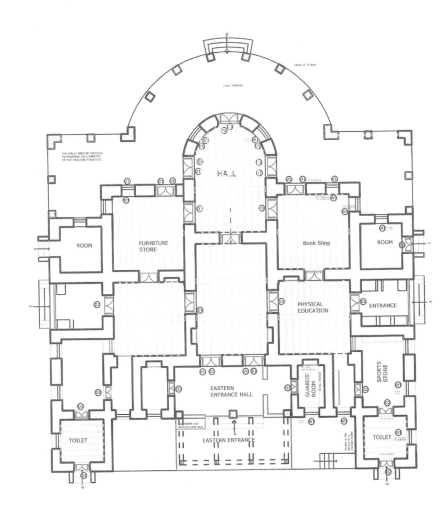

Notice the plan of a residence, with a semi-circular end from Secunderabad Cantonment, presently functioning as Army School.

British Residency

PHASE III C Late Asaf Jahi Nizam VI (1869-1911) and Nizam VII (1911-1948)

1878- Secunderabad Club
1884- Devdi Mukarrab Jung
1884- Mehboob Mansion, Malakpet
1880-90- Khursheed Jah Bahadur Devdi
1890- Monty's Hotel
1896- Secunderabad Clock Tower
1891- St. Joseph's Cathedral
1892- Mehboob Chowk Clock Tower
1894-Paigah Palace, Begumpet (by Paigah Iqbal-ud-Daula, the family of Vikar-ul-Umra)
1908 - Flood in Hyderabad becomes a reason for the new planning
1915- Wanaparthy Palace (also known as Mahabhoopal Manzil by Wanaparthy Samasthana Family)

The city of Hyderabad was surveyed extensively by the City Improvement Board. The Indo-Saracenic architecture of Hyderabad was created by Architect-Vincent Esch, combining the architectural styles of the city existing at that point of time.

The major structures that came up in this period were as follows:
1919- High Court
1921- City College, Osmania General Hospital
1930- State Archaeological Museum
1935- Moazzam Jahi Market
1936- State Central Library

This was the period during which the Qutb Shahi architecture was revived. Saidanima's tomb built in late nineteenth century is a good example of the revival of Qutb Shahi architecture, known as Neo Qutb Shahi.

Various forms of minarets topped with Qutb Shahi miniature dome, define the limits of the structure as a major feature of city's architecture. The minarets ornament the exterior corners.

Advent of cement is another major event to be discussed here, which shaped the city's architecture. The cement factories were set-up by the sixth Nizam in different parts of the state and use of cement was common in the structures, in addition to the use of lime. Huge spans were covered with reinforced cement concrete dome and flat roofs, e.g. dome of Entrance Hall of the Arts College at Osmania University.

The jaalis, the minars with Chevron pattern and Nizam's seal at Public Gardens

ORNAMENTATION in PHASES I, II and III of Asaf Jahi period

The walls have been treated with the ribbed and panel moulding from Mughal architecture. Stone cutting, chiselling was done for the most important components of the structure/complex; for example, the *pietra-dura* on the graves of the noble's family in Paigah Tombs. The imitation of stone jaali was done with lime masonry.

Different types of ceilings have been observed: flat, curved, domed, alcove, etc. The openings and niches also exist in different shapes and forms, the square, rectangular, round and arched. The projections in the structures are supported by wrought iron angles and brackets and stone brackets. Different types of elements have been used in exteriors and interiors to embellish the surface of structural or non-structural members, which are influenced from the phases of past; namely, lime plaster, glazed tiles, mosaic, inlay, stained glass and stucco and surface paintings.

The Dying Wisdom

The Asaf Jahis inherited the natural and built heritage from the earlier rulers. The Koh-e-Tur was chosen by Fakhr-ul-Mulk to make Falaknuma Palace. Bagh-e-am, the hunting grounds for the Asaf Jahi kings, was later converted to Public Gardens. Chowmahalla is a perfect example of this period. The planning of Chowmahalla ia a result of an interesting mix of the natural elements with the built.

Later on, as the British built the Residency Complex (1805) to the north of the river Musi, European style gardens became a fashion. *Devdis* were built with a garden in front; the original site plan of Devdi Raja Rameshwar Rao (Circle II Moazzam Jahi Market, Mahal Wanaparthy Ref. No. 130) is a good example of the influence of European architecture and landscape; a look at the 1914 map substantiates this. The garden of Falaknuma Palace is designed on lines of the Palace of Versailles. Gyan Bagh Palace at Panmandi is another example from this period with water channel, garden furniture, lamps, statues, etc. La Palais Royale had a big fountain in the centre of its courtyard.

In the late Asaf Jahi period, a lot of work was done by the City Improvement Board including the water works of the city. Nizam Sagar, Himayat Sagar and Osman Sagar are the main resources of the water supply. To overcome the problem of floods a bund was made on the River Musi. Osmania Park in front of the Osmania General Hospital is also an effort of the CIB scheme. The balance between the natural and built was thoughtfully maintained.

The baoli in Sitaram Bagh Temple

THE ARCHITECTURAL KNOWLEDGE SYSTEM: With respect to people, place and time

Passing through different phases in history, we understand that the historic architecture of Hyderabad is the result of intermixing of different cultures from different parts of the globe. The structural system of these structures varied over a period of time. To understand the system a historic structure is divided into its main components vertically; these are the foundation, plinth columns, walls, arches, beams and brackets, roofing/slab, lintels and *Chajja*[162]. A brief discussion about the materials of construction needs a reference here along with the building technology.

THE BUILDING TECHNIQUES AND MATERIAL

Over a period of four hundred and thirty years, we see that the material used in the structures of Hyderabad is mainly: stone, bricks and wood, and steel in the later structures. The cementing material is lime and cement (introduced in later Asaf Jahi period). Stone was widely available and it was used for most of the structural components of the building in Qutb Shahi period. The brick also played a major role in the structural and non-structural components of the building. Use of earthen tiles[163] has also been noticed in some structures of the city. As the shape and form of the building varied along with the scale and use of the building, so did the techniques of construction.

A general overview on the historic architecture of Hyderabad is presented here, as a result of the study of two hundred odd heritage structures and sites from built and natural heritage.

THE SRUCTURAL COMPONENTS

Foundation and Plinth: The foundation of the structures have been made with locally available stone, brick, timber, rubble, dressed stone. Above the foundation level, the plinth gave a base to the structure and was made of stone and bricks. The vertical surface of the plinth is found exposed, plastered and pointed in different buildings.

Notice the stone octagonal column with a floral catital standing at the intersection of beams

Columns: The vertical structural member—the column, has been made with stone, bricks and wood as well. At many places monolithic stone columns have also been observed. The column supports the horizontal structural members: the beam and the slab. The composite columns were done with a combination of different materials.

Notice the placement and joining of beam, column and brackets in different structures:

Walls: Method of constructing a wall has varied over a period of time. We find the rubble masonry, dressed stone masonry, brick masonry, and plastered surfaces (over brick or stone masonry) in different buildings.

Beams and brackets: Beams have been made with monolithic stone, wood, steel or box sections.

The brackets were made with wood, stone and steel also. Barckets are made in different shapes, serving mainly the structural purpose and also add to the ornamentation of the structure. Fan shape brackets have been observed in Palace Dhanrajgirji. The elephant trunk-shaped brackets have been observed in some of the Qutb Shahi structures and the wooden brackets in vernacular structures.

Lintels: Lintels are the structural members to support the door, window and ventilators openings. These are made flat, arched and in the shape of segmental arch, with brick, stone and wood.

Roof: Different forms and shapes of the roof have been experimented in history over a period of time: flat roof, pitched roof, vaults and domes. These are made with the help of stone, bricks and binders and reinforcing members. Flat roof has been made with the stone slabs cemented with lime mortar.

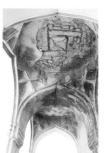
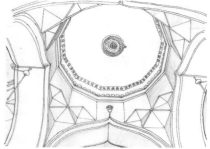

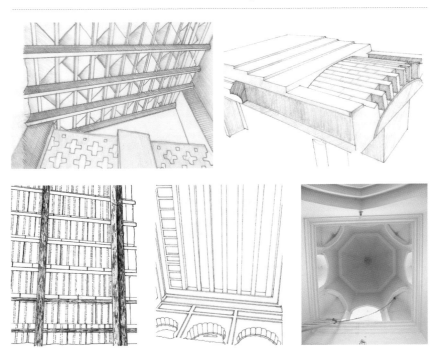

A group of shallow domes took the shape of flat terrace on top. The deep domes provided the domed ceiling and irregular terrace at the top. Roofing was done with the help of steel as a major reinforcing agent with cement in later period.

THE NON-STRUCTURAL COMPONENTS: The term refers to doors, windows, ventilators, wall panels, flooring and ceiling decorations, parapet wall and the ornamental features of the building.

1. Doors, Windows and Ventilators and Niches

The doors and windows in the historic architecture have seen many changes over a period of time. The doors are made to stand in the different shapes of openings with the help of a **post**. The door posts were made with stone in the forts and palaces (refer to the stone post in the entrance door of Khairat Khan's Tomb, Mughalpura dated 1655).

In the residences, the door post is made of wood mainly.

The wooden door at Chowmahalla Palace, ornamented with lime mouldings around

The door and window panes are composed of a frame and panels. The advent of glass changed the formation of doors and windows in the British buildings. The glass panels are fitted in the wooden door and window frames, at some places these panels have etching in different **patterns**. The doors in ENT hospital display an interesting etching pattern on the glass panels. Some of the door panels also display wooden carving of different patterns.

Beautiful door panels in Mahal Wanaparthy display the initials of the patron etched in glass. British Residency is a very good example from the purely European structure. The size of the doors is huge. The doors in the British Residency structure (refer to building No. 49, in Koti area, Circle II) surprise the visitor by its scale. The door panels are louvered at many places. The adjustable louvered panels provide light ventilation and at the same time create a visual barrier (as required by the climatic and social condition of the place). The joint between different materials and different structural members[164] was also treated artistically. Mouldings in lime are made on the wall around the door frame. The wooden beading (technically known as mouldings on the edges of framing, to hold the glass panel in place) has been fixed on the door, where the craftsman could show his skills. A well-crafted beading enhanced the beauty of the panelled door. The scale of the door varied with the typology and use of the structure.

Door fittings also vary with the typology of the structure. The doors of the forts are strong and had nails from one side.

The door hinges from ENT Hospital

The door hinges are big and heavy in the structures inspired by European architecture (refer to the St. Georges Church, Osmania University).

The door heads are designed with the different shapes of pediment. (Refer to the Mahal Wanaparthy and ENT Hospital). Use of such motifs reflects the appreciation of classical forms in structures of Hyderabad. The door handles, latches, etc., are some more interesting features made of different materials and scale over a period of time. The scale and location of the door was also dictated by the requirement of the access and construction type. The external doors are different from the internal doors in terms of size and ornamentation.

The windows and ventilators are designed in the same way as doors. Oriel window is one of the most beautiful features of this section, also known as *jharokha*. They give a festive look to any common or uncommon structure. Amberpet Burj is a good example, where a simple watch tower looks attractive with the oriel window. The gateway of Jhamsingh temple and Jilu Khana Gate at Laad Bazaar are the heritage components with oriel windows needs to be discussed here. The Paigah Tombs display the repetitive use of this feature.

Paigah Tombs - the jaali door

The ventilators are designed with or without the doors and windows. 'Fanlight' is the term used for the ventilator placed over the door or window. The independent ventilators were provided at a much higher level and were operated with chains or strings. The posts/frames of the ventilators are decorated with the mouldings around it. Some paintings have been observed in the ventilators of one of the residential structures of the city (Refer to Wanaparthy Palace in Mozam Jahi Market area, Circle II).

The niche is a very small and another common element of a built structure. They are built with the utilitarian and sometime with ornamentation puroses.

The lime niche in *Devdis* of Hyderabad is quite common. Refer to the niches in Paigah Tombs, La Palais and Devdi Mirdhe Hamid Ali Khan.

2. Wall Panelling

The most common practice of beautifying the plain walls is with the plaster work. The interior surface of the brick or stone wall are decorated with different patterns made in lime. e.g. Classrooms in the first floor of Iqbal-ud-daula Devdi (present use). Walls of the most beautiful and important buildings were done with the timber panelling. For example: Falaknuma Palace and Bella Vista. The height of the wall panel varied from dado level to full height. The panelling was done with thin timber boards fixed with tongue and groove joints in solid timber uprights and cross members. Carving work on different materials was quite popular amongst the city nobles.

The embossed glazed tiles were used to decorate walls up to the dado level; this could be seen in Mahal Wanaparthy.

Other than the wall panelling, wallpaper has also been used in European structures. Decorating the wall surface with lime mouldings was also common. (Refer to the surface decorations)

3. Flooring and ceiling

The flooring of the residential structure was another favourite component for surface ornamentation. Use of stone slabs was most common for the flooring of the lower level. Most of the Qutb Shahi structures have the flooring of big stone slabs, easy to maintain and clean. The flooring underwent a significant change with the advent of European architecture in the city. The coloured and patterned tiled flooring of some of the palaces of the Chowmahalla is borrowed from the European architecture.

Similar type of flooring can be seen in King Koti Palace Complex, Mahal Wanaparthy, some parts of Town Hall (Assembly old structure) and ENT Hospital also. There is mosaic flooring, observed in Raj Bhavan old building, made with broken glazed tile, display beautiful geometrical/floral patterns and similar one can be seen in La Palais Royal, near Paradise Crossing. Wooden flooring is also observed in many of the city's palaces (Khursheed Jah Devdi, British Residency).

Discussion of ceiling decoration is as interesting as flooring. Looking at the heritage sites of the ealier dates from the city's history, the ceiling was not flat in most of the structures. The arches carried the dome with the help of arch netted pendentives/squinches and the dome rose from the squinches (with or without a drum). Different geometrical and floral patterns were made on the (interior and exterior) curved surface of the dome. The drum of the dome was ornamented with a series of floral and vegetal patterns (both in interior and exterior).

The ceiling decoration varied from Qutb Shahi to the British period, since the technique of construction of roof also changed. British Residency (Ref. No. 49, Koti area, Circle II) is a good example of the decoration of curved and flat ceilings surfaces. The ceiling was decorated richly with plaster work; alternatively a false ceiling was made with a moulded iron sheet (refer to Director of Industries Building, Ref. No. 63 in Abids area, Circle II).

In Khursheed Jah Devdi one can experience the beauty and functionality of the wooden ceiling (made with wooden battens) with a central piece, known as pendant, dropping down vertically from the centre of the ceiling.

Devdi Mirdhe Hamid Khan[165] at Mehboob Chowk displayed excellent surface painting on the ceiling. Raja Bhagwandas Pavilion is another good example for wooden ceiling. The columns, beams, doors, windows, *jharokhas* and brackets all together make this very attractive and the only example of the existing wooden palaces in Hyderabad. The ceiling of the *devdi* is too low. Traces of paints can be seen on different wooden members. In some of the vernacular structures of the city, the pitched roof has been made with terracotta tiles which display beautifully patterned surface in the ceiling; for example, I. Parakash Building in Secunderabad, (Ref. No. 11, Circle IA).

The ceiling picture of Chowmahalla

4. Parapet walls and compound walls

The parapet wall acts as the crown of the structure and enhances the beauty of the superstructure. In Qutb Shahi structures the horizontal band of the parapet wall has been balanced by introducing vertical architectural elements. It appears as a lace to the structure. At many places the elements of the parapet walls of the Qutb Shahi structures are found to be similar to the one in Mughal architecture (Khairat Khan's Tomb and some of the tombs in the Qutb Shahi Tomb Complex). Most of the Qutb Shahi structures display a double parapet wall. With the advent of British architecture, the pattern of the parapet changed. The pillars of the parapet wall (called pedestal in the classical architecture) are topped with different shapes of urns/flower vases. See Mahal Wanaparthy, Chowmahalla, Purani Haveli. The structures built in Asaf Jahi period took a queue from the landmarks of earlier periods. The parapet of Saidanima's Tomb displays the elements of the Qutb Shahi, Mughal and British.

5. Staircases

The style of staircase changed with the age and the use/typology of the building. The staircases found in the forts are simple and functional, made with stone slabs, without railing as they were made as a part of movement pattern. Minarets of the Qutb Shahi structures have the winding staircase going to the top of the structures. Staircases in Charminar, Purani Idgah and Premamati's Mosque fall in this category.

The marble staircase with classical railing in ENT Hospital

The palaces had the grand staircases. In the houses of nobles the staircase was an object of status. The staircases have been embellished with expensive railings and the newel post[166]. The grand staircase of the British Residency (Ref. No. 49 Koti area, Circle II) with a dome on top is another beautiful example of staircases from European architecture in Hyderabad. The structures made with European influence adopted the interiors from the pattern books, which were available with European officers. The grand *devdis* had a main staircase, the embellished one. The other one used to be at the back for the service.

6. Surface decorations: Lime stucco, glaze tiles, mosaic[167], inlay and architectural painting.

Lime stucco art developed over a period of time in Hyderabad structures. Started with Qutb Shahi structures, developed in European and Asaf Jahi structure, the tradition lives even today, in modern structures: as an imitation of lime with plaster of paris in different parts of a residential and commercial structures. Stucco was done on different components of a building with different designs. The lime mouldings of British Residency have been repeated in many residential structures in the city and in Paigah Tombs also (refer to the Egg and dart moulding in British Residency). Lime *Jaali* was made for the screen walls in Paigah tombs copying the patterns from Mughal architecture.

Three different types of flowers can be seen in the first row, then a barided pattern followed by another type of flowers in the next row, all are done with vegetable colours

The famous Qutb Shahi Lime work in the Mosque atop Charminar. Notice a multi-cusped arch with a flower vase kind of object used for apex ornamentation

A crown/fruit-like object used for the apex ornamentation, giving a way to another feature like entwining creepers. Notice the medallion complementiong the apex ornamentation.

The glaze tiles were used for the colour embellishment in the Qutb Shahi period, which even existed in Mughal architecture in the northern part of the country. The best example for interior glaze tile is the Badshahi Ashurkhana. Glazed tiles were used in the tiles in the exteriors also.

The arch intrados at Chowmahalla

Presently, one can witness some colourful remaining tiles in the exterior surface of the tomb of Mohammmed Quli Qutb Shah IV, in Qutb Shahi Tombs complex.

Another way of decorating the surface is inlay. Small and thin pieces of a regular stone (marble, sandstone, granite, etc.) or semi-precious stone are assembled together in the grooves of big stone slab to make the inlay pattern. Similar technique is adopted in wood to make a wood inlay, along with ivory and/or mother-o-pearl. The graves in Paigah Tombs complex display beautiful stone in-lay, which is influenced by Mughal architecture from the period of Shahjahan. Architectural paintings have also been observed in different residential structures namely Mirdhe Hamid Khan Devdi and Raja Bhagwandas Pavillion.

The prayer wall of Badeshahai Ashurkhana displays the glaze tiles, suffered a severe damage during the Musi floods of 1908.

7. The furniture: the built-in and loose

This section discusses about the movable and immovable furniture items of the city's famous heritage structures. City's *devdis* are famous for the lavish lifestyle and interiors, taking a cue from European mansion houses. The Nizam's palaces have the best display of built in furniture. The grand wardrobe of the Purani Haveli Palace is famous because of its size and quality. It was once the largest continuous walk-in wardrobe. It is 240 ft long lined both side of the room. The Salarjung Museum and Chowmahalla Museum both offer a huge collection of the built in and loose furniture used by the kings and nobles of Asaf Jahi era.

The site museum of Golconda has remains of the crockery used by Qutb Shahis which is the proof for the grandeur of the interiors of Qutb Shahi palaces. The Nizam could boast on the cup-boards and tables of Falaknuma palace, where he could host the grandest dinner to a hundred dignitaries at a time. The Chowmahalla also had a large collection of cutlery and crockery in the cup-boards, which can be seen in the present Chowmahalla Museum.

8. Other external and internal architectural details

The entrances: The lime stucco in front pediment of Asman Jah Devdi and Falaknuma Palace, etc.

The gateways and name plates: The magnificent gateways of Public Gardens, Chowmahalla, Mahbub Mansion at Malakpet, etc., are some of the important heritage components from the city's built heritage.

The original name-plates still exist in many of the historic residential structures. Many of the historic structures at AOC Secunderabad Cantonment also have the original name-plates.

Metalwork: the grills, the entrance gates, garden fixtures and furniture
Some of the very attractive metalwork can be experienced in Chowmahalla Palace Museum. Beautiful fountains can be seen in the internal courtyards of Sardar Mahal, Old City.

The metal railing at La Palais, Secunderabad

Some of the very attractive metalwork can be experienced in Chowmahalla Palace Museum. Beautiful fountains can be seen in the internal courtyards of Sardar Mahal, Old City.

Use of stained glass is common in the windows of the historic churches (refer to the churches of Secunderabad and Abids).

Lighting: The fancy chandeliers of Nizam's palaces fall under this category. The best ones are in Falaknuma, the Venetians and Belgian, one of them is the largest one of Hyderabad. Chowmahalla Museum also witnesses very attractive chandeliers.

Services–electrical and plumbing: These components are best preserved in Falaknuma Palace. The electrical switch-boards in Falaknuma Palace were among the largest in British India.

The section of electrical and

The Chandeliers of Chowmahalla

plumbing will be left incomplete without discussing the baths of Hyderabad, known as *hamam*. The three storeyed Qutb Shahi palaces in Golconda had a piped water supply with the pipes made of terracotta. The Hamam Complex in Qutb Shahi tombs also needs a reference here. The hot and cold water used to run through different water channels.

Later on, the Europeans bought some beautiful Victorian fittings to India, which were fixed in the palaces of Hyderabad. These fittings can still be seen in Falaknuma palace, Purani Haveli and Chowmahalla.The seats, the lighting fixtures, the statues, can be seen in the Dhanrajgirji Palace.

Chapter 5

The Efforts to Conserve the Natural and Built Heritage of Hyderabad[168]

This chapter introduces the reader to the contributions of individuals and organisations that are known to have promoted the cause of heritage conservation in the city. It also lists some of the city's heritage structures that have been conserved in the past and the present; this is followed by a discussion on the ethics of conservation and re-use of historic structures.

In addition to its glorious past and architectural history, Hyderabad has a significant tradition of conservation as well. The archaeological department of the Nizam's dominions was set up at the instance of Sir Akbar Hydri, and the preservation of the buildings was taken up under the supervision of Sri Ghulam Yazdani, the first director of the Archaeology Department. There was no notification made for the historic structures as they were well maintained by the king and his nobles. However, when the Hyderabad State merged with the Indian Union, some major monuments went into the jurisdiction of the Archaeological Survey of India; thus the Charminar and Golconda Fort of the Hyderabad, among others, became the nationally protected monuments.

Because of inadequately defined policies, ineffective regulations and a lack of general awareness, many of the components of the city's invaluable heritage resource, have been lost over a period of time. Diwan Devdi, the house of Salarjung family, was allowed to decay; palaces of great nobles were sold to make way for housing colonies. Sometimes, even the road widening also became a demolition drive. This notwithstanding, even the relics – the leftover walls and the gateways of the once magnificient complexes – contribute to the historical character of the city.

There is the brighter side of the story as well. Some concerned citizens of Hyderabad did notice the heritage loss of the city. Consequently, in 1976, for the first time, a listing of the heritage components of the city was undertaken by the Institute of Asian Studies, followed by yet another study by the Institute of Economics, Hyderabad. Forty-seven historic components were identified. Later, in the year 1982, HUDA prepared a draft bill for the conservation of historic areas and historic buildings, a set of regulations were enforced. This draft bill of HUDA became the first attempt at conservation legislation in India. In 1984, a report on Urban Conservation of Hyderabad, by HUDA, was published. The National Commission of Urbanisation (NCU) got a report prepared on Urban Development in 1988. Government of Andhra Pradesh appointed a Heritage Conservation Committee (HCC) for Hyderabad, under the 1995 regulations. Conservation was by now had become a significant issue. The HUDA study identified the structures. A few more heritage precincts were included in the new Government Order, No. 13, and the Draft Master Plan 2020 now had in it a list of 137 structures and 9 heritage precincts. Another 14 structures were added later, under GOMs No. 102, MA and UD (refer to the appendix).

Apart from the government initiatives, the efforts of the NGOs and the individuals also need to be discussed here.

- In 1930s the Idara-e-Adbiayat-e-Urdu started celebrating Quli Qutb Shah Day annually, for which the credit goes to Dr Mohinuddin Quadri Zore. Following this programme, the Golconda Society was formed which organised the first Golconda Festival in 1980s. It was contributed to build the public awareness.
- INTACH participated in a project known as Relating Heritage along with Tourism and Urban Development in 1996.
- A publication was brought by Society to Save Rocks, listing the rocks along with the flora and fauna of the city.
- Department of Tourism along with some professionals worked on the old city's built heritage and came up with an idea of conducting Heritage Walks.
- Another organisation the Forum for Better Hyderabad was formed by some sensitive citizens to raise the voice against the destruction of heritage. Regular case filing and follow-ups are done by the Forum.

- INTACH Hyderabad is also working for the inclusion of more structures in the list of heritage components. But greater, perhaps, is the need to monitor the state of preservation of the components that are already listed.
- Heritage Walks have been restarted from October 2009, in the Old City.

The structures saved and re-used in past:

Chowmahalla: Presently functioning as a Museum, one of the best and latest attractions of the city.

Purani Haveli: A palace of Nizam, presently functioning as Museum.

British Residency: presently functioning as Women's College in Koti.

Falaknuma Palace: Taken over by Taj Group of Hotels and Resorts.

Asman Garh Palace: A school is functioning in this palace.

Devdi Khurshed Jah: A girls' school is functioning here.

Paigah Palace: Previously functioned as HUDA Office, currently taken over by the US Consulate.

Khazana Building: A Qutb Shahi structure re-used as State Museum by the State Archaeology Department.

9. **Taj Mahal Hotel:** A small residential unit, re-used as a hotel.

10. **Utsav Hotel:** Another residential unit in Secunderabad area, dating back to British period, re-used as a hotel.

11. **Country Club:** A Paigah *devdi* re-used as a club.

12. **Baitul Ashraf:** being re-used as a Function Hall in Masab Tank locality.

13. **La-Palace- Royale:** A residential structure re-used as a Function Palace.

14. **Aiwan-e-ali and Manjhli Begum ki Haveli:** re-used as Function Palace.

15. **Errum Manzil:** Functioning as an office complex for Government Organisations.

16. **ENT Hospital:** A government hospital is functioning in this magnificent palace.

17. **Bashir Bagh Guest House:** Currently functioning as Lok Ayukta Building.

18. **Golden Threshold:** Residence of Sarojini Naidu, currently put to the institutional use.

Not only the heritage buildings listed here, many more structures exist in the city. Some of the residential structures are being used by their successive owners and stand in a fair shape. A lot of efforts have gone into saving the built and natural heritage, yet we need to work more effecively to maintain the city's historic architecture. Some suggestions are given by different scholars.

There is a need to sensitise and aware all the government officials, policy-makers and decision-makers, journalists and political associations.

The financial benefits should be given to the heritage owners. Finacially viable solutions in the form of the appropriate re-use of the heritage structures need to be worked out as early as possible. It will deter the owners from pulling down the structures.

Enough powers are required to be given to the authority administrating the heritage structures (listed or protected), so that the heritage can be saved without any delay. For heritage (natural and built) related disputes at least one judicial bench of the State High Court should be dedicated.

Mere beautification projects will not help to improve the city's life. There is a need to understand the ecology, than superficial manifestation of nature.

Environmental Impact Assessment should be done for a new project or extention to the existing project.

Maqbara Mirza Kalyani

There is a need to create an organisation at all-India level on the lines of English Heritage of England, who will take care of the regional and local heritage with different chapters.

Any new allotment of land (either to the government or to any individual/group) should be done only after proper on-site inspection and off-site checking of records. The unique physical features[169] and archaeological remains need to be restored.

Different government organisations (ASI, State Archaeology, GHMC, HMDA, HMWSSB, APSEB, BSNL, etc.) should be working together in harmony for the citizens. As a result, the money and energy spent in providing the infrastructure to the public will not result into disturbing the existing architectural character of the city.

Why conserve?

It is very easy for any city to loose its ages old heritage components which had been giving character and identity to it. In turn it is not very difficult to retain and enhance and improve the quality of life along with the built and natural heritage components. This is an invaluable national assest for us. Other than the emotional and cultural values these components possess the use value too, which makes the conservation financially viable. These values could be further explained as written under:

Use Value: the functional, economic, social and political values.

Emotional Value: Identity, wonder, continuity, spiritual and symbolic.

Cultural Value: Documentary, historic, archaeological, aesthetic and symbolic, architectural, townscape, landscape and ecological, scientific and technological.

Skilful rehabilitation (also known as Adaptive Re-use) of the historic structures can be economical, often costing only two-thirds of the new structure of the same area and saving the cost of renewing the infrastructure. Re-use can save the fabric of the city, in a way will help in maintaining the city's age-old identity wrapped in different layers of history.

A

Apex ornamentation: The apex of the arch hold a fruit-like object, with a bewildering design of entwining creepers[171] spreading both sides of the apex of the arch. A main feature of the Qutb Shahi architecture.

Annulated Shaft: A shaft of the column with rings at intervals.

Arabesque: Intricate overall pattern of geometric forms used in the panels of different elements.

Ashlar masonry: Masonry composed of stones larger in size than bricks, properly bonded, having dressed, joints laid in mortar.

B

Baoli: The man-made water body, a part of the historic water network of any city/ fortress/palace or complex. Baolis were mostly made in the form of a stepped tank on different scale that contained water all over the year.

Barbicans: The outer defense work of a castle or town, frequently a watch-tower at the gate.

Bastion: One of the series of projections from the main curtain wall of a fortress placed at intervals in such a manner as to enable the garrison to keep off the besiegers attacking the intervening stretches of wall. Bastions are pentagonal, semi-circular or triangular.

Battlement: A parapet having a series of indentions or embrasures, between which are raised portions known as merlons. Archers or soldiers could shoot through the embrasures (gap) between the protecting merlons.

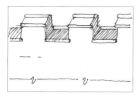

Bangladar Roof: Bangla are the pavilions vaulted with the curved roof characteristic of the Bengali peasant hut. Bangladar roof is a curved roof. If the curve of the roof is in one direction it is called *do-chala*, the other one with two directions is *chau-chala*.

Bell Tower: A tower in the church, carrying the bell.

Buttress: a wedge-shaped masonry construction to support the wall of a structure.

Chajja: A projecting stone feature above the arches to protect from rain and sun, generally slanting and broad, supported by brackets. It is a characteristic feature of Mughal architecture.

Chatri: A kiosk or pavilion with four, six or eight pillars, generally with a cupola roof supported on brackets and lintels. See *Chatri* in Puranmal Samadhi.

Clerestory: An upper zone of the wall pierced with windows that admit light to the centre of a lofty room.

Console Brackets: A decorative bracket in the form of a vertical scroll, projecting from a wall to support a cornice, a door or window head, a piece of sculpture, etc.

Cornice: A decorative border around the top of the walls in a room or outside of the wall.

Coupled Columns: Columns set as close pairs, with a wider intercolumniation, between the pairs.

Crenellated: having battlement.

Crown Moulding: Any moulding serving as a corona (overhanging vertical member of a cornice), or otherwise forming the crowning or finishing member of a structure.

Cyma recta cornice and dentils: Cyma Recta, a moulding of double curvature, concave at the outer edge and convex at the inner edge.

The dentil is a series of small square shape, closely placed blocks (looks like teeth).

Chaitya Arches: Profile of the arch inspired from barrel-shaped form of the Buddhist Chaitya Hall.

Door Post: is a piece of wood, steel or stone that is set in ground to an upright position to support the door.

Dormer: A structure projecting from a sloping roof usually housing a window or a ventilating louver.

Festooning: A decoration with chain of flowers. (refer to the street façade of Aman Jah Bahadur Devdi)

Flat arch:

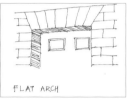

Flowing tracery: see tracery.

Fluting: a pattern of curves cut around outside.

Fluted Column: Flute is a groove or channel, semi-circular, elliptical or angular in section used decoratively along the shaft of a column or/and in domes. See coupled column also.

Gable: The upper part of the end wall of a building, between the two slopes of the roof that is shaped like a triangle.

Tri-foliated gable: the gable with a shape of three arcs.

Gargoyles: the water spouts in the shape of an animal or human being.

Gopuram: It is a monumental gateway in south Indian temple architecture.
Gothic pointed arches: pointed arches, very much part of Gothic architecture.

Grecian Horns: An element used in the Qutb Shahi period is said to have its origin in Greece. It has a curved bracket type shape topped with a cupola, used in Qutb Shahi structures of Hyderabad.

M

Mansard Roof/Gabriel: A roof with double slope in which the upper part is less steep than the lower.

Medallion: An ornamental motif on both sides of the arch.

Miniature balcony: A balcony around the shaft of the minaret is an ornamental feature of Qutb Shahi architecture. See the balcony in the sketch of the minar.

Miniature Minarets/Minars: A main feature of Qutb Shahi architecture in the parapet of a structure, used for ornamentation.

Mouldings: A member of construction or decoration so treated as to introduce varieties of outline or contour in edges or surfaces, whether on projections or cavities, as on cornices, capitals, bases, door, window and ventilator jambs and heads, etc. Mouldings may be of any material, but almost derive at least in part from wood prototype (as those in classical architecture).

Mosaic: A pattern formed by inlaying small pieces of stone and tiles. Mosaic can also be made with wood, ivory, metal, semi-precious stones and jewels, etc.

Multi-tiered arches: The arch with a number of other same arches designed with a common centre making a beautiful appearance altogether; a typical element of the Qutb Shahi architecture.

Osman Shahi arches: Pointed arches introduced in later Asaf Jahi period.

Pediment: A surface used ornamentally over the main entrance, doors or windows, usually triangular, may be curved also. It was originated in Classical Architecture.

Bas Relief: It is the pattern made with lime on the triangular recessed part of the pediment.

PEDIMENT

Tryglyphs and metope: are the parts of the pediment.

Dentils: another ornamental feature with pediment.

Pendentive: A spherical triangle which acts as a transition between a circular dome and a square base on which the dome is set.

Pilasters: An engaged pillar, may be constructed as a projection of the wall itself.

Papyrus Capital: A column from the Egyptian architecture. The capital of the column has the form of papyrus leaves.

Pylons: Massive columns; sometimes holding the entrance gate.

R

Ribbed Dome: A dome displaying the ribs.

S

Scroll: An ornament consisting of a spirally wound band, either as a running ornament or as a terminal, like the volutes of the Ionic capital or the scrolls on consoles and modillions.

Segmental arch: The arch is in the shape of the part of an arc, a segment.

Spout: A short channel or tube used to spill water from gutters, balconies, exterior galleries etc., so that the water falls away from the structure without spoiling its surface.

Stucco: A type of decorative plaster work.

Squinches: Arches placed diagonally at the internal angles of the square space in the phase of transition to convert it from the square to octagon (or polygon with sixteen edges) to support the circular dome.

Stained glass: The glass is given a desired colour in its molten state or by firing a stain into the surface of the glass after forming. It is mainly used in decorative windows.

Sub aerial denudation: Top surface of the rock becoming bare.

T

Topiary work: The clipping and trimming of the plants, trees and shrubs, usually evergreens, into ornamental and fantastic shapes.

Tower: A structure characterised by its relatively greater height and slender proportions.

Tie bars: In roof framing, a horizontal timber connecting two opposite rafters at their lower ends to prevent them from spreading.

Turret: Turret is a diminutive tower, characteristically corbelled from a corner.

Tracery: The curvilinear openwork shapes of stone or wood creating a pattern within the upper part of a window. The mullions of the window are treated as to be ornamental. This is one of the main features of the Gothic architecture.

Flowing tracery: This is the tracery in which continuous, curvilinear patterns dominate.

Appendix

<u>**The Heritage sites identified by different Organisations**</u>
Many of the Hyderabad heritage sites and components have been identified by the ASI, State Archaeology and HMDA. Some more sites have been identified by INTACH and Society to Save Rocks. These government and non-government organisations have been discussed under:

A Archaeological Survey of India
B State Archaeology and Museums
C Hyderabad Metropolitan Development Authority
D Indian National Trust for Art and Cultural Heritage
E Society to Save Rocks

A. ARCHAEOLOGICAL SURVEY OF INDIA
The Archaeological Survey of India (ASI), under the Ministry of Culture, is the premier organisation for the archaeological researches and protection of the cultural heritage of the nation. Maintenance of ancient monuments and archaeological sites and remains of national importance is the prime concern of the ASI. Besides it regulates all archaeological activities in the country as per the provisions of the Ancient Monuments and Archaeological Sites and Remains Act, 1958. Hyderabad has two sites protected by ASI, these are:
1. Charminar
2. Golconda Fort.

B. STATE ARCHAEOLOGY AND MUSEUMS
The Department of Archaeology and Museums is a research-oriented academic institution, the aim of which is to preserve ancient culture for the posterity through various activities such as conducting explorations, excavations at ancient habitational and archaeological sites, conservation and preservation of excavated sites and monuments, conducting village-wise survey for registration of antiquities, identification of archaeological sites and collection of epigraphical material and identification of historical monuments

for their protection. Establishment of museums in all the District Headquarters with a view to educate the people about our culture and its development through displaying artifacts in general and in particular of A.P. for knowing the cultural milieu of A.P. for which the Department is functioning with seven branches headed by the Commissioner.

Monuments listed by the State Archaeology and Museums (printed on the Circle maps with numbers S-1, S-2, etc.)

- Mecca Masjid
- Badshahi Ashurkhana
- Old Gate of Dabirpura
- Mushirabad Mosque
- Toli Masjid
- Gunfoundry
- Khazana Buildings
- Shamsheer Kotha
- Mausolea of Qutb Shahi Kings
- Taramati Baradari
- Premamati Mosque
- Akkanna's Sarai
- Shaikhpet Mosque and Sarai
- Hakim's Tombs
- Mia Mishk's Tombs
- Khairat Khan's Tomb
- Khairati Begum's Tomb
- Mon's Raymond's Tomb
- Akkanna Madanna's Temple, Kukkatpalli
- Grave and Mosque of Princess Hussaini Begum, Janwada
- Fortification and Baradari
- Armenian Cemetery
- Ancient Gateway, Puranapul
- Kulsum Begum Mosque
- Shams-ul-Umra Tombs
- Old Idgah
- Dargah Hazrata Saidanima Saheba
- Sir Ronal Ross Building

C. HYDERABAD METROPOLITAN DEVELOPMENT AUTHORITY (HMDA): Formed in 2008, earlier known as Hyderabad Urban Development Authority has declared a list of notified Heritage Buildings and Heritage Precincts vide GO MS No. 102 MA dated 23 March 1998 and GO MS No. 407 MA dated 6 September 2002. HMDA also has a Heritage Conservation Committee constituted by the Government of Andhra Pradesh.

As per the first list, these 137 Heritage buildings are

Grade I (No. 1 to 24)
1. Parsi Dharamshala
2. Clock Tower, Secunderabad
3. Amberpet Burj
4. Nizamia Observatory
5. Clock Tower, Sultan Bazaar
6. Gate Portion, Dewan Devdi: Two Gates
7. Kaman Chatta Bazar
8. a) Charkaman
    b) Machlikaman
    c) Kalikaman
    d) Sher-e-Batil-ki-Kaman
9. Gate portion, Shahi Jilu Khana
10. Aliabad Sarai
11. Puranapul Bridge
12. Gate portion, Devdi Akram Ali Khan
13. a) Gate portion, Dargah Nooruddin Shah
     b) Ancient Gateway, Kukatpally
14. Osmania Arts College
15. a) Malwala Palace, main courtyard
     b) Secondary Courtyard and Residential quarters
16. Pavilion in Bhagawandas Garden
17. I. Prakash Building
18. Manjhli Begum ki Haveli
19. Mushk Mahal
20. Allauddin's Building
21. Devdi Mehdi Nawaz Jung

22. Gandhi Medical College
23. Golden Threshold
24. Ameen Manzil.

Grade IIA (No. 25-34)
25. Spanish Mosque (Jama Masjid)
26. St Mary's Cathedral
27. St John's Church
28. Sitaram Bagh Temple
29. Jhamsingh Temple Gate Portion
30. Mosque near Jhamsingh Temple
31. St. George's Church
32. Jama Masjid, Charminar
33. Darush Shifa and Mosque
34. Air and Land Warfare Building

Grade IIB (No. 35–80)
35. a) Chowmahalla (Main Palace)
    b) Other Palaces - Chowmahalla (except Afzal Mahal which will remain
       in Grade I)
36. Dargah Yousufain
37. Afzal Gunj Mosque
38. Dargah Hazrath Shujauddin
39. Moghulpura Tombs
40. Dargah Syed Shah Mir Mahmood Wali
41. Qila Kohna and Mosque
42. Clock Tower and Police Station, James Street
43. Hyderabad Public School
44. Paigah Palace (Vikhar-ul-Umra Palace)
45. Vikhar Manzil
46. Devdi Nazir Nawaz Jung (Chiran Fort Club)
47. Erram Manzil
48. King Koti Complex
    a) Hospital (old)
    b) Usman Mansion (Demolished)
    c) Nazri Bagh

49. Residency Complex (Women's College, Koti)
50. Mahboob Mansion
51. Asmangarh Palace
52. Purani Haveli Complex
53. Shahi Khilwat Khana
54. Baradari of Nawab Khursheed Jah Bahadur
55. a) Falaknuma Palace (Main Palace)
    b) Other Palaces (Falaknuma Palace)
56. Devdi Iqbal-ud-Doula (Shah Gunj)
57. Victoria Memorial Orphanage
58. Bella Vista (Administrative Staff College of India)
59. Dhanrajgirji Complex
60. Nizam College
61. Osmania General Hospital
62. City College
63. Directorate of Industries
64. Princess Esin Women's Educational Centre
65. Monty's Hotel
66. Jubilee Hall
67. E.N.T. Hospital
68. State Central Library
69. State Archaeological Museum
70. Lady Hyderi Club
71. Moazzam Jahi Market
72. Aiwan-e-Ali
73. Victoria Maternity Hospital
74. High Court
75. Government Unani Hospital, Charminar
76. Vilayat Manzil (Country Club)
77. Andhra Patrika Building
78. Homeopathic Hospital
79. Sardar Mahal
80. Nizam Club

Grade III (No. 81–137)
81. Devdi Asman Jah
82. Tomb Fakhr-ul-Mulk
83. Vijay Marie Church

84. Puranmal Samadhi
85. St Joseph's Cathedral
86. Parsi Fire Temple
87. Mahboob Chowk Mosque
88. Azha Khana-e-Zehra
89. Maharaja Chandulal Temple
90. Kishan Bagh Temple
91. Clock Tower, Fateh Maidan
92. Clock Tower, Mahboob Chowk
93. Gate Portion, Shamraj Bahadur
94. Ritz Hotel (Hill Fort)
95. D. Lakshmaiah's Residence
96. D. Pentaiah's Residence
97. Lakshmi Paper Mart's Building
98. Mohanlal Malani's Residence
99. Raza Ali Bunglow
100. Nanu Bhai G. Shah's Building
101. Raja Bhagwandas Building
102. Façade Baitul Ghouse
103. Façade Hifazath Hussain
104. Goshamahal Baradari
105. Jawahar Bal Bhavan
106. Prem Chand's Residence
107. Shyam Rao Chungi's Residence
108. Dilkusha Guest House
109. College of Nursing
110. Yousuf Tekhri
111. Khusroo Manzil
112. Devdi Ranachand and Ahotichand
113. Asman Mahal
114. Baitul Ashraf
115. Devdi Bansilal
116. Devdi Imaad Jung Bahadur
117. Panjmahalla (Lingampally)
118. Parwarish Bagh
119. Adil Alan Mansion
120. Central Bank Building
121. Mini Bal Bhavan

122. Ali Manzil
123. Taj Mahal Hotel (Old Block)
124. Ravi Bar
125. Hyderabad Central Building Division's office
126. Roshan Manzil
127. Central Cooperative Training College
128. a) Mahboobia Girls High School and Junior College
    b) Madrassa-e-Aliya
129. Reddy Hostel
130. Mahal Wanaparthi
131. Baquer Bagh
132. Devdi Nawab Shamsheer Jung
133. Devdi Maharaja Kishan Pershad Bahadur
134. A. Majeed Khan's Residence
135. Old M.C.H. Office, Dar-ush-Shifa
136. Greenlands Guest House
137. Raj Bhavan Old Building.

Additional 14 buildings as Heritage Buildings are [172] (printed on the Circle maps with numbers N-1, N-2, etc.)
1. St Georges' Grammar School Complex (Grade II B)
2. Old Jail Complex (Grade II B)
3. P. Ramachandra Memorial Hall (Grade II B)
4. CV Padma Rao Memorial Hall (Grade II B)
5. Muthiala Memorial Hall (Grade II B)
6. Wesley Church Complex (Grade II B)
7. St Mary's Presbytery, St Anns School (Grade II B)
8. Mr Krishna Reddy's Building (Grade III)
9. Bhoiguda Kaman (Grade I)
10. IAS Officers' Association Building (Grade II B)
11. Mitti ka Sher (Grade I)
12. Nampally Sarai (GradeII B)
13. Sheikh Faiz ki Kaman (Grade I)
14. Ghode ki Qabar (Grade I)

HERITAGE PRECINCTS
1. Charminar Area
2. Golconda Area

3. Falaknuma Palace Area
4. Kasu Brahmanand Reddy (KBR) Park and valley up to Hotel Banjara Residency
5. Park on Road No. 1, Banjara Hills and Valley
6. Additional areas around Durgam Cheruvu Lake.

HERITAGE PRECINCTS – ROCKS
1. Hillocks around Durgam Cheruvu Lake, Jubilee Hills
2. Rock Park, on Old Bombay Road near Dargah Hussain Shah Wali
3. 'Bear's Nose' inside Shilparamam, Madhapur
4. 'Mushroom Rock' inside the University of Hyderabad Campus
5. 'Cliff Rock' between Road No. 45 and 46, Jubilee Hills
6. 'Monster Rock' near Film Nagar, between Road No. 70 and 71, Jubilee Hills
7. 'Tortoise Rock' in Nandi Hills layout near Jubilee Hills
8. 'Toadstool' next to Blue Cross, Jubilee Hills
9. 'Obelisk' on Road No. 66, Jubilee Hills.

The Non-Government Organisations

THE INDIAN NATIONAL TRUST FOR ART AND CULTURAL HERITAGE (INTACH): was founded in January 1984 with a view to create general awareness about the rich cultural and natural heritage of India. It was hoped that the Trust, once formed, would help a revival of interest amongst the people, to look at their culture with the respect and dignity it rightly deserves. As a membership based national non-government organisation the charter of INTACH enjoins it to involve people in the conservation of this heritage. Towards this end it seeks to carry out activities, which are oriented to education and communication.

INTACH Heritage Awards instituted in 1996 have good response in creating public awareness for conservation and re-use of historical buildings.

SOCIETY TO SAVE ROCKS
The Society to Save Rocks aims to preserve and protect the spectacular ancient granite formations of the Deccan Plateau, India—a natural wonder of stony ridges and hillocks shaped into picturesque balancing forms.

To prevent the indiscriminate destruction of this natural, historical, and environmental heritage, a group of artists, photographers and environmentalists from Hyderabad has been working for the protection of this rocky landscape since 1992. In 1996, they formed themselves into a registered society, and since then, the Society to Save Rocks has expanded to include many other citizens, from students to housewives to businessmen and bureaucrats (300 members).

The Society wants to impress upon landowners, developers and the government that our beautiful granite boulders could be preserved in houses, gardens, colonies and park areas.

CENTRE FOR DECCAN STUDIES
It is a research organisation from Hyderabad. Its aim is to promote and undertake the study in the field of Deccan Geography, History, Archaeology, Environmental Studies, Urban and Rural Development, Literature, Religion and the Social Sciences. The 'Deccan Studies' is the regular bi-annual Journal from the Centre.

FORUM FOR A BETTER HYDERABAD
It is another local organisation, which has ten working groups, namely, (1) Urban development, slums and other related matters, (2) Heritage, culture, etc. (3) Rock Formation and Ecology, (4, 9 & 10) Urban Parks, Forests, Birds and Wildlife, [5] Urban Lakes and Water bodies, [6 & 7] Urban Transport, noise pollution, Auto Pollution, Industrial pollution, etc. and (8) Solid Waste Management. Each group has a convenor to take up the activity or issue of the respective group.

Endnotes

Chapter 1

[1] Afzalgunj Mosque and Mecca Masjid

[2] These are not the Circles designated by the GHMC for the administrative purposes.

[3] *Heritage component refers to a structure that is a part of a larger (existing or now –nonexistent) heritage site.*

Chapter 2

[4] A detailed listing of the natural heritage of the city has been discussed under the HERITAGE PRECINCTS-ROCKS in the appendix.

[5] Noted by the British Writers Burrows C.B. and A.Claude (late 19th century)

[6] As per the World Heritage Convention at UNESCO in 1972 'natural features consisting of physical and biological formations or groups of such formations which are of universal value from the aesthetic and scientific point of view' belong to natural heritage.

Chapter 3
CIRCLE I

[7] At the time of British rule, it was known as Alexandra Road.

[8] Imbrication is a weather-tight covering that is formed by overlapping rows of shaped tiles, shingles, or the like, using discontinuous joints perpendicular to the lap.

[9] Pattern in the form of rings is seen on the shaft. Refer to the pictorial index

[10] A feature from renaissance period in art and architecture, a part of animal figure forms the water spouts.

[11] Same as Serai.

[12] Paradise Hotel is famous for its Hyderabadi dishes and the Paradise Café is famous for its Irani Tea and Osmania Biscuits.

[13] One can directly plan to go to the MG Road, and see this structure from outside by clubbing it with structures on SP Road in Begumpet trip. One can plan to come back from Park Lane and enjoy shopping here. The trip can be continued from the crossing identified with a statue of Mahatma Gandhi.

[14] as seen from outside.

[15] To be specific, it displays the Roman architecture.

[16] On the first floor wall, the broad fluted pilasters adorn the corner along with round pilaster in the

centre, and the small console brackets below the roof projection. The fluted pilasters are set perpendicular to the round one.

[17] A typical feature of Qutb Shahi architecture

[18] There is a *Samadhi* of the famous Sri Nandmuri Tarak Ramarao (NTR) in this park.

[19] Due to security reasons the trip map for this section has not been printed in this book.

[20] Known as 'Parade' at the time of British.

[21] In 1948, during the Police Action of Hyderabad.

[22] The central gallery is called nave and the side ones are known as aisles.

[23] Its form is like a big fish in the waters of Andaman, built by the British.

[24] Bollarum has a unique story about its name. When the British were laying out the railway line through this town, an officer asked a person what was the name of the place to set up a station there. The person was an ardent worshipper of Rama but he couldn't speak English, so he greeted the gentleman by saying 'Bolo Ram' which eventually became Bollarum, also spelled as Bolaram or Bolarum.

[25] A part of the British cantonment, Alwal got its name after people from Alwar, Rajasthan settled here in the late 1800s.

[26] The locals tell the story about the origin of the temple and the temple is quite famous.

[27] Also known as Moroccan arches.

[28] The latest ownership could not get confirmed.

[29] Art Deco is the international art design movement originated in early 20th century. It is followed by a group of buildings of the city built in post-Independence period.

[30] The HUDA office at Begumpet was taken over by the US Consulate in 2008, and the HUDA had to shift its office into three different locations at Taranaka, West Maredpally and Greenlands.

[31] The *Jagir* granted to Khairat-un-nisa Begum daughter of Ibrahim.

[32] *The prince and the princess occupied separate apartments, as was the custom; The prince was on the ground floor and the princess on the first floor apartments, for the reasons of privacy (Rani Sharma 2008).*

[*] Sir Akbar Hydri was the Prime Minister of Hyderabad between 1936-1941

[33] Tomb Fakhr-ul-Mulk and Ancient Gateway, Kukatpally are situated at a distance from Raj Bhavan Road, but they can be easily visited in this trip.

[34] The ancestors of the Fakhr-ul-Mulk family belonged to Toos, in Persia.

CIRCLE II

[35] Afzalgunj is the market named after the Nizam V, Nawab Afzal-ud-Daula.

[36]The central voussoir of an arch. Usually, the keystone is more elaborate in terms of ornamentation, but here it is done with more simplicity.

[37]It was said to be drawn on a stamp size paper.

[38] The temple at Paradise Crossing, Secunderabad is the oldest of all.

[39]Refer to Raja Bhagwandas Pavillion (Ref. No. 16) in Golconda circle.

[40]Moin-ud-Daula was appointed minister-in-charge of the Industries Department and also a member of the Executive Council.

[41]The stepmother of Nawab Moin-ud-Daula.

[42]One has to follow the route from Secunderabad to Liberty Junction, little ahead of Gandhi Medical College site, under the fly over, and take a U-turn from the crossing.

[43] Today Bashir Bagh Colony stands at the site of the Bashir Bagh Palace.

[44] The previous form of the structure was printed in the reports of City Improvement Board totally different from the one that exists today.

[45]He was also responsible for constructing Nizamia Observatory.

[46]The main façade of the structure is visible only in parts due to the temporary construction put up in front of it.

[47] *Madrassa* is the institute for higher education, usually residential, in which traditional Islamic sciences were taught.

[48] Osmanian or Osman Shahi is a type of arch observed in the structures built during the period of Mir Osman Ali Khan, the seventh Nizam.

[49]Department of State Archaeology and Museums is located opposite the street in which Gunfoundry is located. It is housed in an old residential structure along with some newly constructed blocks. This place is a treasure of information for the research scholars of history, art, architecture and archaeology.

[50]Cathedral is the principal church in a diocese.

[51]The dome displaying ribs. (see pictorial index)

[52]As per another source, it was completed in 1877.

[53]As referred by Claude Campbell. He was of British origin and his book 'The Nizam's Dominions' carry a lot of information on Hyderabad's built, natural and cultural heritage. Hyderabad has been discussed there not only at city level but as State of the Nizams.

[54]Said to have been given to a developer for the new construction in and around the heritage structure.

[55]The Kothi is another residential typology, simply means a big posh house, quite similar to mansion houses. Kothi became Koti later on.

[56] *Purda* or Pardaa means a curtain in Urdu.

[57]*Subedar*- the Governor

[58]Hexastyle-a set of six columns

[59]The seventh Nizam had two sons, Mukarram Jah and Moazzam Jah.

[60]The title of *Balwant* was conferred on Raj Rameshwar Rao I by the Nizam in 1843. Again in 1905, Nizam VI conferred upon Raja Rameshwar Rao II the title of *Mahabhoopal*.

[61]He was member of the city's Municipal Board.

[62]The porch was pulled down in order to provide more space for the theatre, built right in front of the palace.

[63]It was started as a doll house for the Nizam's daughter. Later, it was converted into the State Museum.

[64]The auditorium owned by the Government of Andhra Pradesh.

[65]As per Rajkumari Indira Devi Dhanrajgiri.

[66]*Kabr* or or Kabar refers to grave.

[67]Khairatabad was named after the princess Khairat-un-Nisa. The princess kept indifferent health; on her father's request, Hussain Shah Wali built the Hussain Sagar Tank.

CIRCLE III

[68]As described by Prof Sherwani in History of Mediveal Deccan Vol II Page 294

[69]Growth of vegetation on the tomb is damaging this beautiful edifice.

[70]The rapid urbanisation has changed the face of Hyderabad's natural and built heritage, yet there is a lot to be saved, restored and to feel proud of.

[71]The first five sites-starting from Errum Manzil, can also be clubbed with the Begumpet trip after visiting Raj Bhavan Road structures.

[72]Correctly pronounced and written as Iram Manzil in historic sources.

[73]Known as Iram Manzil in the old records of the city.

[74]That was a normal practice in those days.

[75]Originally, the area of the lake was much more than the exiting one.

[76]The entry to the heritage component is restricted at present.

[77]Refer to the appendix for the definition of Heritage Buildings, Heritage Precincts and Heritage Precincts (Rocks)

[78]*Khanqah*:refers to a house where a group of people and initiates gather around a master. It has facilities for assembly, prayer and communal living.

[79]As suggested by the Society to Save Rocks

CIRCLE IV

[80] A pointed arch composed of reverse curves, the lower concave and the upper convex.

[81] The fort has religious value among Hindus and Muslims because of various religious structures. For Hindus Bonalu festival is celebrated at Sri Jagdamba Mahankali Temple, atop the Golconda Fort. The festival celebrated in the city of Hyderabad starts from this temple.
[82] The site for the Golconda Precinct is declared by the HMDA.

[83] According to the recent findings of Prof. M.A. Nayeem this half-finished tomb was built by Abul Hassan Tanashah. The grave here, however, is that of Syed Ahmed, also known as Nizamuddin.

[84] As per the local legends Majzoob (the holy madman) stayed next to one of the gateways, probably the Fateh Darwaza. He was requested to move out by another sufi saint Yousuf Sahib - a soldier in Mughal army at the time of Mughal sieze. The fort was believed to be protected by this holy madman

[85] As per the city's scholars these are incomplete minarets.

[86] Karvan Sahu came up because of the camp of the traders.

[87] *Rangrez* means the dyer, so Rangrezpura meant to be a settlement of the dyers.

[88] *Langar* was a festival, particular to Hyderabad, celebrated in the month of Muharram. The Langar procession comprised a march past of the whole military before the minister and the Nizam.

[89] Another Jama Masjid stands very close to Charminar, was built later.

[90] These gateways could not be traced on the site.

[91] Also described by Sherwani in *History of Medieval Deccan* (1974).

[92] The *minar* seen in centre of the front view marks the *quibla* wall.

[93] Mian Mishk is known as Mia Mushk also, who got the Mush Mahal constructed in Attapur.

CIRCLE V

[94] The city was also called Baghnagar based on the Urdu word *Bagh* refering to 'garden'. According to a legend the city was called Bhagnagar after Bhagmati, Mohammed Quli Qutb Shah's beloved wife; the city is said to have got its name Hyderabad from *Hyder- Mahal*, another name of Bhagmati.

[95] Kaman refers to arch and arched gateways. These *kamans* are very much part of the civic architecture of Hyderabad.

[96] It is also held that the construction of the structures Charkaman, Dar-ush-Shifa, Badeshahi Ashurkhana and Jama Masjid were complete by 1591, the year in which Charminar was built.

[97] These Qutb Shahi multi-cusped arches are different from the Mughal multi-cusped arches; they carry a fruit-like object on its apex and a ribbon-like pattern radiating in opposite direction. Due to inadequate maintenance, these interesting features are not distinct.

[98] There are a few more arched structures nearby.

*Both the components are from south-eastern part of walled city but are being discussed here for the ease of the visitor.

[99]Malwalas were the treasurers of the Nizam. The increasing pressure of commercialisation in the city has taken a toll on their magnificent devdi, the Malwala Palace is lost, including this large, majestic gateway, shown in the picture.

[100]Ali Jah was the second son of the third Nizam, Nawab Sikander Jah.

[101]beyond Ali Jah Kotla the Itebar Chowk Road is known as Mir Jumla Tank Darwaza Road. The tank does not exit any more.
[102]One mile is equal to 1.6 kilometres.

[103] According to Prof. MA Nayeem, and also the 1914 survey map, there were thirteen gates and thirteen posterns: Names of these gates are: Chaderghat Drawaza, Dilli Darwaza, Afzal Darwaza, Champa Darwaza, Puranapul Darwaza, Doodh Baoli Darwaza, Gazi Banda/Fateh Darwaza, Aliabad Darwaza, Lal Darwaza, Gowlipura Darwaza, Mir Jumla Darwaza, Yakutpura Darwaza, Dabirpura Darwaza

[104]*Imambara* and Ashurkhana both refer to the mourning hall for Muslims

*This is the part of north-eastern quadrant of the walled city but will be discussed in the trip of north western quarter.

[105]Laakad Kot used to be the old palace of Salarjung; it does not exist anymore. The Salarjung Museum stands on this site today.

[106]There is a structure called Bohron ki Sarai here.

[107]The mosque reflects the Mughal and Qutb Shahi architectural styles. As one visits Chowmahalla and sees the Mecca Masjid in the background (to the to the north-west), the front and rear *minars* display a balanced composition of both styles (refer to Chapter 4)

[108]Jilukhana- is the entrance courtyard, visitors would alight a horse or elephant etc.

[109]The southern-most boundary at the Aspan Chowk was probably named after the royal stables that were located in the Moti Gali and Aspan Chowk Road Crossing.

[110] a title given to the Paigah nobles.

[111]In Asaf Jahi period water was served from this structure.

[112]Bordering this quadrant the land was given to some of the regiment of the Nizam's army. The word 'barracks' was pronounced as Barkas locally and this area was referred to as Barkas. The Arab soldiers settled here and the Maratha soldiers in Brahmanwadi and Shah Ali Banda.

[113]Hanuman Temple is a good example of local temple architecture, it is a landmark for the residents of the Old City. In Khoya Gali the local shopkeepers sell khoya - a sweet made from milk, in the early hours of the day.

[114]The Shad Mansion and Khana Baag were used for parties and gatherings. Khayam Mahal was used as residential quarters for the Chandulal family.

[115]Raj Rayan Bahadur died in 1914; his elder son Raja Shamraj Bahadur was sixteen years old then. The ancestors of Raja Rayan were treasurers and accountants to the Mughal emperor Shahjahan.

They continued their services as peshkars to the Asaf Jahi kings. In 1935 Raja Shamraj Bahadur was made the minister of the Public Works Department.

[116]One kilometre to the south of Falaknuma, to the right of the Srisailam Road, are situated the Chandrayagutta and Keshava Temples; several shrines, about six hundred years old, can also be located between the rocks of this steep hill.

[117]This road meets the Inner Ring Road after driving three kilometres from Kishan Bagh Crossroads (in the south-west).

[118]Pittis were the bankers in the Asaf Jahi period, popular for their generosity.

[119]This feature originally appeared in the Elizabethan architecture of Britain. The gable sometimes, takes the shape of a plain triangle, or a tri-foliated arch. This feature is common in vernacular architecture of the city.
[120]Rediscovery of Qutb Shahi architecture in Asaf Jahi period is termed as Neo-Qutb Shahi architecture by the scholars.

[121]Nizam's Dominions - refers to different regions under the Asaf Jahi Rule.

[122]Alam - a standard - used by Shia Muslims.

[123]This is due to the pressure of increasing land rates and population along with the migration of people from different cities.

CIRCLE VI

[124]It was a small village in the outskirts of the city named after Malik Yakoot. Malik Yakoot was a faithful servant of Sultan Abdullah Qutb Shah. He was granted this Jagir and built his residence and garden here.

[125]This locality dates back to the period of Nizam II. A *jagir* was granted to Begum Suroor Afza Bai. She was the wife of Nawab Arastu Jah Bahadur, Prime Minister of the then Nizam. The Nawab built a beautiful palace with a garden and a tank here and named it Suroornagar after his Begum.

[126]The mosque, said to be a part of the same complex, could not be located. However, a temple does exist in the fortress.

[127]This site is far away from the group of structures standing in Dilsukhnagar locality but may be covered in this trip.

[128]Refer to Circle III - Masab Tank.

[129]*Amalaka*- a feature in the structures built with the Hindu temples architecture.

[130]As per the Urban Conservation Study HUDA - This study is also known as Ford Foundation work. In this Urban Conservation report of 1988 the committee had proposed to convert it into a tourist hotel. Currently the structure is not in a good condition and needs immediate attention and protection. The physical and structural condition of the building is not very good due to neglect. Most of the structural and non-structural components of the palace are fallen a prey to the vandalism.

[131]Named after Syed Mir Momin Peshwa of Golconda, this locality was founded in 1591.

[132]The pattern on the surface of the pediment made in lime plaster.

[133]*Bangladar* roof with the curve in all four directions (refer to the pictorial index)

[134]These windows stand above the parapet wall, converting the semi-open space-verandah into a room.

[135]Refer to Circle V- Charminar, Mir Alam Tank.

[136]It is three kilometres from Charminar, towards the south-east.

CIRCLE VII

[137]Amberpet can be accessed from Sivam Road to the north or, from Kachiguda to the west side.

[138]Also known as Mahalaqa Bai Chanda, the same veteran singer whose baradari is located in Maula Ali.

[139]*A senior eunuch from the Qutb Shahi court named Ruby was asleep one night. A man in green came to him in a dream and told him he was being called by Maula Ali, the husband of the prophet's daughter Fatima, and the most revered figure in Shi'a devotion. Ruby followed the mysterious figure in green and was led to a place where Maula Ali was seated on the summit of a hill, with his right hand resting upon a rock. Ruby fell down before the figure, but he could not say anything, he woke up* (Dalrymple 2002).

[140]If one is approaching from the north side of the city, via the AOC, there is the Ram Krishna Puram (RK Puram) Flyover. This is the place from where one can enjoy the topographical beauty of the city of Hyderabad. On the left side are the rocks that fall under the jurisdiction of AOC; the one at the right is the Maula Ali. Five Kilometres from here is Radhika Theatre Crossing. A right turn from here leads to Maula Ali.

[141]Taking this road which turns to the right again, one gets back to the entrance steps of the Maula-Ali shrine.

[142]In the years of 1734-1758 and 1762-1803, as per the document procured from the present site.

[143]Kesari is one of the several names of Hindu Monkey God Hanuman. Kesari subsequently changed to Keesara after which the village is presently known.

Chapter 4

[144]"Dying Wisdom"(1997- Centre for Science and Environment) is the title of the book describing the rise, fall and potential of India's traditional water system. It is used here to discuss the sustainable practices of collection and supply of water from natural sources.

[145]In 1724 the first Nizam founded the Asaf Jahi dynasty, but the II Asaf Jah, Nizam Ali Khan shifted the capital to Hyderabad in 1763.

[146]Sultan Quli of Turkman tribe of Iran was the governor of Golconda under the Bahmani Kings and declared himself independent in 1518 as the Bahmani kingdom was becoming weak and was likely to fall.

[147]The style evolved in this period was later revived as Neo Qutb Shahi architecture in Asaf Jahi period.

[148]Also known as Mohammed Qutb Shah.

[149]Jamsheed (also known as Yar Quli Jamsheed was succeeded by Subhan Quli, Daulat Quli and then by Ibrahim. The first two were there for a very short period.

[150]as per Prof. MA Nayeem

[151]This system of water supply is changed over a period of time. The growth of the city has turned the storm water channels of yesteryears, into *naalas*, feeding into the main water bodies.

[152]Aurangazeb died in 1707, and the first Nizam established his supremacy and founded the Asaf Jahi Dynasty.

[153]The best example of this period could be observed in Mecca Masjid, started by the Qutb Shahi king and completed by Aurangazeb, displays the Mughal flavour in the top part of the minarets, dissimilar to the Qutb Shahi counterparts existing in the city.

[154]Nasir Jung, Muzzaffar Jung and Salabat Jung, ruled between1748-1763, they were not known as Asaf Jah.

[155]Second Asaf Jah-Asaf Jahi lineage goes back to Samarkand. The first king was from the generation of Khwaja Alam Sheikh and was born in Mughal India.
[156]Refer to Circle VII, Ref No. S-36

[157]A typical Qutb Shahi feature, see pictorial index.

[158]*Jharokha* window is an important feature of the Mughal architecture.

[159]Built by the fourth Resident Major Kirkpatrick (1797-1805).

[160]The style of architecture started by Andrea Palladio was known as Palladian architecture.

[161]Jack arches are segmental arches, spanned and supported on steel joists spanned at regular interval.

[162]Brackets and *Chajja* can be ornamental also.

[163]Smaller size domes are constructed with earthen tiles.

[164]Cornices are made on the ceiling where the walls meet the slab.

[165]Paint is fading constantly in the absence of restoration.

[166]The post at the end/starting of the staircase, usually attached to both the handrail and the string of the staircase.

[167]Arrangement of different pieces of the coloured stone or any other building material to achieve a design is known as Mosaic.

Chapter 5

[168]This chapter is written with the help of the material collected from individuals and organizations that are working for the cause of natural and built heritage.

[169]The built and natural heritage components, the forest land and land under the department of archaeology, needs to be checked on map and on-site as well.

The Pictorial Index

[170]The pictorial index has been prepared with the help of various source materials.

[171]As described by Prof. Sherwani in History of Medieval Deccan, Vol II, p. 294

Appendix

[172]These Heritage Buildings/ components have a reference number as N-1, N-2 etc. in the map, as they are a part of the new list.

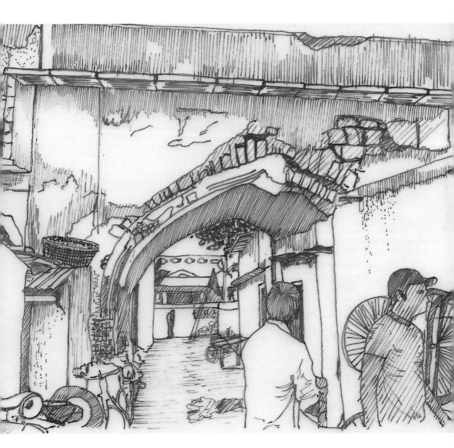

Gateway near Jama Masjid, Charminar

Bibliography

- Banagiri, Vanaja (ed.), *Hyderabad Hazir Hai - Writings from the City of Nizams*, Rupa and Co., 2008
- Bilgrami, H. and S. A. Asgar, *Landmarks of Deccan Hyderabad*, Hyderabad: Government Central Press, 1927; rpt., Manas Publications, Hyderabad, 1984
- Campbell, Claude A., *Glimpses of the Nizam's Dominions*, London: CB Burrows, 1898
- Chandraiah, K., *Hyderabad 400 Glorious Years*: K. Chandraiah Memorial Trust, February 1998
- Dalrymple, William; *White Mughals - Love and Betrayl in Eighteenth Century India*, Delhi: Penguin Books, 2002
- Fielden, Bernard, *Guidelines for Conservation - A Technical Manual*, Delhi: INTACH, 1989
- Harris, Cyril M. (ed); *Historic Architecture Sourcebook*: Mc-Graw-Hill Book Company, 1997
- *Heritage Capital Hyderabad*, Mumbai: Indian Express Group, 2001
- *Hyderabad*, Hyderabad: Sangam Books and Orient Longman Limited, 1991
- Indian Resources Information & Management Technologies Limited, Hyderabad: *Guide Map of Greater Hyderabad*, Hyderabad: Kala Jyothi Process (P) Ltd, 2005
- Khan, Raza Ali, *Hyderabad 400 years (1591-1991)*, Hyderabad: Zenith Services, 1990
- Luther, Narendra, *Hyderabad a Biography*, Delhi: Oxford University Press, 2006
- Mudiraj, Sri K. Krishnaswamy, *Pictorial Hyderabad*, Hyderabad: Privately Printed, 1934; Reprinted- Karshak Art Printers, Hyderabad, 2007
- Nayeem, M. A., *Splendours of Hyderabad - Last Phase of an Oriental Culture 1561-1948*, Mumbai: Jaico Publication House, 1987
- Prasad, Dharmendra, *Social and Cultural Geography of Hyderabad City - A Historical Perspective*
- Quarni, Khwaja Owais, *Quarni's Sketches of Hyderabad*, Hyderabad, 1990
- Sastry, V.V. Krishna, *Select Monuments of Hyderabad*: The Director of Archaeology and Museums, Andhra Pradesh, Hyderabad

- Sherwani, H.K., P.M. Joshi (ed); *History of Medieval Deccan* (1295-1724) Vol I and II, Government of Andhra Pradesh, 1973
- Shorey, S.P., *In Search of Monuments*, INTACH Hyderabad
- *The Chronology of Modern Hyderabad 1720-1890*, Commissioner Andhra Pradesh State Archives and Research, 1998
- *The Paigah Tombs - A Companion Guide*, Department of Archaeology and Museums, Government of Andhra Pradesh, 2003
- The *Qutb Shahi Tombs*, Department of Archaeology and Museums, Government of Andhra Pradesh

Articles and Papers

- Bawa, V.K., 'Saving the Architectural Heritage of Hyderabad', Intercity Conference on Citizens Action for Heritage Conservation, Birla Science Centre Hyderabad, 2000
- Chinoy, Poly Naoshir, 'The contribution of Parsis to the administration of the Nizams of Hyderabad', *Islamic Culture - An English Quarterly*, July 1997, The Islamic Culture Board, Hyderabad
- Doshi B.V., 'Vision 2020: Cyberabad' - *Architecture - Time Space and People*, Mumbai, May 2004
- Naidu, P. Jogi, 'Studded Bangles of Hyderabad', *INTACH Heritage Annual 2007*, INTACH Hyderabad
- Reddy S. Jeevananda, 'Hussain Sagar Lake', *Forum For a Better Hyderabad Journal*, Annual Number, 2004-05
- Shahid, Sajjad, 'The City Conquers the Citadel', *Hyderabad The Power of Glory*, Deccan Books, Deccan Chronicle
- Shahid, Sajjad, 'The Architecture of Hyderabad', *INTACH Heritage Annual 2008*, INTACH Hyderabad
- Shorey, S.P., *'Heritage Conservation Efforts Hyderabad'*, *Architecture +Design*, Nov-Dec 2000
- Varma, D.N., 'Water Management and Gardens of Qutb Shahi Capital of Golconda and Hyderabad', Vol III, Number 2, July – December 2005, *Deccan Studies Journal*

Reports, Brochures, Maps and Drawings

- Ali, Neda'A Abdul-Ameer, 'Traditions and Transformations in the Core of Islamic Cities: Structure of Urban Spaces' - Thesis, M.Arch, Urban Design, School of Planning and Architecture, New Delhi, India

- Charminar, Hyderabad, Archaeological Survey of India, Hyderabad - a Brochure
- Ed. Anil Agrawal, Sunita Narain: State of India's Environment- A Citizen's Report: 'Dying Wisdom' 1997, Centre for Sience and Environment, New Delhi
- Forum For a Better Hyderabad annuals
- Golconda Fort, Hyderabad, Archaeological Survey of India, Hyderabad - a Brochure
- Heritage Walks of Old City - Hyderabad by Andhra Pradesh Secretariat, (1990s) - Brochures 8 Nos
- *INTACH Heritage Annuals*, INTACH Hyderabad
- Maps from Town and Country Planning Office, Hyderabad, 1914
- Reports, Maps and Drawings from HMDA Heritage Cell, State Archaeology Department
- The Flood of 1908 at Hyderabad, An Account of the Flood, its Causes and Proposed Prevalent Measures, Hyderabad (Deccan)
- Vaastu Shilpa Consultants, Ahmedabad, 'Hyderabad: Restructuring the historic core, Proposals' - Final Urban Design Proposal Stage II Report, Nov 1999.
- Vottery, Madhu, 'Developing a Methodology for the Appropriate Re-use of a Heritage Structure'- Thesis, M.Arch, Architectural Conservation 2005, School of Planning and Architecture, New Delhi

Oral History Refrences:

Bhoopal, Sreeram: Son of Raja Ram Linga Reddy from Sirnapally Samasthana and Janamma from Wanaparthy Samasthana. He worked for Hyderabad Civil Services which later became IAS.

Brahma, Somen: Brigadier Brahma served as the Commandant of AOC Secunderabad. He has a good knowledge about the history of the structures of the Secunderabad Cantonment.

Bawa, Oudesh Rani: An Urdu Scholar, born and brought up in Old City, Hyderabad, also studied in Moscow. She is close to CPI and has a good knowledge of Hyderabad.

Bawa, V.K.: A retired IAS Ofiicer, Founder Vice Chairman of HUDA and President of Centre for Deccan Studies. An eminent Historian, Dr Bawa has written two books on Hyderabad: *Hyderabad under Salarjung-I and The Last Nizam*

Chinoy, Poly Naoshir: Daughter of Naushir Chinoy, one of the famous Hyderabadi Parsi. She worked as an English Professor in Osmania University.

Devi, Rani Kumudini (late): Daughter-in-law of Raja Rameshwar Rao-II, Wanaparthy Samasthana. She was a companion to the Princess of Berar.

Dhanrajgirji, Rajkumari Indiradevi: Daughter of Raja Dhanrajgirji, a nobleman and philanthropist of Hyderabad. She has written a book *Memories of the Deccan*.

Jones, Ivan Ernest: Retd. Lt. Col. Jones was born in Ferozepur in 1926. He joined Indian Military Academy, Dehradun and was commissioned in 1948 in Indian Army Ordinance Core. He worked with Prince Muffakkam Jah as his Private Secretary between 1982 and 1996.

Khan, Aminuddin: The administrator of HEH the Nizam's Private Estates. He is an Industrial Psycologist by profession, a management consultant and a novelist.

Luther, Narendra: Retired as the Chief Secretary of Andhra Pradesh (IAS). He has written several books on Hyderabad in Urdu and English. He has been living in Hyderabad for more than forty years.

Qayum, M.A.: Retired as the Deputy Director of State Archaeology and Museums. He has been writing columns in Urdu daily on Historic structures of Hyderabad.

Rao, Vikram Dev: The grandson of Raja Rameshwar Rao II, and son of Rani Kumudini Devi. Mr Rao has a keen interest in photography and social service. He is secretary of Sivananda Rehabilitation Home, Kukatpally, catering to Leprosy, TB and AIDs patients.

Reddy, Anuradha: Daughter of Sri Sreeram Bhoopal, interested in photography. She has a good knowledge of historic sites of Hyderabad.

Shahid, Sajjad: A Consulting Engineer, comes from a well known family of Hyderabad. Sajjad has a keen interest in Deccan History. He is an active member of CDS and INTACH and writes regularly on historic structures of Deccan.

Index

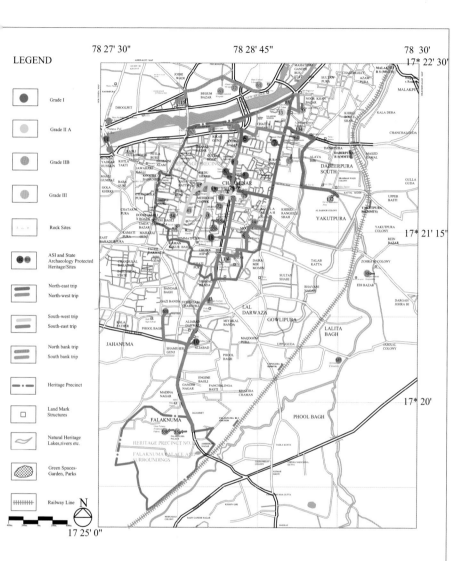

LEGEND

78 27' 30"   78 28' 45"   78 30'
17* 22' 30"

●	Grade I
○	Grade II A
●	Grade IIB
●	Grade III
▭	Rock Sites
◉◉	ASI and State Archaeology Protected Heritage/Sites
▬	North-east trip
	North-west trip
▬	South-west trip
	South-east trip
▦	North bank trip
	South bank trip
- ▪ -	Heritage Precinct
□	Land Mark Structures
〰	Natural Heritage Lakes, rivers etc.
▨	Green Spaces- Garden, Parks
▥	Railway Line

17* 21' 15"

17* 20'

N

17 25' 0"

CHARMINAR AND SURROUNDINGS

HERITAGE PRECINCT NO.12 and 14

DILSUKHNAGAR AND SURROUNDINGS

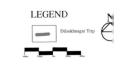

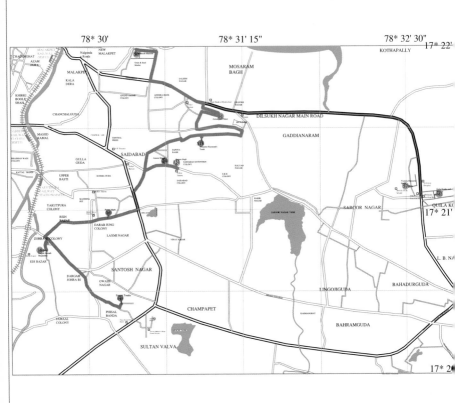

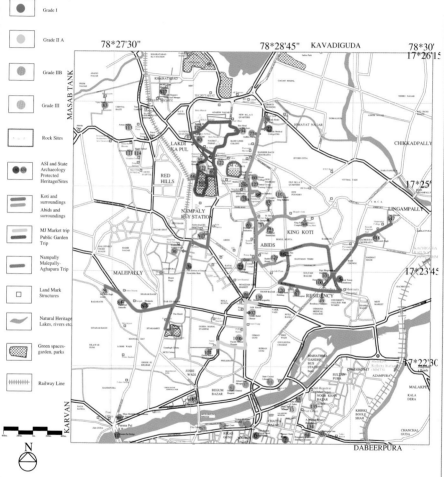

LEGEND

- Grade I
- Grade II A
- Grade IIB
- Grade III
- Rock Sites
- ASI and State Archaeology Protected Heritage/Sites
- Koti and surroundings
- Abids and surroundings
- MJ Market trip Public Garden Trip
- Nampally Malepally-Aghapura Trip
- Land Mark Structures
- Natural Heritage Lakes, rivers etc
- Green spaces-garden, parks
- Railway Line

KOTI AND SURROUNDINGS

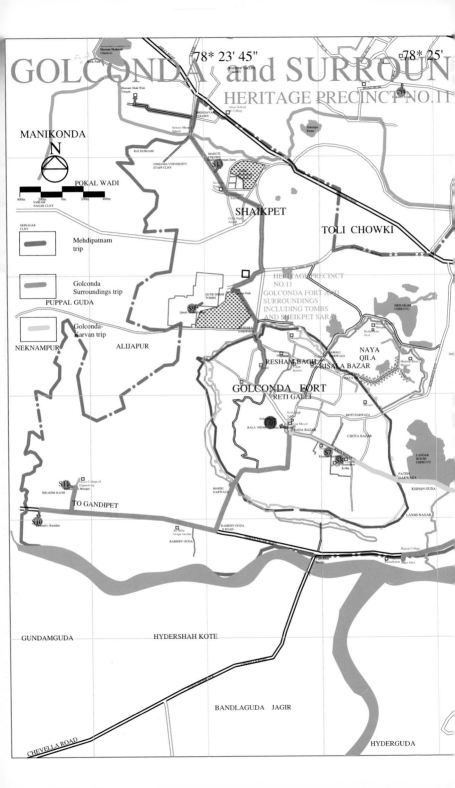

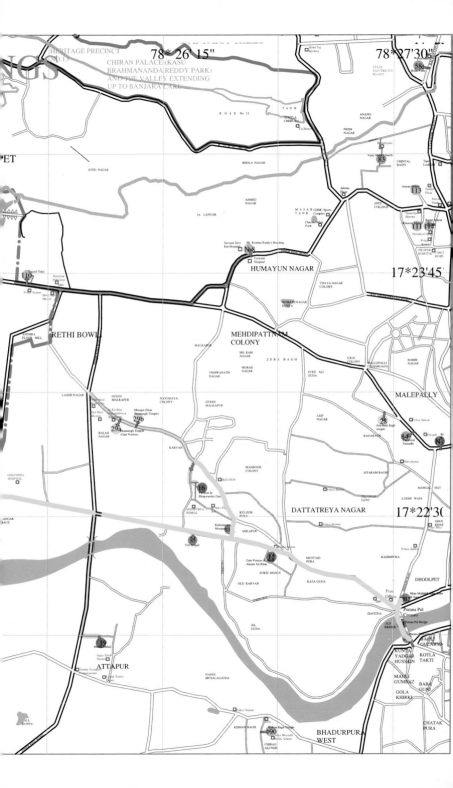

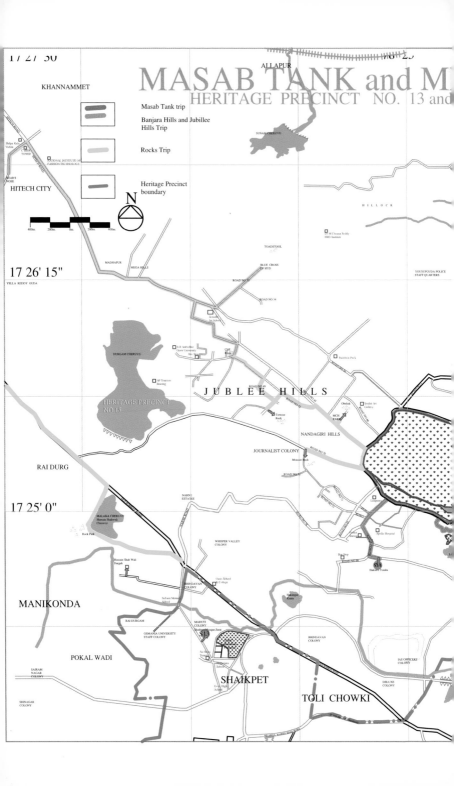

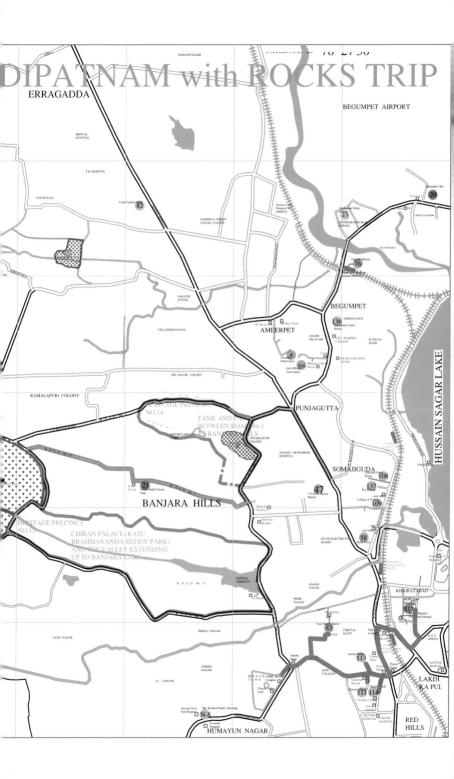

LEGEND

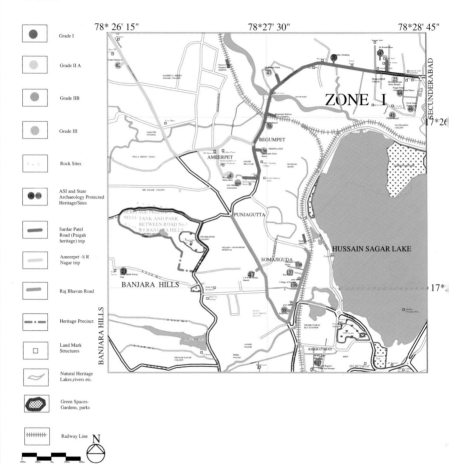

●	Grade I
●	Grade II A
●	Grade IIB
●	Grade III
	Rock Sites
●●	ASI and State Archaeology Protected Heritage/Sites
▬	Sardar Patel Road (Paigah heritage) trip
▬	Ameerpet -S R Nagar trip
▬	Raj Bhavan Road
▬▪▬	Heritage Precinct
□	Land Mark Structures
⌇	Natural Heritage Lakes,rivers etc.
▦	Green Spaces-Gardens, parks
▥	Railway Line

78* 26' 15"   78*27' 30"   78*28' 45"

ZONE I

BEGUMPET

AMEERPET

PUNJAGUTTA

SOMAJIGUDA

BANJARA HILLS

HUSSAIN SAGAR LAKE

KHAIRATABAD

N

BEGUMPET AND SURROUNDINGS

SECUNDERABAD AND SURROUNDINGS

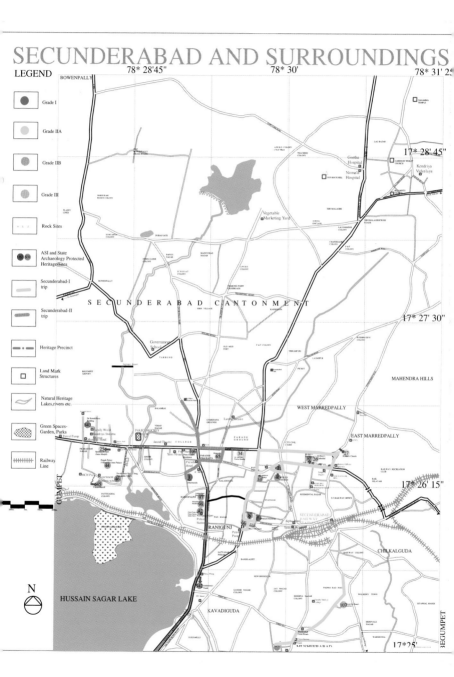

LEGEND

●	Grade I
●	Grade IIA
●	Grade IIB
●	Grade III
	Rock Sites
● ●	ASI and State Archaeology Protected Heritage/Sites
	Secunderabad-I trip
	Secunderabad-II trip
—	Heritage Precinct
□	Land Mark Structures
	Natural Heritage Lakes, rivers etc.
	Green Spaces-Garden, Parks
+++++	Railway Line

HUSSAIN SAGAR LAKE

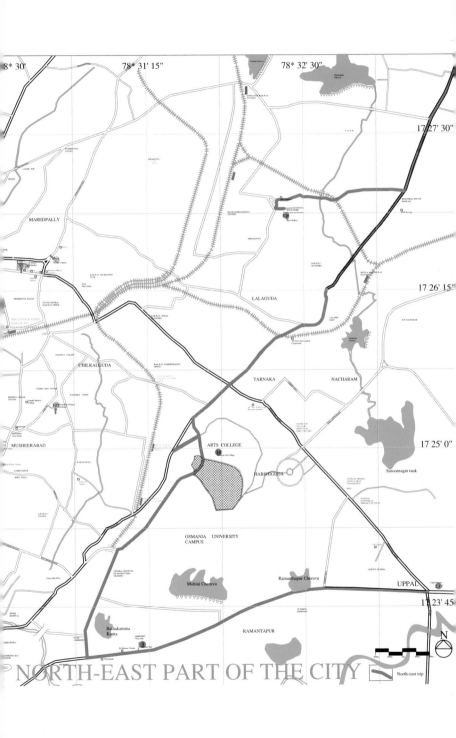

8* 30'   78* 31' 15"   78* 32' 30"

17 27' 30"

MAREDPALLY

LALAGUDA

17 26' 15"

SECUNDERABAD
RAILWAY

CHILKALGUDA

TARNAKA   NACHARAM

MUSHEERABAD

ARTS COLLEGE

17 25' 0"

HABSHIGUDA   Saroornagar tank

OSMANIA   UNIVERSITY
CAMPUS

Mohini Cheruvu   Ramanthapur Cheruvu

UPPAL

17 23' 45"

Bathakamma
Kunta

RAMANTAPUR

N

NORTH-EAST PART OF THE CITY

North-east trip

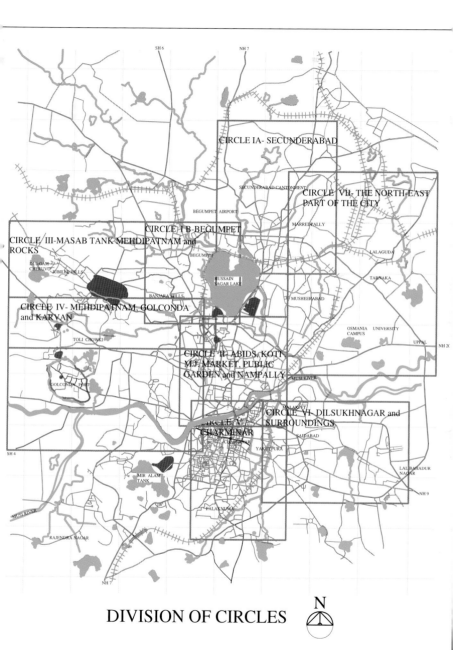

DIVISION OF CIRCLES

N

HISTORY OF AREAS

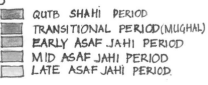

QUTB SHAHI PERIOD
TRANSITIONAL PERIOD (MUGHAL)
EARLY ASAF JAHI PERIOD
MID ASAF JAHI PERIOD
LATE ASAF JAHI PERIOD.